EXPERIMENTING

WITH ETHNOGRAPHY

EXPERIMENTAL FUTURES:
Technological Lives, Scientific Arts,
Anthropological Voices *A series edited
by Michael M. J. Fischer and Joseph Dumit*

EXPERIMENTING
WITH ETHNOGRAPHY

A Companion to Analysis

EDITED BY

ANDREA BALLESTERO AND

BRIT ROSS WINTHEREIK

DUKE UNIVERSITY PRESS DURHAM AND LONDON 2021

© 2021 Duke University Press
This work is licensed under a Creative Commons Attribution-
NonCommercial-NoDerivatives 4.0 International License,
available at *https://creativecommons.org/licenses/by-nc-nd/4.0/*.
Printed and bound by CPI Group (UK) Ltd, Croydon, CR0 4YY
Designed by Amy Ruth Buchanan
Typeset in Arno and Trade Gothic by
Westchester Publishing Services

Library of Congress Cataloging-in-Publication Data
Names: Ballestero, Andrea, [date] editor. |
Winthereik, Brit Ross, [date] editor.
Title: Experimenting with ethnography : a companion to analysis /
edited by Andrea Ballestero and Brit Ross Winthereik.
Other titles: Experimental futures.
Description: Durham : Duke University Press, 2021. |
Series: Experimental futures | Includes bibliographical
references and index.
Identifiers: LCCN 2020028571 (print)
LCCN 2020028572 (ebook)
ISBN 9781478010746 (hardcover)
ISBN 9781478011996 (paperback)
ISBN 9781478013211 (ebook)
ISBN 9781478091691 (ebook other)
Subjects: LCSH: Ethnology—Research—Methodology. |
Anthropology—Research.
Classification: LCC GN345 .E974 2021 (print) | LCC GN345 (ebook) |
DDC 305.80072/1—dc23
LC record available at https:// lccn.loc.gov/2020028571
LC ebook record available at https:// lccn.loc.gov/20200285721

Cover art: Beatriz Milhazes, *Popeye*, 2007/2008. Acrylic
canvas, 199 x 139 cm. © Beatriz Milhazes Studio. Pho   on
Águas & Pepe Schettino. Courtesy of the artist and Pace Gallery.

This title is freely available in an open access edition made
possible by generous contributions from the Center for Digital
Welfare at IT University of Copenhagen, the Massachusetts
Institute of Technology, Rice University, and the University of
California, Davis.

ACKNOWLEDGMENTS IX

INTRODUCTION Analysis as Experimental Practice
Andrea Ballestero and Brit Ross Winthereik 1

PART I BODILY PRACTICES AND RELOCATIONS

1 Tactile Analytics: Touching as a Collective Act
Patricia Alvarez Astacio 15

2 The Ethnographic Hunch
Sarah Pink 30

3 The Para-Site in Ethnographic Research Projects
George E. Marcus 41

4 Juxtaposition: Differences That Matter
Else Vogel 53

PART II PHYSICAL OBJECTS

5 Relocating Innovation: Postcards from Three Edges
Endre Dányi, Lucy Suchman, and Laura Watts 69

6 Object Exchange
Trine Mygind Korsby and Anthony Stavrianakis 82

7 Drawing as Analysis: Thinking in Images, Writing in Words
Rachel Douglas-Jones 94

8 Diagrams: Making Multispecies Temporalities Visible
Elaine Gan 106

PART III	**INFRASTRUCTURAL PLAY**	
9	Ethnographic Drafts and Wild Archives	
	Alberto Corsín Jiménez 123	
10	Multimodal Sorting: The Flow of Images	
	across Social Media and Anthropological Analysis	
	Karen Waltorp 133	
11	Categorize, Recategorize, Repeat	
	Graham M. Jones 151	
12	Sound Recording as Analytic Technique	
	Brit Ross Winthereik and James Maguire 163	
PART IV	**INCOMMENSURABILITIES**	
13	Substance as Method (Shaking Up Your Practice)	
	Joseph Dumit 175	
14	Excreting Variously: On Contrasting as an	
	Analytic Technique	
	Justine Laurent, Oliver Human, Carolina Domínguez	
	Guzmán, Els Roding, Ulrike Scholtes, Marianne de Laet,	
	and Annemarie Mol 186	
15	Facilitating Breakdowns through the Exchange	
	of Perspectives	
	Steffen Dalsgaard 198	

16   Analogy
Antonia Walford 209

17   Decolonizing Knowledge Devices
Ivan da Costa Marques 219

18   Writing an Ethnographic Story in Working toward
Responsibly Unearthing Ontological Troubles
Helen Verran 235

19   Not Knowing: In the Presence of . . .
Marisol de la Cadena 246

AFTERWORD 1   Questions, Experiments, and
Movements of Ethnographies in the Making
Melanie Ford Lemus and Katie Ulrich 257

AFTERWORD 2   Where Would You Put This
Volume? On Thinking with Unruly
Companions in the Middle of Things
Clément Dréano and Markus Rudolfi 262

REFERENCES 267

CONTRIBUTORS 287

INDEX 295

We are grateful to all the people and institutions that made this book possible. The Independent Research Councils of Denmark (funding ID 0602–02551B) supported Brit's visits to UC Davis and the Ethnography Studio at Rice University in 2016. During these visits we had our first conversations about crafting a book that focused on analytic practices in creative and critical ethnography. Marisol de la Cadena hosted Brit and her family during her stay at UC Davis and has been family and friend to both of us, enthusiastically encouraging the writing of this book since its very beginning. Gracias! Thanks also to Helen Verran for providing years of support and for beginning a conversation on methods with Brit years earlier, a conversation that traveled from Melbourne University to the Ethnography Studio at Rice.

The Anthropology Department, the Humanities Research Center, and the School of Social Sciences have supported the Ethnography Studio since its arrival at Rice University in 2012. A special thank-you goes to Nia Georges, Altha Rodgers, and Addison Verger for helping us materialize our ideas and for supporting the Studio as a unique pedagogical and collaborative space. Joe Vicich has lent his graphic talents to give the Studio a distinct graphic aesthetic. The Ethnography Studio has been built by a number of amazing graduate-student coordinators over the years: Kristin Gupta, Tim Quinn, and Gebby Kenny; Mel Ford and Katie Ulrich; Baird Campbell and Eliot Storer; Adam Webb-Orenstein, and Katelyn Parady. Over the past decade, all our faculty guests and student participants, from various departments and universities, have not only provided inspiration but contributed energy and labor to the Studio's unique sense of collegiality and creativity. Thank you all for everything you give!

We also thank all members of the ETHOS Lab at the IT University of Copenhagen (ITU) for their continuous inspiration on why experiments in analysis matter. Thanks to the Navigating Complexity students; you have figured as an important imagined audience for this book. Also at ITU, we thank all members of the Data as Relation project: John Mark Burnett, Marisa Cohn, Rachel Douglas-Jones, Mark Elam, Christopher Gad, Morten Hjelholt, Michael Hockenhull, Bastian Jørgensen, James Maguire, Christina Neumayer, Mace Ojala, Irina Papazu, Lise Røjskjær, Lucca Rossi, Jannick Schou, and Laura Watts. Anna Sommer has provided incredible administrative support. Thank you to the Data as Relation advisory board: Geof C. Bowker, Casper Bruun Jensen, Adrian Mackensie, and Evelyn Ruppert.

Also, our gratitude goes to the Velux Foundation (funding ID 12823) for cofunding editorial assistance and for making Andrea's workshop on analytic moves in Copenhagen possible. The Technologies in Practice research group continues to be an amazing nest from which to fly out and come back. Thank you all for such inspirational research and pedagogy.

Without the editorial assistance and reviewing efforts of Clément Dréano, Lea Enslev, Mel Ford, Markus Rudolfi, Caroline Anne Salling, and Katie Ulrich the book would still be in the proverbial drawer. Thank you for your incisive thinking and for embodying the best possible form of collaborative writing. Kregg Hetherington offered a careful reading of the introduction and provided sharp insights on the project as a whole. Marilyn Strathern remains a crucial inspiration for this book, and we cannot thank her enough for her thoughts and words, and for sharing tea and biscuits with us along with a wondrous conversation on the pasts and futures of ethnographic thinking.

At Duke, Gisela Fosado and Alejandra Mejía kept the project going with patience and wisdom as we aligned more than thirty contributors from various continents, career stages, and academic backgrounds. Susan Albury led the production project, helping us navigate all of the challenges a volume with so many contributors creates. Also thank you to Michael Fischer and Joe Dumit for welcoming this contribution into the Experimental Futures book series. Crucially, we were able to enroll the support of Rice University, University of California Davis, ITU Copenhagen and MIT to make this publication open access. We want to recognize their support for open scholarship. We are very excited for the book to circulate as widely as possible through as many academic exchange networks as possible.

For each of the authors who put their energy and creativity into this book, we are profoundly thankful. Your generosity in responding to the somewhat unorthodox structure of this project is evidence of what is best in the academic worlds we inhabit and build every day. Thank you for signing up with openness, flexibility, and humor. And most importantly, thank you for your academic friendship; we have learned immensely from each of you.

Finally, Rob, Frijol, Sigga, Jonathan, and Thomas, who were and continue to be there, creating worlds and revealing the rich relations upon which we live, flourish, lose, and experience global pandemics.

ANDREA BALLESTERO AND
BRIT ROSS WINTHEREIK

Analysis as Experimental Practice

This collection grapples with analysis as a constitutive process of ethnographic work. It picks up where most discussions on ethnography as a form of knowledge production stop: the point at which we are called to specify how we perform analysis. If analysis is the practice of immersing oneself in ethnographic materials in order to transform them into insights that are not automatically apparent, how exactly does that alchemical process play out? Contributors in this book take a radically ethnographic approach to answer this question. They examine their own analytic practices and thinking habits to offer conceptual and practical insights into analysis as a practice that unfolds in concrete social, material, and political contexts. That is, instead of developing a universalized discussion of analysis as an abstract category of thought, each chapter engages with analysis as a concrete mode of action, laying out the specific moves of a particular analytic experiment. Put differently, each of the contributors theorizes the process of analysis by performing it. The result is something akin to a guide, a companion for the reader to borrow thinking habits they can adjust and make their own.

In this introduction we frame the analytic experiments the contributors offer by laying out the distinct approach the collection follows. To begin, let's consider a familiar (but hypothetical) figure: an ethnographer. She is going through her research materials once again. She is immediately immersed in the worlds she wants to learn more about and in the worlds out of which she conducts her inquiry. Those various worlds may overlap geographically, or they may not. She thinks alongside collaborators of various sorts: friends, interlocutors, authors, ancestors, advisors. She goes through sound files, notes, memories, stories, found and constructed objects. She mobilizes categories that she has inherited: kinship, religion, technology, law, embodiment, colonization, territory. She borrows other categories: biopolitics, capital, cyborg, naturecultures, governance, becomings, rhizome. Additionally, in the past ten years, our ethnographer has encountered new ethnographic labs, studios, and collaboratories where experiments with media, narrative genre, and the creation of new publics proliferate. And yet, amid all of that richness of resources, she is still after something that remains unruly and often is collapsed into preexisting theoretical concepts: an explicit take on analytic practice.

Our ethnographer is after a form of analysis that creates an opening for making sense of something that she cannot fully anticipate, despite having a fleeting sense of its presence. During her training, there was little discussion about how to establish and navigate that analytic opening. She learned to mobilize categories such as scale, time, process, and relations to craft a theoretical parallax or a provocation (Ballestero 2015). She learned techniques for interviewing, notetaking, coding, categorization, and data visualization (LeCompte and Schensul 1999; Bernard 2006; Lave 2011). She has also learned to think about the affective power of literary moves and poetic licenses (MacGranahan 2020; Pandian and McLean 2017). But the opening she is after is elusive. It is difficult to pinpoint because it can emerge at any phase of the research process and can take a variety of forms. Throughout her training, our hypothetical ethnographer was told that such an analytic opening could appear serendipitously, emerge after long periods of staring at the blank page, irrupt in conversations with colleagues, hit her emotionally in the field, or transpire from cyclical recodings of her notes and rewritings of her narrative. Furthermore, to generate said opening, she might even have to "go back" to the field to conduct follow-up research. She has also heard many ethnographers praise beautiful writing, detecting an intrinsic ascription: if you have literary skill, analytic power follows.

Our hypothetical ethnographer may observe that these takes on analysis can result in a dual and contradictory mystification. On the one hand, they can turn analysis into an ethereal process that depends on a creative and affective spark, made explicit only through the craft of writing, and that can never be systematized without exhausting it. On the other hand, they can turn analysis into a mechanical procedure that flattens the richness of our ethnographic encounters, creating a subject-object partition through practices of capture, breaking down, and dissection (Holbraad et al. 2018, 19). This book challenges both forms of mystification and does not assume analysis has to be an intractable creative process or a violent mechanistic procedure. Rather, we argue that analysis is a creative and organized process of generating insights. It is a process that can be full of space for imaginative thinking while resolutely grounded in a distinct understanding of empirics that is thoroughly ethnographic. In our rendering, analysis is a practice by which we can intensify the conceptual creativity and relational commitments that sit at the core of ethnography in its best forms. Thus the purpose of this book is to offer ways to perform this form of analysis in a way that allows us to stay steadfastly bound to the creative and inventive edge of ethnographic knowledge production. Our aim is to refuse to black-box analysis as something that is, in the best case, inaccessible, happening in the background as you do other things, and in the worst case, a violent imposition of hegemonic thought. Quite to the contrary, the authors in this collection take analysis as a process that entails careful and deliberate crafting. This process is one with fieldwork experiences, interpersonal relations, institutional and organizational settings, and the material, historical, and conceptual infrastructures on which all research depends.

OPENING ANALYSIS

As you go through the chapters in this collection, you will see that the contributors operate under the assumption that analysis is an exercise in seeking an unanticipated insight—something that could have not been predicted with existing categories yet nevertheless depends on them. Collectively, contributors see analysis as a means to approach something that lies beyond the "predictable and the uncertain" and sits in the "space of excess, of telling us more than we knew to ask" (McGranahan 2018, 7). This does not imply that analysis is always about pursuing the new. It does mean, however, that analysis seeks ways of noticing that which seems to be there in one's materials and relations but cannot be immediately articulated as such. In this sense, ethnographic analysis shares a lot with what the Nigerian poet Ben Okri (1997) refers to as the quickening of the unknown. Jane Guyer (2013) elaborates on Okri's usage of the notion of quickening by noting how it does not refer to speed but rather to something else, to the enlivening of an unknown, marking its presence by drawing it into recognizable existence. Veena Das (2018) uses the language of concepts and the production of anthropological texts to make a similar point. She notes that ethnographic analysis flourishes when it works through "singular concepts [. . .] whose mode of generality is different from that of comparison between different objects or cases" (10). A singular concept is not meaningful because it illustrates a typified series, for example, a new ethnographic example of coming-of-age rituals, human-nonhuman relations, or settler colonialism. Rather, the power of singularity lies in how ethnography enlivens a concept itself, becoming its flesh (Das 2018, 10) and thus bringing it into existence in a different manner than how it previously was. In this sense, "what counts as empirical [in ethnographic knowledge production] already bears the imprint of the conceptual" (11), and, at the same time, what is conceptual is given life and existence through the empirical charge of ethnographic relations. Thus ethnographic analysis at its best enlivens thought and concepts through a type of singularity that cannot be reduced to an example or an instantiation of a predetermined category.

This notion of analysis as the process of enlivening concepts frames a necessary question that ethnographers in anthropology do not discuss often: By what specific procedures or habits of thought does that quickening, enlivening, or opening happen? If analysis is a concrete process of opening our insights, we should see it happening in particular times and places and through concrete means (e.g., writing, conducting fieldwork, following protocols, reorganizing materials). Concretely, this enlivening unfolds in a condition of immersion that yields an ethnographic effect (Strathern 1999). Immersion in the worlds that we want to make sense of, and immersion in the act of producing knowledge, with all its inherited instruments (Helmreich 2007), and political entanglements and implications. But immersion can easily become drowning if it is not crafted with embodied and theoretical skill. It is not uncommon for ethnographers to have a moment of feeling drowned by the rich and extensive reach of ethnographic relations that our work enacts. Each of the chapters in this book offers one concrete way to dwell in generative immersion rather than drown.

Along with fieldwork, theory, writing, and method, analysis is part of a semantic cloud that orients research design, fieldwork, and narrative composition. The necessity or impossibility of establishing borders between these concepts has historically generated deep intellectual discussions.[1] In this book we do not focus on this kind of boundary-making, for numerous reasons. First, the contributors come from various intellectual traditions and would arrange those concepts, and their boundaries, in very different configurations according to their own epistemic commitments. Thus, presenting a unified theory of what analysis is and where it sits in relation to method or writing would imply a kind of homogeneity that does not adequately capture the rich diversity that this collection highlights. Another reason for avoiding establishing boundaries is that we deliberately engage analysis as a historically specific exercise that channels our attention to grasp something in the world that at first seems elusive. We do not take analysis as an abstract category in need of definition but consider it a historically and materially grounded practice. Consequently, we have designed the book so that each chapter enlivens the concept of analysis through the singularity of the concrete historic form the author gives to analytic practice. As a result, we bracket what for some is a necessary place to begin: the question of what analysis is. Instead of asking "what is analysis," this book engages with the question of "*how* is analysis," and it offers nineteen answers.

Finally, asking "how is analysis" instead of "what is analysis" prevents us from reducing analytic practice to a transitional stage between fieldwork and theory, something to get over quickly, a mere point of passage before settling on an empirical finding or category. That rush to pass through analysis feeds into the desire to produce insights that travel quickly, usually in the form of a concept or argument, so that they can be "applied" to other cases. Through nominalist categories or propositional statements, these traveling insights promise to move seamlessly across contexts and among readers, losing in the process the lively power of their singularity. Each of the chapters in this collection expands the duration of analysis through concrete experiments designed to draw on ethnographic liveliness, quicken conceptual power, and open space for that which could not be anticipated. These experiments open up space to cultivate the incredible power of ethnographic knowledge forms while embracing the interpersonal commitments of our research practice as inherent to its analytic power.

THE TIMESPACE OF ANALYSIS

It is possible to think that in order to "make space" for this kind of analytic singularity it is necessary to "make time," that is, to carve out hours in the calendar. But making space does not necessarily mean adding more hours to the workday or more days to the research schedule. As ethnographers ourselves, we are in no way strangers to the pressures of the neoliberal university or to the demands for quick, actionable knowledge outside of it. Furthermore, the SARS-Cov2 pandemic that began in 2020 once again sharply revealed the gendered, classed, and racialized conditions that structure not only social relations but academic inquiry globally. Nevertheless, we do not argue for a return to some idealized era when thinking was supposedly an intrinsically slow and egalitarian practice. What we are proposing are a series of techniques to help craft the conditions for enlivening analytic insights through experiments that create a distinct timespace. An example might help bring our point home.

Let us think with the well-known notion of the dazzle, an idea that Marilyn Strathern (1999) put forward twenty years ago to describe being grabbed by an image from fieldwork and being unable to let it go. The notion of being dazzled has traveled widely, and many refer to it to capture powerful moments when ethnographic research puts in front of us something that arrests our imagination, a situation in which we are entrapped in the net of another world (Wagner 2001; Corsín Jiménez and Nahum-Claudel 2019). Although this notion has been widely embraced, something is lost when the "dazzle" is transplanted into a new ethnographic context. The dazzle was a singular response to a particular ethnographic encounter; it was not meant to become an abstract concept to be dis-embedded and re-embedded as if it could be seamlessly transplanted into any context. For Strathern, the notion of the dazzle was a way of suspending the grip of the ethnographer's theoretical models, halting what she already knew and what she thought she should focus on, in the face of an encounter that required she make sense of it on its own terms. The idea of being dazzled offered a timespace for the bodily labor of analysis to unfold—the tasks of organizing interviews, composing index cards, crafting vignettes. This kind of labor pauses the thinking body, slowing down thoughts that rush ahead to make the encounter fit under preexisting categories. As Strathern notes, the dazzle created suspension to deal with the problem that "as soon as you drop one theory, another rushes in. [This is the problem:] that one never has an empty head. There's always something to fill it with and it'll be common sense if it's nothing else."[2] Ultimately, it is by crafting this kind of suspended analytic timespace that one can precipitate that sense of immersion that allows one to approximate the elusive ethnographic insight, to precipitate the enlivening of our sense-making process.

It is this notion of a timespace for suspension that this collection puts at the center of the systematized but messy labor of analysis. This entails committing oneself to analysis-as-craft, in kinship with the Greek concept of *technē*. In this rendering, analysis is a practice where bodies, instruments, theories, debts, curiosities, and responsibilities coalesce around the desire to make something present, to draw something into being. This practice depends on cutting-edge and rudimentary tools: it can be achieved with index cards, data visualization software, handwriting, and satellite images alike. What is inescapable, though, is that analysis-as-craft is not invention out of thin air, nor is it flat reproduction of the already known. It cannot be reduced to developing better observational skills, precise data collection techniques, or more accurate abstractions. Nor is it enough to write evocative texts. It is not about choosing a theorist in advance or claiming to have no theoretical preferences. Analysis transpires at the intersection of many of these and according to the specific problems and questions at hand.

The contributions in this book embody this idea of analysis-as-craft and translate it into a series of techniques to generate suspension, to expand the timespace of analysis. Each of the techniques you will encounter is an experiment to wonder, a process that depends on a "certain duration so that doubt and confusion can endure long enough to allow qualitative leaps and contradictions in our sense-making" (Ballestero 2019, 32). This kind of wonder is possible when conditions for structured play are put in place (Fortun 2009). Furthermore, we understand these conditions as ways of "staying with the trouble" (Haraway 2016) and directing our analytic movement athwart (Helmreich 2009). They are the conditions of possibility for finding companion concepts (Winthereik 2019), embracing unwanted afterlives (Murphy 2017b), and experimenting with kinky forms of empiricism (Rutherford 2012). Each technique offers an opportunity to co-labor (De la Cadena 2015) with what peers and interlocutors share with us.

ANALYTIC PRACTICE IN COMPANIONSHIP

We invite readers to think about this volume as a companion to analysis. A companion text sits somewhere between handbook and guidebook, and this collection fulfills that sense of the term. It has been conceived as a resource to turn to for concrete suggestions on how to begin or continue ethnographic analysis. But companionship is also a particular type of relationality. It is a form of copresence that entails proximity during highs and lows. Not devoid of asymmetries or completely smooth, companionship entails a persistence across the waves of events that populate our lives. This book came into being in that kind of companionship.

In spring 2016 we held a workshop through the Ethnography Studio (www.ethnographystudio.org) that Andrea runs. The workshop explored notions of intervention and collaboration through the Skyspace, an

FIGURE I.1 *Twilight Epiphany* (2012), the James Turrell Skyspace at the Suzanne Deal Booth Centennial Pavilion at Rice University. Photo by Florian Holzherr. Courtesy of Rice Public Art.

installation by artist James Turell (figure I.1) at the Rice University campus.[3] We had already initiated a conversation to connect the Studio with the ETHOS Lab (https://ethos.itu.dk/) that Brit led at the IT University of Copenhagen, and this was the first opportunity for a joint event. One of the reasons why we chose the Skyspace stemmed from what ethnographers learn early in their practice: they have to work with what is there. They cannot always catch a spectacular event or craft an experimental setup while doing fieldwork. The Skyspace offered an opportunity to experiment with how to think with something that was just there, however spectacular it is.

As an art piece, the Skyspace becomes breathtaking at dawn and dusk when a light show transforms, softly but continuously, the ceiling of the structure by changing its color and with it the visitor's perception of the sky that is visible through an opening at its center. Our workshop did not take place at any of those times. Thus, the time we spent inside the Skyspace was not exactly breathtaking. Like so many instances of ethnographic research, nothing eventful seemed to happen while we were there. We—Andrea, Brit, and a group of graduate students—stayed inside the installation for approximately fifteen minutes; some of us sat on the granite benches designed for audiences to see the light show, while others climbed to the second level. We were all trying to be fully present, as ethnographers would. As we attuned our senses to our surroundings what we captured was the sound of motorized lawn mowers circling the structure, the sirens of ambulances rapidly approaching the medical center across the street, and the conversations among students from the music school briskly cutting across the installation to make it to class on time. Any unique insight about intervention, collaboration, or noticing (the keywords in the title of the workshop) that we wished to generate out of the experience would need considerable intellectual labor to be drawn out. And yet, despite its lack of dazzle, being there was not a completely flat experience. Our imagination was cautiously enlivened with potentialities as we noticed threads: the aesthetics of higher education in the US, the burdens of labor on immigrant bodies, the motorized lawn mower as a technological device, the rhythms of sound, and the practice of listening.

After the workshop was over, as we debriefed, the conversation circled back to the questions of what role analytic practices have in ethnography and how they help open up ethnographic encounters that (1) are far from exceptional occurrences, (2) feel more like unremarkable events waiting to be untangled, and yet, (3) tease our imagination with something that needs to be deciphered even if it cannot be immediately articulated. Our thinking about this kind of ethnographic encounter was inspired by feminist and STS (science and technology studies) scholars who have taught us that the world is not a flat or passive entity available for reflection at the will of a disembodied and "objective" explorer (Daston and Galison 1992; Harding 2015; Noble 2016; TallBear 2019). Considering these epistemic affinities and the fact that both of us did ethnographic fieldwork in what could be classified as unremarkable settings (e.g., office spaces, meetings, documents, laboratories), we wondered about the techniques we used to craft the sense of exceptional analytic openness that we so often experienced in our ethnographic work. We quickly arrived at a rich array of resources that anthropologists have developed to address the three issues that dominate discussions about ethnography: fieldwork, theory, and writing (Clifford and Marcus 1986; Hammersley and Atkinson 1995; Boellstorff et al. 2012; Nielsen and Rapport 2017; Estalella and Criado 2018; Hegel, Cantarella, and Marcus 2019). And yet, we craved resources that focused on analysis as a practice that does not fall into cognitivist or mechanical territories but can, nevertheless, be engaged as an organized and methodical process.

In searching for those resources, we were struck by many ethnographers using their creativity to design techniques to conduct the kind of analysis that captured our imagination. Those techniques, however, had remained unpublished for the most part and did not circulate as widely as resources on qualitative methods or ethnographic writing have. Our own experiences in the Ethnography Studio and ETHOS Lab were evidence of this: while we had designed a number of analytic experiments with our students, they remained unpublished and circulated only within small circles. At that moment, we could think of two exceptions: the "Implosion" exercise as conceived by Donna Haraway and developed by Joe Dumit (2014), and Kim Fortun's (2009) "Figuring Out Ethnography" memo system. Both of these had indeed traveled widely in anthropology and STS, filling an important gap and becoming part of many methods and research-design courses. We knew that many more analytic experiments like those were happening around us; a good number of researchers were developing analytic techniques and collaborations to engage ethnographic materials in generative and open-ended forms. Many of those were connected to a proliferation of centers, labs, and studios that have emerged recently, and yet, there were no sources where they could be consulted.

That is how this book emerged: out of the desire for a companion to analytic practices that preserves the open-ended and creative forms of thinking we were fond of and that brings together many of the inventive techniques ethnographers have produced to recapture analysis. We reached out to colleagues whose work we had found particularly inspiring and invited them to join us in creating the companion we wished for. The invitation was not without requirements. First, we asked the contributors to produce pieces that were shorter than a standard academic text—no more than four thousand words. We also asked them to include in their chapters a description or example of how they used the technique they were sharing.[4] The texts had to show by doing. And finally, we requested they condense their technique into a set of instructions, something we decided to call an "analytic protocol."

ANALYTIC PROTOCOLS

Our decision to use the concept of an analytic protocol links this collection to the tumultuous history of experimental spaces in laboratories and experimental settings (Rheinberger 1997; Latour 1999; Tilley 2011; Kowal, Radin, and Reardon 2013; Davies et al. 2018; Wolfe 2018). In those spaces, a protocol is the experimenter's purported practical guide to generating new insights while following standardized steps from one iteration to the next.

But that connection does not imply that the authors in this book replicate the premises that shape the use of protocols in those settings. In particular, we wanted to work with the figure of the protocol while also refusing to reproduce the violent, extractivist, and essentializing legacies it carries. As we finish this book, the protocol has become part of our everyday lives as governments depend on its form to handle contagion and reshape social interactions in public spaces. At the time we were conceiving this book, however, we moved carefully wanting to generate straightforward, almost telegraphic, sets of instructions—something like condensed versions of broader analytic trajectories that offered orientations but could never be taken as comprehensive, totalizing. We also knew that a protocol is probably an imperfect name for what the authors are offering. Calling a technique designed to open up analytic possibilities a "protocol" can potentially bring to mind a sense of closure, of decontextualized repetition. And yet, we committed to it as a way to work from within its constraints to show how fixed structures provide space for improvisation and inventiveness.

As we deploy the notion of a protocol, we also refuse the fiction of pure replicability, rejecting any connotations of a protocol as a device to close off variation. Instead of disciplined reduction to secure replicable results, the protocols the authors have crafted set up conditions to create analytic timespace. The protocols help suspend the rush. They create the conditions to slow the urge to swiftly elucidate an ethnographic puzzle or pin down a slippery encounter. They do so by increasing analytic duration, enlivening ethnographic singularities. Protocols invoke a sense of organized reflection that, we argue, is essential for the unruly creativity of ethnographic analysis to flourish. Thus, although the idea of a protocol might elicit suspicion, we want to hold on to that feeling. We mobilize it to explore the power of ethnographic thinking in suspension of both "assumptions and disbelief" in order to allow different arrangements and possibilities to emerge (Choy and Zee 2015). After all, suspicion and suspension share a lot and warrant joint consideration. The urgent demands we face require this kind of creativity.

As you go through the pages in this companion to analysis, you will feel summoned by some protocols but not others. You might decide to experiment with a technique that does not seem to fit very well with your questions, or, conversely, you might want to go directly to the ones that intuitively make sense. Regardless of where you choose to begin, the techniques and their protocols will give you a starting point for creatively adjusting them according to the specific questions at stake. The power of the techniques these protocols embody is that they are deeply explorative and experimental while also being structured and methodical.

We have grouped the protocols into four clusters according to how they carry out the work of suspension. In part I, you will find the techniques that center on forms of bodily labor, representation, or both. The chapters in part II all involve handling, comparing, and designing physical objects. Part III contains techniques that gain their efficacies through infrastructures, digital or otherwise. And last, in part IV you will find techniques that toy with incommensurabilities and with the (im)possibility of overcoming them during analysis. Two afterwords close the collection in lieu of a conclusion. Written by four researchers that were PhD students at the time, the afterwords frame the analytic techniques in the context of their pedagogical trajectory, crafting their own ethnographic projects for the first time. One of the pieces engages the chapters from a pre-fieldwork perspective and the other, post-fieldwork. The overall organization of the book is a temporary grouping, a transitional order that does not exhaust the techniques, what they have in common, or what makes them different. We hope you enjoy playing with the possibilities this companion to analysis opens. Each chapter and its protocol is an invitation to cultivate the unique analytic power of ethnographic knowledge production. We extend each chapter as a lasting invitation to enliven the singularity of analysis in your own research and pedagogical practice.

NOTES

1. In the US tradition, this was already a worry of Boas, who early on challenged the role of preexisting categories as ordering devices because they reduced cultural traits to isolated examples, erasing their real meaning, which had to be elucidated via their historical integration into particular cultural wholes. Since then, the articulation of empirics, method, theory, and writing has been at the core of anthropology's debates around knowledge production.

2. Marilyn Strathern, personal communication, November 2017.

3. The workshop consisted of several parts: a preparatory visit to the artwork by Andrea and Brit, a short introductory presentation for students, a collective visit by workshop participants to the Skyspace, and a discussion in the Anthropology Department's seminar room.

4. We subjected ourselves to the same restriction and kept this introduction within the four-thousand-word limit as well.

PART I

BODILY PRACTICES AND RELOCATIONS

....

CHAPTER 1

PATRICIA ALVAREZ ASTACIO

Tactile Analytics

Touching as a Collective Act

Playing with the small, knitted swatch of alpaca wool in my hand, I lost track of time. The small piece of textile had become a riddle for me. The swatch was made up of rice stitches overlaid with a large diamond shape that formed a braided design. I kept feeling the weave, the tautness of each knot, rubbing my fingers back and forth. But at first my touch was blind to the culture and craft of the artisan's work. It would take me months to learn to feel the material qualities of alpaca wool, to appreciate the knowledge conveyed through touch. The knitted surface was as important as the design; it interlaced sociocultural negotiations, histories, and layers of meaning (Alvarez Astacio 2015). To appreciate the density of this surface, I had to learn a different form of touch that could recognize the ontological complexity of this material surface. At the very least, I need to recognize the gap between my own conditioned tactility and that which is materialized in alpaca textiles.

Within the fashion industry, alpaca wool is considered a luxury material; it is softer, lighter, and stronger than cashmere or sheep wool. Alpaca wool garments and accessories are especially valued for their ability to trigger imaginaries of pristine Andean indigenous communities. They are marketed as eco-friendly, long-lasting, and resistant to stains, odors, flames, and wrinkles. Alpaca wool is indeed a high-quality material, valued by twenty-first-century consumers and contemporary indigenous artisans in the highlands, but for different reasons.

Between 2010 and 2012, I spent twenty months following the supply chain of alpaca wool from artisanal workshops in the rural highlands of

Huancavelica and Cusco to fashion markets in Lima. I came to realize that in the Peruvian highlands the value of alpacas and their wool goes beyond economic remuneration.[1] Artisans insisted on how special this material was and what made it valuable *to them*, rather than focusing on what made the alpaca wool valuable to trendy shops in Lima, London, or Paris. Alpaca wool, I learned, is a material that traverses disparate systems of value and ontological realms. These different worlds and systems of signification are encoded in ways of touching that required me to learn to touch differently. How do we take touch seriously? How do we learn to experience and decipher what is coded in tactility? How could I approach such diverse forms of touch from my own limited tactile knowledge? Was there a method that could help me?

Sitting in the artisanal workshop, I wrapped the knitted square of alpaca wool around my fingers until they felt too warm. I laid it on the palm of my hand, focusing on the empty spaces between knotted threads. With my finger I traced pathways along the striated surface of the weave, hoping to uncover something. I tried to recognize the subtleness of the artisan's skill. I stretched the wool and let it fall back into its original square shape. The swatch was undeniably soft, with a bouncy, cushion-like feel. Almost unconsciously, and against the instruction of the artisans who encouraged this exercise, I kept bringing the swatch close to my eyes, hoping that my sight would aid my touch and reveal what I should be able to know through my skin.

FIGURE 1.1 Close up of alpaca crochet textile detail being made for a garment. *Entretejido* (2015) film still.

The quiet laughter of the women around me pulled me away from my microscopic inspection; the artisans were amused by my clumsy interaction with the wool. I was missing the point of the exercise. Without stopping her knitting, Mama Carmelina said, "Señorita, you need to touch, feel the wool, to understand it." I was failing to allow a tactile conversation with the wool to unfold. If I wanted to come into contact with the multiple ontological worlds and the political, aesthetic, and economic systems of value this wool had traversed, I needed to learn a new skin-based dialogue—one beyond the primacy of sight—that demanded an experience different from how my senses had been acculturated.

As my research continued, the synesthetic connection between touch and sight became clear. This was not the hapticity I was used to, the one espoused by impressionist painters seeking to represent a touch that penetrated the reality of representation itself (McLuhan 2005), nor the one found in our consumer culture that treats touch as a medium of sensory persuasion deployed to generate affectivity, intimacy, immediacy, and a pleasurable encounter with products (Ewen 1990; Green and Jordan 2002; Howes 2005; Postrel 2004).[2] I wasn't being asked to touch with my eyes or to translate through my eyes what I was touching. This tactile encounter wasn't meant to be intimate and immediate, but to be complex, collective, and full of history. Touch is a complex *multi*sensory way of knowing. Yet, I felt illiterate, dependent on the crutches of the pleasure of the softness, the immediacy of the experience, or a kind of rational analysis of pure technique.

Knowing well that I was confronting a limit—what Marisol de la Cadena (2015) calls the "incommensurability of radical difference" and Laura Marks describes as "the limits of sensory translation" (2000)—I faced the problem of engaging ethnographically and analytically with this way of knowing that I barely had words to convey or translate into more quotidian forms of analysis. How could I delve analytically into this sensorial world? How can we approach the textural without giving primacy to our Western knowledge-eye? How can we stop "seeing" as both a visual act and a way of knowing, and open ourselves to feeling as an act brimming with knowledge, affect, and social and individual memory?

TEXT, TEXTURE, TEXTILE

Back at home, my fingers curved over my laptop's keyboard while I tried to recall my sensorial encounters in the Andes, I turned to my samples of alpaca and wool textiles I had brought back with me from the field. They now felt differently than they had in the Andean workshops. During my time with the artisans, I had become the official wool detangler, repeating the exercise described above a multitude of times as I learned different stitch patterns and how to recognize some of the alpaca types by touch. Now, my tingling fingertips remembered this training, triggering memories including the sensorial. The usual modes of representing such knowledge felt inadequate, too removed. I began looking for different ways to trigger a sensorial recollection that might stimulate an analytic process.

The words *text*, *texture*, and *textile* all share the same Latin root, *textere*, "to weave." Rather than regarding text as weaving, weaving is treated as something else to read. The Western Enlightenment tradition we have inherited defines touch, smell, and taste as "lower" senses, pathways to pleasure and emotion, not knowledge. Knowledge is the realm of sight and sound, the senses of rational thought. Still today, our education system prioritizes sight and hearing as the routes to knowledge, relegating the lower senses as external to learning processes (Classen 1999). Scholars have thus treated textiles hermeneutically, focusing on unpacking the symbolic and social meanings of textiles or providing detailed descriptions of techniques. Even popular knitting magazines and YouTube tutorials approach weaving through the logic of reading. You can look at diagrams, or read or listen to step-by-step instructions on when to loop or pull, with little regard for the subtleties of hand movement or material qualities. Such methods foreclose the recognition of multisensory ways of knowing through touch and reinforce that the epistemological value of tactility is obtained through vision-language.

Using tactile practices as another form of field notes did not mean I was simply reading the textiles or reviewing my notes; I sought a more complex and active analysis that included the specificity of the fiber, the embodied practice of weaving, sensible tactile elements, and their semiotic resonances. Moving beyond interpretation, I wanted to immerse myself in touch—even if only to touch a limit. This was my attempt to treat knowledge as multisensorial and to engage my acculturated perceptual system in more "attuned" ways (Ingold 2000), reminding myself that "the senses are a source of social knowledge" (Marks 2000).

But I still struggled with how to achieve this tactile immersion. Readings across anthropology and science and technology studies of the senses gave me a deeper understanding of how forms of knowledge can insist on analytical extension into our senses and bodies. Anthropologists have

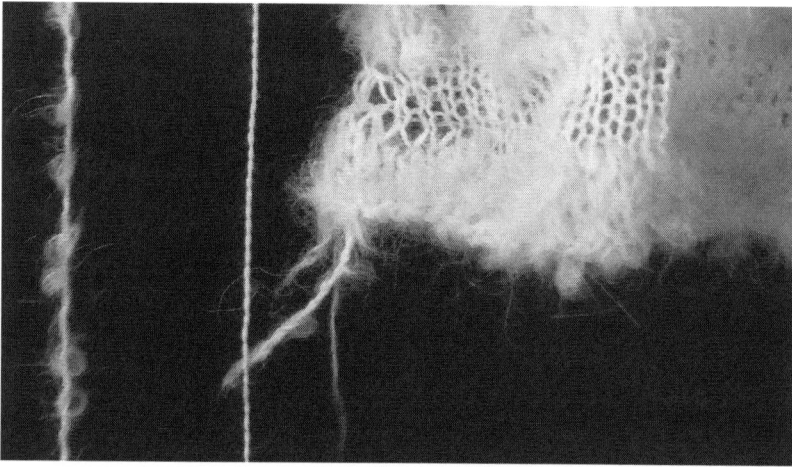

FIGURE 1.2 Close up of the threads and textures of alpaca wool textile. Photo by author.

long explored how sensory experience is not natural or precultural, but permeated with social values specific to historical and cultural settings (Howes 1991; Classen 1993; Feld 1996; Stoller 1997; Geurts 2002). Contemporary ethnographies on various forms of scientific knowledge production further compelled me to engage in my own "haptic creative" explorations (Myers and Dumit 2011). As ethnographers realized that *forms of knowing* in the sciences rely as much on the sensorial abilities of scientists (and other practitioners) as they do on technological instruments and detached forms of observation and data analysis, new methods and analytics were called for.[3] Ethnographers had to learn "how to *move with and be moved by* the energetics, affects, and movements" (Myers 2012) they encountered in their research, from the development of molecular models and interactive cave automatic virtual computerized active visualization environment systems to submarine soundscapes, atmospheric environments, and cellular, bacterial, plant, and mycological research (Helmreich 2007; Myers and Dumit 2011; Paxson 2013; Myers 2015; Tsing 2015; Choy 2016, 2018). The need for these new forms of sensorial engagement is reflected in Michelle Murphy's statement: "I am looking for words, protocols, and methods that might honor the inseparability of bodies and land, and at the same time grapple with the expansive chemical relations of settler colonialism that entangle life forms in each other's accumulations, conditions, possibilities and miseries" (2017a, 498). The need articulated by these scholars to train their sensoriums, to "read with our senses attuned to stories told in otherwise muted registers" (Hustak and Myers 2012), resonated with what felt like my own tactile analytic limits. Myers's (2014) invitation for us to cultivate our inner plant as a way to "consider trying on the habits, comportments, and sensitivities of other bodies" and the deployment of improvisation techniques by Dumit (2017) and his colleagues (Dumit, O'Connor, Drum, and McCullough 2018) sparked ideas of how to begin making sense of my own encounters with alpaca wool and tactile knowledge.

Moreover, many of these scholars also bridge the gap between the hard sciences and social sciences by bringing the scientific literature into conversation with anthropology. This nexus between the scientific literature and anthropology clearly helped further their methodological and analytic explorations. Thus, turning to the literature on the neuroscience of the somatosensory system was another significant strategy in helping me move past the analytic impasse I was facing and think otherwise about what's encoded in a touch. Both biology and anthropology affirm that we are synesthetic beings. Sensory information flows through and across various senses.[4] Today, touch—the first of the senses to form in utero—is considered to be part of the larger, more complex somatosensory system. Through our skin, the most complex perceptual structure in the body, we obtain information about pressure, pain, temperature, position, movement, and vibration.

I learned that tactile information travels to the brain through two pathways, which helps explain the limits of coming into touch with a different onto-material world and the dissonance I felt between my tactile memories from the field and touching the same alpaca textiles when I was at home. Through one route we obtain facts about touch: vibration, pressure, location, the fine texture of objects. The cortex builds tactile images that allow us to recognize the objects around us.[5] The second pathway communicates and determines the social and emotional content associated with touch. This information is coded in an area of the brain involved in higher-level functions associated with social bonding, allocating attention, reward-based learning, decision-making, ethics and morality, impulse control, emotions, and social evaluation. Because of this socioemotional pathway, touch can feel physically different on the basis of things such as social context, one's previous experiences, knowledge, and ethical stances. Thus the same stimuli, for example alpaca wool, can feel different because of the ways in which information about affect and social context are part of what and how we touch.

Our skin is the common border between the world and our bodies; it brings about the mingling among things in the world (Serres [1985] 2008). More than a vehicle for pleasure and displeasure, touch is a mode of being in the world. Jane Bennett (2010) invites us to consider the vitality of matter as a way of reflecting on the many ways bodies are "enmeshed in a dense network of relations" (13). Although she doesn't consider other ontological regimes, staying within a squarely Western framework, her conceptualization of a dense network of relations cuts across ontological and epistemological regimes, communicating a realm beyond words and visual representations. As Barad (2012) points out, the indeterminacy of touch means that we are also in touch with a realm of possibilities (past, present, future) and affective entanglements (social, political, historical). This immediacy of textural perception immerses us in a field of active narrative, a conceptual realm beyond the dualities of object and subject (Sedgwick 2003).

Touch is felt, but not fully grasped; its knowledge and experience exist at the limits of our usual representational practices. The immediacy and intimacy of touch are laden with interwoven strands of information and affect. Touch is never just about individual experience. The immediate reciprocity of sensation particular to any given encounter is also social and historic. To take multisensory forms of knowledge (like touch) seriously, we can't only stay in the realm of reading and interpretative analysis. Analytic attention to touch reminds us that it is not a passive act. Every touch always touches back.

RESENSING EXPERIMENTATIONS

Because I was studying an aesthetic terrain where the textures of knitted alpaca wool are laced with meaning and where tactile knowledge was deeply important, my first impulse was to turn to my own creative and aesthetic practices in order to open up my representational analytics. In the field, filmmaking is a central part of my research practice. This multimodal approach allows me to take advantage of the specificities of diverse mediums in order to engage my research material differently, including learning to listen with my skin. Multimodal approaches expand the purview of visual anthropology by deemphasizing the centrality of a finished product

PLEASE
TOUCH

FIGURES 1.3 AND 1.4 Stills from the interactive installation *Sintiendo el Tejido/Sensing the Woven* by the author in collaboration with Mozhdeh Matin and Cristina Flores Teves, presented at the 2012 Ethnographic Terminalia exhibit Audible Observations in San Francisco's SOMAarts Gallery.

(e.g., a film or installation). In doing so, we are encouraged to reflect on the possible mediums available and consider how we "work to engage and collaborate along media forms our interlocutors find relevant to their lives" (Collins, Durrington, and Gill 2017, 142). It is about being open to engaging in varying processes of knowledge production that can lead to multiple outcomes, meaningful interventions, unexpected collaborations, and innovative methods and analytic forms. More than a novel form of disseminating or representing anthropological knowledge, it can be seen as a *politics of invention* through which to open new ways of knowing and learning together, of rethinking anthropological practice so as to enact "new relations, new narratives, new possibilities" (Dattatreyan and Marrero-Guillamón 2019, 220). But multimodality can and should do more than provide a more diverse methodological and technological toolkit.

Alongside the potential created by new tools and methods, especially technological and digital ones, we must consider the *bad habitus* that multimodal interventions can reproduce, for example through the "reification of power hierarchies and privilege of technoscience that these tools and methods may enable" or by "dressing up neocolonial practices of extraction, inclusion and appropriation in a new language" (Takaragawa et al. 2019, 518). Thus, understanding our technologies (materially, socially, politically, economically) should shape how we critically engage with our practices in order to avoid causing "a mere stir within the same frame" (Chen and Minh-Ha 1994, 439).[6] For Pink (2013) the real potential of multimodality lies in new conceptualizations of ethnography, ethnographic knowing, and empathetic research practices. Keeping these considerations central to my praxis led me to approach multimodal work not as a way of narrowing the gap between documentation and lived experience, but as a way of opening up analytic ways apt for delving into touch. In an improvisational spirit, the camera surprisingly became an instinctual tool I could turn to as a means of immersing myself within my own tactile limits. The media work that emerges through these processes is not only illustrative but also a research product in its own right, which works dialectically with my scholarly writing and forms part of a broader analytic process.

Guiding me through what I couldn't understand through my hands, I developed a haptic visuality with my camera. Its images helped me play, replay, and explore the feel and material qualities of alpaca wool, embedded with the skill of artisans and excess semiotic and material meaning (see figures 1.1 and 1.2). The incommensurability of this sensorial encounter, exceeding translative processes, let loose and came to the fore in the editing room. The indexical excess of cinema and the hapticity of film helped me to explore this sensuous dimension of alpaca, to consider the resonant gaps between the immediacy of tactility, feeling the *longue durée* of history materialized and the limit of touching another ontological realm through a fiber. Unpacking the meaning(s) of wool was not the main intent; rather, I started focusing on exploring its uneasy meaningfulness as part of multiple yet interconnected worlds.

Although cinema can be used to deepen a haptic-optic encounter, bring our "fingereyes" (Hayward 2010) to bear, it still lacks the physicality of material and direct tactile encounter.[7] My desire to engage publics with woolen materiality animated me to collaborate with a Peruvian fashion designer and an artisan on an interactive installation (see figures 1.3 and 1.4). The installation reflected on how alpaca wool travels from the highlands to high-end boutiques, bringing Quechua-speaking herders and artisans together with fashion designers and anthropologist-artists like myself. The installation comprised three alpaca woven sculptural garments that deconstructed the weaving process. Each object represented a site along the supply chain: one of raw wool and a large swatch, another an unfinished sweater, and the last a completed sweater.

My collaborators were interested in exploring the disconnect between the consumption of objects and their socioeconomic production histories. We sought to reconnect objects to these histories, to move past the popular use of textures in advertising as mere ways of creating a pleasurable encounter with products, by inviting a tactile-auditory engagement with an object of consumption. As participants interacted with the objects, they activated touch-based sensors, triggering an audio landscape recorded at each production site. We wanted to mobilize an immediate experience of touch and soundscape that envelops the social interactions that make the existence of these garments possible.

Because our bodies grasp somatosensory stimuli differently depending on social context, we were interested in how participants in the US would connect to the tactile knowledge shared by my Peruvian interlocutors and how they would reflect on their own engagement with such garments. I often conversed with participants during their interactions, keeping records of their experiences and impressions. Some would discuss their knowledge of the Andes, woven together with intimate memories of their grandmothers who knit. Others reflected on the garment industry, highlighting an estranged intimacy unnoticed while out shopping, despite their knowledge of the labor and environmental issues that plague the industry. It was through this experience that I realized how such a performative engagement encouraged people to transform touch into a public and collective act. In doing so, the interaction with textiles ignited a skin-led dialogue that enmeshed knowledge, experience, material, individual and larger histories, and sociocultural processes. This experience also inspired me to use workshops as an analytic trigger outside my field site, drawing from some of the tactile exercises artisans taught me to do. I quickly realized that these workshops allowed me to stage sensorial interactions and analyses that aren't directed by data. What began as a methodological tool to help me trigger analysis became a collaborative space in which to collectively explore, analyze, and think through diverse modalities of sensory perception and multisensory ways of knowing. Although I later tailored these workshops to engage other objects and sensory experience such as smell, here I discuss an exercise related to touch.

The following "tactile essay" is an attempt to engage with touch as a collective experience rather than as an individual and immediate act. The aim of this 90- to 120-minute-long exercise is to produce a shared experience among participants through a guided sensorial exploration. Using a series of five to eight objects organized sequentially, participants will jointly create, or weave, a narrative that sparks the sensorial but also produces analysis with social, cultural, and political implications. In designing this exercise, I wanted to bring the entire body to bear in a collective reengagement with our sensory modalities and be open to potential analytic forms that can emerge.

An organizer needs to select and sequentially arrange a series of objects that will serve as the material basis of this "essay." The materiality of the objects will loosely shape discussion as they catalyze sensation. The sequentially arranged objects should be shielded from participants, who should not see what they are touching. Here, sight is decentered in order to minimize overreliance on visuality and ensure participants' focus on the objects' material and sensorial qualities. As participants blindly interact with the objects in the predetermined order, the meaning(s) obtained from this exercise will comprise impressions, associations, memories, sensations, interpretations, embodied reactions, and existing knowledge. All of these elements will come together later during a group discussion, forming a multilayered weave that accounts for and opens the door to a sensorial analytic that can go beyond interpretation. Participants might even enter into the realm of speculation, something that I have found can open the conversation into newer areas and expand our understanding of sensorial experience. Thus, although each participant will individually interact with the sequence, "meaning" will be woven through a collective discussion comprising associations, sensations, impressions, affects, and even memories. The goal is not just to come to any definitive conclusion about the object sequence or its significance.

I have done this exercise in various settings, including as a course assignment in which students had to select and organize the objects and lead the discussion. The selection and organization of objects done before the workshop is the most time-consuming part of this exercise. Here are two brief examples. I have done this exercise by selecting a sequence of textile-objects made from the same material but composed of different types of threads and knit swatches, and made through different manufacturing techniques. The dialogue that surged from students' blind interactions with these textiles touched on the themes of affect, consumption, materiality, and memory. A student who ran her textile essay as part of a senior seminar sought to stage an immersive engagement that explored the connection between affect, sensory modalities, and place. Focusing on the Santa Cruz beach boardwalk, her sequence of objects included a teddy bear, a jar containing salt water, a jar containing sand (to be touched after the water), followed by wet cloth. Among the other objects, she had stale fried food meant to be smelled. Dipping our fingers into the salt water and then into the sand made the sand stick to our hands, inflecting with a particular texture everything else we touched, including the subsequent discussion.

PROTOCOL

- Select a series of objects according to your interests and the conversation you want to have about the nuances of sensory modalities.
- When selecting the objects, be attentive to the types and combinations of shapes and textures. Consider the feelings, sensations, and meanings that can be elicited through textures, shapes, sounds, or even smells.
- As you organize the objects in a pointed yet open-ended sequence, think about how one sensory interaction can enhance, diminish, or alter the impressions of those that come before or after in the sequence.
- Have all participants sit in a circle.

- Without showing the objects to participants (you can ask them to close their eyes or place the objects in a box), begin passing around each object according to the order of the sequence.
- You may give instructions on how participants should interact with each object and emphasize that each participant should linger on the act of touching, concentrate on a specific attribute, or both.
- Prompt participants as they interact with an object: focus on particular qualities of the material; be attentive to feelings and sensations; keep track of memories, associations, or meanings that initially arise; and investigate how the memory of sensory stimuli changes as they move from object to object.
- Make sure everyone interacts with every object in the appropriate order.
- When everyone has interacted with the complete sequence of objects, ask participants to write down their responses and impressions.
- Begin the discussion.
  - Ask participants to reflect on the experience in general.
  - Solicit reactions to each object in sequential order.
  - Allow participants to respond to each other.
- Once everyone has shared their initial impressions with the group, reveal the objects to jumpstart the second part of the conversation.
  - Ask participants whether they identified overarching sensations or feelings and whether seeing the objects affected this. If so, how?
  - Guide this second part of the discussion beyond personal stories that come up: zoom out to the group to contemplate larger social, cultural, historic, political, and economic dimensions.
  - Be attentive to the moments and ways in which the conversation moves between symbolic associations and material descriptions.
  - When personal memories come up in the discussion, encourage the participants to engage with their own mnemonic association in order to allow a larger, more social weave of impressions to unfold.

- Dwell on the tension between the immediate and intimate felt experience and the object and its sociocultural history. Direct comments on materiality, for example, toward economic considerations: Does the object feel industrial or handmade, or a combination of both? What impressions or affects does the material composition elicit?
- Discuss how the objects convey information to us about a production history.
- Discuss how materials create particular textures, sounds, and so on, and how these affect sensation: What meanings were linked to which textures, sounds, smells?
- Delve into the relationship between meanings and felt sensations.
- You may wrap up the conversation by discussing how participants started sensing and arriving at certain meanings and associations: How did their sensations, impressions, memories shift and change as they went through the sequence? What about after they saw the objects? How did juxtaposition affect sensory experience? What happens during these sensory interactions across objects? How do objects speak to us, and under what constraints?

NOTES

1. Alpacas have been vital in sustaining human development at high altitudes. Many important cultural aspects circulate around alpacas, their care, and the products obtained from them. These animals are steeped in local ontologies existing in relation to *apus* (earth-beings), and other-earthly realms (*Ukhu Pacha*); they move between the realm where spirits communicate and human worlds (Flores 1968).

2. Some scholars argue that touch resists objectification, problematizing the relationship between touch and representation. Mazzio (2005) points out that touch is simultaneously physical and psychological, unmediated and immediate; it resists stasis and has no spatial medium. These qualities make it resistant to representation. For Classen (2005), being surrounded by many representations of touch that do not allow us to touch anything produces a sense of alienation.

3. Sensorial abilities involved in such systems of science-based knowledge production include kinesthetic, haptic, aural, and other synesthetic engagements or synesthetic reasons (Paxson 2013). I also want to point out how these scholars not only look at scientists but also account for other practitioners who engage with scientific knowledge, such as artisanal cheese makers or those involved in various institutional regulatory agencies, for example.

4. For example, perceptions of flavor arise from the central integration of peripherally distinct sensory inputs (taste, smell, texture, temperature, sight, and even the sound of foods). Discussion in relation to images can be found in Hamilton 2014.

5. Sight can also be synesthetic, as through it we can discern textures, vibrations, and so on. As Deleuze and Guattari (1987, 429) point out, the concept of hapticity, with all its limitations and criticism, also invites the assumption that the eye itself may fulfill a nonoptical function.

6. Minh-Ha referred here to the need for ethnographic filmmakers to question standard cinematic methods and techniques that were sustaining how ethnographic films continued reproducing a Western view of other cultures. Her provocation resonates in relation to our contemporary discussions on multimodality.

7. For Hayward (2010), the concept of fingereyes helps "articulate the in-between of an encounter, a space of movement of potential . . . the inter and interchange of sensations" (581). Although she uses this term to discuss cross-species encounter, it resonates with encounters with inhuman materials as it seeks to approximate the "transfer of intensity, of expressivity in the simultaneity of touch and feeling" (581).

The Ethnographic Hunch

This chapter is about the ethnographic hunch: that moment in research when I encounter something—a situation, something someone has said or shown me, a moment in a fieldwork video recording made by a co-researcher—that deepens what I think I know, sparks an ethnographic-theoretical dialogue, turns around my thinking, and creates a strand of investigation through my research, analysis, or both. Such insights are dispersed, not part of predetermined analytical processes or systems, yet in my experience they are among the most important moments in ethnographic analysis. Anthropological ethnography should value the sensibility of the researcher in configuring diverse materials, modes of knowing and feeling, and temporalities in order to make meanings that can be used in the world. Rather than taking refuge in an analytical structure that is supposed to compute findings for them, researchers require the crucial ability to identify meaning and significance as part of their research process. Such hunches are an expression of a particular form of anthropological sensibility and must be treated with both care and confidence. They are what enables anthropologists to produce novel and deep insights, which disciplines that depend on procedures and predetermined systems of analysis and theoretical structures cannot access. Hunches do not exist in isolation, however; in fact they need to be played out as part of elements in a rigorous and reliable process of fieldwork, analytical interrogation, or both. In this chapter I discuss the idea of the ethnographic hunch in order to reflect on how ethnographic analysis happens for a lone ethnographer and in team-based ethnography.

In my research the ethnographic hunch is part of a configuration of ways of knowing that emerge with research participants and co-researchers. My projects, which are usually collaborative, are designed to address a set of research questions, which are explored ethnographically, sometimes in combination with other methods. Here, the research questions and the specific things we think we need to find out are one element of the research. We should not, however, assume that we can be confident that we are already aware of everything we need to know before starting to explore the worlds from which we expect such knowledge to emerge. Themes and questions we did not realize we needed to investigate tend to emerge along the way, often through ethnographic hunches.

The idea of the ethnographic hunch also helps explain how the research anthropologists do—while often with relatively small samples in contrast to quantitative studies—is systematic and in-depth, and achieves rigorous and deep analyses. It does not just find things out; it also follows these things through, often in collaboration with research participants and co-researchers, interrogating them across the experiences of participants and having an unfailing ability to detect patterns in how the same or similar things manifest across groups of participants.

In what follows I first discuss the question of analysis in anthropological ethnography. Then I explore the significance of thinking anthropologically through the ethnographic hunch by using three themes: serendipity and the hunch as it emerges in fieldwork and analysis; how the hunch is related to comparative analysis; and how it enables us to create wider shared concepts. In doing so, however, I take a step away from the way the hunch would be used in traditional anthropology and call for an interdisciplinary anthropology that engages the hunch for team-based interventional projects.

ANALYSIS IN ANTHROPOLOGICAL ETHNOGRAPHY

Anthropologists in particular and ethnographers in general have found it difficult to explain how we do "analysis." While writing the book *Doing Visual Ethnography* ([2001] 2021), I realized why. In the proposal for the book, I had naively planned a chapter about analysis. I was aware that in anthropology there is an insistence that analysis starts during fieldwork and that it is not a distinct phase. Once I began to write the book, however, I realized that the situation was more complex, and a chapter about ethnographic analysis would be irrelevant. Instead, I started to rethink by asking myself what actually happens when I try to make sense of research materials. For example, in my PhD research about women and bullfighting

(Pink 1997), I had spent several months doing fieldwork, and I lived near to where I performed that fieldwork. I worked with my many handwritten field notes, analogue photographs, media cuttings, videos, novels, and other miscellaneous materials—that is, materials of many different categories and correspondingly different qualities and affordances. The process of analysis had already begun during the fieldwork, and many of my notes were analytical. Moreover, the process of analysis, which also put my research in dialogue with theory, was part of the process of writing. It did not have a set process to follow, as does the grounded theory used by sociologists or conversation analysis used by social psychologists. Nor did it apply an existing theory to the materials and then use that theory to structure the analysis, as often happens in some cognate disciplines. Instead it involved creating narratives and correspondences between different categories of materials, and though I was guided by theoretical principles, I was ready for the materials to challenge existing theory. This ethnographic-theoretical dialogue is always central to the process of research design, ethnography, analysis, and dissemination. Thus the researcher and her or his creative capacity stands at the center of the process of making sense of ethnographic materials in anthropology, in contrast to the centering of the process by which the analysis is done.

This vision of the lone researcher, however, is not the only way to do anthropology, and my focus is on team ethnography, which has recently become the dominant mode of my own ethnographic practice. Team ethnography is inevitably collaborative, and it means that fieldwork, analysis, and writing might be shared, and that responsibilities for different tasks take various configurations. In team ethnography the mode of research-analysis continues as we encounter materials produced by others. For example, in my work with Jennie Morgan—each of us on a different side of the world while Jennie undertook fieldwork in the UK and I was in Australia—we developed a mode for 24-hour short-term ethnography, applying an ethnographic-analytical-theoretical dialogue. Each night Jennie, in the UK, would send me field notes and commentaries when she finished her ethnographic research about worker safety and health in a health care unit, and I would receive them in the morning in Australia. I would then read her materials and send back comments, which Jennie would receive when she woke up the next day. As such we developed the themes and strands of the research as we went along, and we used them to guide the ethnographic process (Pink and Morgan 2013).

Some researchers have interrogated the question of analysis in ethnography, again not necessarily based on the lone ethnographer model. For example, the ethnologists Tom O'Dell and Robert Willim (2013) focused in on the sensoriality of transcription as an analytical and performative practice. Their work shows how the qualities of transcribed text, when treated as sensory and performative, take us into an experiential mode of engagement, rather than being a separate stage of analysis. Kerstin Leder Mackley and I have discussed analysis in interdisciplinary contexts, outlining how our video ethnography research about domestic energy demanded two analytical routes: we followed our participants' narratives, identifying themes that emerged in the ethnography and were reinforced through the sample of twenty participating families; and we also used a set of predetermined categories and questions, which we had specifically designed to create bridges that would help us discuss our findings and develop a meta coanalysis with the engineering and design disciplines we were collaborating with (Leder Mackley and Pink 2013). The first set of themes was driven by ethnographic hunches. The second set was negotiated in relation to the literature, the project's goals, and our shared interests with colleagues from other disciplines. A theme from the first set can be adopted into the second if it can be made meaningful across disciplines and research practices. Such analytical work is complex because it involves both immersion in the principles of one's own discipline and engagement with positions that might be very different from one's own. To achieve this, we need to both maintain a critical anthropological perspective and use that perspective to constructively shift thinking through shared categories in collaboration with others who might think differently from us.

The ethnographic hunch has a pivotal role in bringing such modes of critique forward. Moreover, the ethnographic hunch signifies an openness to knowing, feeling, and thinking differently through our contact with other people's worlds. Here the hunch is not owned by just one anthropologist, as it would be in a traditional mainstream anthropological process, but rather it is codeveloped in dialogue.

SERENDIPITY AND THE HUNCH: MOMENTS OF EMERGENCE

Anthropological knowing has frequently and long since been characterized as serendipitous (Okely 1994), whereby ethnographers often stumble without warning onto the thing that they later realize is what they really needed to know. Many researchers have reflected on how ethnographers know in fieldwork (e.g., Hastrup and Hervik 1994; Kulick and Willson 1995; Halstead, Hirsch, and Okely, 2008; Melhuus, Mitchell, and Wulff, 2009). Yet discussions emerging from conventional, reflexive accounts of the experiences and fieldwork relationships of the lone ethnographer are no longer sufficient for contemporary contexts in which anthropologists work in teams and through differently engaged modes of practice.

Therefore, although serendipity is important in anthropological work (see, e.g., Pink [2001] 2013, [2009] 2015), it does not simply emerge through the fieldwork encounters that make a monograph or article by a single author. Rather, the serendipity of anthropology happens from fieldwork to teamwork—the sharing and viewing of other researchers' materials, discussion, checking things out with each other, and following through. It is not just the serendipity of fieldwork and our relationships with people who participate in research with us that matter (although of course they still do). Serendipitous ways of learning equally emerge from the relations that constitute research teams and participants and their different modes of presence in fieldwork, analysis, and writing.

With reference to serendipity in the anthropological process, the ethnographic hunch refers to those moments when we realize that we have found something significant for the course of our research. This moment is different from those of understanding and sharing with a participant and from the incremental process through which we come to learn about other people's lives. The ethnographic hunch is when we realize something that we think is more universal, that we will continue to find throughout our research process—an enduring theme that will guide the course of the research and analysis as we go along. For example, during my long-term PhD fieldwork, when I worked as a lone ethnographer, I experienced several such moments. For instance, early on in my fieldwork I realized how being photographed in public together with other people significant to that context was one of the ways in which participants represented, confirmed, or made comments about fields of local social relations. I therefore followed this through the research, maintaining an interest in how people became copresent in the local public photography that related to my research topic.

The ethnographic hunch can emerge at any moment in the research process. It might be during fieldwork or during analysis—whether shared with participants or co-researchers or done alone—of the materials and memories that are part of what I have elsewhere called the "ethnographic place" (Pink [2009] 2015). Ethnographic hunches are already framed by theory to some extent, just as our theoretical commitments frame everything that we interpret. Yet, as part of the ethnographic-theoretical dialogue, the ethnographic hunch participates in critiques or modifications of existing theory. This is not inspired by the ethnographic hunch alone, but occurs because the course into which it will guide the research/analysis will systematically build up a case for a revision to existing theory.

The ethnographic hunch can also be thought of as happening when we realize that something not previously visible has been rendered knowable through the ethnographic or analytical encounter. One example occurred after a video ethnography research encounter with a participant in his home, during a research project about energy demand reduction in the UK. As my co-researcher Kerstin Leder Mackley and I walked out of the house toward the car, I knew something very interesting had occurred during our meeting with the participant. He had shown us around his home, detailing how he had insulated it himself against the cold and showing us the now neatly wallpapered walls, which hid the detail of his work from view, and the attic floor, which was covered in insulation materials and provided evidence of the work. As we sat in the car, about to pull away from the curb, I realized that he had been showing us the invisible architectures and infrastructures of his home. I've described this elsewhere:

> As we left Alan's house, our researchers started to discuss how Alan's home was full of "invisible architectures"—those that he knew about behind the walls, but also the digital infrastructures that from his "always on" wifi which supported the ways in which digital media were used. What made this even more interesting was that these invisible infrastructures were precisely those things that made his home "feel right" for him and his family. That is, they created a specific sensory aesthetic or "atmosphere" of home that he also carefully maintained as he set out on his route through the night time home. (http://energyanddigitalliving.com/stories-from-the-home/)

By touring the home with the participant and delving into its history and what its walls meant to him, we had been able to imagine what was behind the wallpaper, in terms of the work he had put into it, his affective investment, and the materials he had used. It became clear to me that to understand energy demand, we needed to attend not to what we could see when we looked at the walls and floors of people's homes, but to what they could sense when surrounded by this materiality (see Pink et al. 2017). Video, although a visual medium, played a key role in enabling and bringing to the fore those things that we cannot normally see, because it invited participants to show us their homes, their feelings, and their everyday activities.

The ethnographic hunch might also emerge in a moment of encounter with research and other materials, or during a conversation with other members of a research team. Such instances take us further from traditional modes of anthropological research toward greater teamwork and shared research materials over distance. For example, within the Natural User Experience (NUX) project, I sat in my office with two co-researchers, Alex Gomes and Renata Zilse, who were visiting from Brazil so we could complete the analysis and reporting of our project together. The video, photography, and audio transcription materials we were working with had been produced with our wider research team of five junior researchers, who were also based in Brazil. In this large research team we played various roles, and two of mine were to develop the design anthropological strand of the research, which I piloted with the research team in Brazil, and to participate in analyzing the materials. In this project, in which we researched technology use while commuting, we used GoPro video cameras mounted on participants' heads while they drove, and then in-depth interviews based on a preanalysis undertaken by the junior researchers. While viewing these materials I was struck by the extent to which some participants continually used their smartphones during their commute to work. As I and my colleagues have outlined elsewhere (Pink et al. 2019), smartphones were used before and during the journeys, predominantly to send WhatsApp text, voice, and emoji messages; to plan routes by using the Waze or Google Maps apps; and to create an atmosphere in the car by playing music. Our core research questions in this project were not initially about safety; however, while viewing the videos produced by the participants, we discussed how they were staying safe by using the smartphone in a particular way that created a balance between road safety and their need to access the apps that were important for their personal safety. Taking this as a theme in the analysis, in consultation with the team I worked through the video materials to understand how this balance manifested in participants' sensory engagements with the technologies and how their uses of technology and their experiences of safety were articulated during the interviews (Pink et al., n.d.).

An ethnographic hunch is not the end of the analytical story. Rather, it usually signifies the beginning of an analytical trajectory, which need not necessarily be contained within just one project.

The analysis in the NUX project (introduced above) was impacted by the findings of another project in which we researched participants' use of smartphones while commuting, although from a different perspective. In the NUX project we were specifically interested in participants' experiences of smartphones, using the drive of everyday commuters as context through which to understand the experience of smartphone use. In the Human Expectations and Experiences of Autonomous Driving (HEAD) project, which I undertook with a different team based in Sweden, we were initially interested in people's experiences of driving, in particular their use of automated features in their cars and their imagined future driving experiences in a world of autonomously driving (AD) cars. During one of the projects within HEAD, described elsewhere (Pink, Fors, and Glöss 2018), my co-researcher Vaike Fors and I interviewed and drove with a participant while I video recorded. During this encounter the participant used his smartphone continually, before and during the drive, to plan the route and make a voice call. Building on that encounter, during our next two meetings with participants, I began to interrogate the ways that they used their smartphones in relation with their cars, and I continued to do so through my co-analysis of the research materials with Mareike Glöss, who undertook the remainder of the fieldwork. As we discussed in our ensuing article, for participants it was essential to have their smartphone with them as they drove, and because they were safety conscious, those who used their smartphones for in-car calling tended to have them mounted on the dashboard. Although little research exists about the ways in which the car-smartphone relationship is evolving, our research suggested that the two were becoming inextricably related (Pink, Fors, and Glöss 2018).

Once we began our analysis of the Brazilian materials, the differences between the ways drivers in Sweden and in Brazil used their smartphones in the car stood out to me, enabling me to extend the analysis further to reflect on the global inequalities and local circumstances that are at play in the rollouts of new automated and connected technologies.

The ethnographic hunch is thus not necessarily just a moment in fieldwork that creates a research theme in one particular site or project. Rather, it can lead us to invest in analytic categories that might transcend projects. In this sense we might think of what Henrietta Moore (2004) calls the "concept-metaphor." Concept-metaphors, as Moore explains them, ". . . are a kind of conceptual shorthand, both for anthropologists and for others. They are domain terms that orient us towards areas of shared exchange, which is sometimes academically based. Concept-metaphors are examples of catachresis, i.e., they are metaphors that have no adequate referent. Their exact meanings can never be specified in advance—although they can be defined in practice and in context—and there is a part of them that remains outside or exceeds representation" (2004, 73). She goes on to note: "Their purpose is to maintain a tension between pretentious universal claims and particular contexts and specifics" (Moore 2004, 74). Moore writes of concept-metaphors that represent significant categories such as gender, the self, and the body; however, "smaller" categories can also play a role in creating novel thinking about things that occur across different spheres of life. In a context where digital data are part of our everyday worlds, we need new categories for understanding what data are and what data can mean that exceed those used in science and technology fields. In a recent project focused on self-tracking and personal data, I realized during an encounter with a participant that we could consider both wearable technologies and the digital data produced with them as being "broken," both when the technologies did not work and when the data were cut off, and when they did not fit into the category intended by the makers of the technology. Before this I had been reading about theories of breakage and repair, and they offered me a point of inspiration through which to consider data as "broken." To test the idea, I held a workshop with colleagues who were also involved in ethnographic work on data. From this workshop emerged an article, which I cowrote with Minna Ruckenstein, Robert Willim, and Melisa Duque (2018), in which we discussed three examples from different countries and projects—self-tracking data, the work of data scientists, and sound data—which could be made sense of through the shared concept-metaphor of broken data. In this example, the ethnographic hunch began during a research encounter and was then explored, discussed, debated, and adapted through discussion with colleagues in order to create a category of analysis that was meaningful for us all. Thus, we took a different step away from traditional anthropological research and analysis to follow the hunch across projects in a new form of teamwork.

- Recognize a hunch: A hunch is when your practical experiences in an ethnographic setting and your thoughts start to cohere. You will know when it happens because you will start to obtain conceptual clarity about what you have learned through ethnography. In the examples discussed throughout this chapter, the hunch was recognized when I realized conventions existed for the public bullfighting photography I was participating in; when it became apparent that invisible architectures were present within a research participant's home; when I was determining to follow through hunches about the relationship between cars and smartphones in Sweden and Brazil, and while further comparing these hunches; and when during discussion with colleagues I realized that we could follow broken data across our initially separate projects.
- Follow the hunch: Following a hunch involves being attentive to new ethnographic encounters and moments of knowing that support your hunch. You will begin to seek them out and to gradually see how similar experiences play out or how other things happen that endorse your hunch, thereby enabling you to create a narrative and argument through your research. In the examples discussed in the chapter, I followed a hunch by following a series of different photographic encounters through fieldwork; by exploring the otherwise "invisible" elements of other research participants' homes; by focusing on the car-smartphone relationship with subsequent research participants; and by seeking out the various ways that broken data might manifest across different projects.
- Create the conditions for a hunch to emerge: For a hunch to come about, you need to be attentive and open to making connections. Analytical work in ethnography involves creating relationships between things of different categories, affordances, and qualities. You cannot create conditions for a hunch, but by being open to seeking out the things, processes, and connections that are not immediately obvious, your sensibility to bring things together in order to create novel or previously imperceptible understandings

will enable the hunch to emerge. In the examples discussed here, I never expected or anticipated the hunch; it came about in moments where deep insights or patterns in research began to cohere. We depend on our anthropological sensibilities and training to do this. For instance, when something significant seems to happen around photographic encounters, we ask what social patterns might be related to them; when an invisible element of the materiality of home emerges, we ask what human experiences, feelings, and activities might be related to it; when a specific human-technology relationship emerges, we ask how this is related to other things and processes in the same environment; and when data appear to be used in ways that are not intended, we are open to seeking alternative ways through which we can conceptualize their use.

The Para-Site in Ethnographic Research Projects

The following three paragraphs introduce an experimental exercise that was invented at the inception of the Center for Ethnography at the University of California Irvine (UCI) in 2006.[1] This exercise lies within and in relation to the production of (primarily) dissertation research projects by graduate students. This brief chapter reports on the first of eight such experiments conducted during the Center's first five years.

Although the design and conduct of ethnographic research in anthropology is still largely individualistic, especially in the way that research is presented in the academy, many projects depend on complex relationships of partnership and collaboration at several sites, and not just those narrowly conceived as fieldwork. Anthropology departments preserve the binary here-and-there-ness of fieldwork, despite the reality of fieldwork as movement in complex, unpredictable spatial and temporal frames. This is especially the case when ethnographers work at sites of knowledge production with others who are patrons, partners, and subjects of research at the same time. These others not only have their own stakes in what lone ethnographers learn among them, but they have interested and differential coauthorship in the concepts and relations that the ethnographer invents (by method or design).

In the absence of formal norms of method covering these de facto and intellectually substantive relations of partnership and collaboration in many contemporary projects of fieldwork, we at the Center for Ethnography encourage, where feasible, events in the Center that would blur the boundaries between the field site and the academic conference or seminar room. Might the seminar, conference, or workshop under the auspices of a Center event or program also be an integral, designed part of the fieldwork?

Hybrids between research reports, or reflections on research, and ethnographic research itself, events would be attended by a mix of participants from the academic community and from the community or network defined by fieldwork projects. We term this overlapping academic/fieldwork space in contemporary ethnographic projects a "para-site." It creates a space outside (alongside? lateral to? adjacent to?) conventional notions of the field in fieldwork in which to enact and further certain relations of research essential to the intellectual or conceptual work that goes on inside such projects. It might focus on developing those relationships, which in our experience have always informally existed in many fieldwork projects, whereby the ethnographer finds subjects with whom he or she can test and develop ideas (these subjects have not been the classic key informants as such, but the found and often uncredited mentors or muses who correct mistakes, give advice, and pass on interpretations as they emerge—whom I have termed, somewhat awkwardly, "epistemic partners").

We invite graduate students engaged with ethnography at UCI and elsewhere to propose projects in which the Center event can serve as a para-site within the design of specific research endeavors. This theme signals an experiment with method that is directed to the situation of apprentice ethnographers and in turn stands for the Center's interest in graduate training and pedagogy as a strategic locus in which the entire research paradigm of ethnography is being re-formed.

The model exercise that I report in what follows is as relevant and useful today as it was in the early 2000s when the Center for Ethnography was established. That was a period when—following the openings offered by such efforts as the "writing culture" critique, postcolonial and feminist critiques, and the proposal of "cultural critique"—an anthropology of globalization and a critique of neoliberalism were being formulated. This effort continues, but macro themes have since shifted (toward the ecological, the environmental, and the planetary); collaboration with regimes of expert knowledge, especially in science, medicine, and technology, and with activist movements has regularized; and forms of ethnographic reporting and representation have more routinely succeeded the classic monograph or paper in ethnographic journals. Still—and certainly in terms of the ethnographic research form of the *rite de passage* that qualifies anthropological scholars—the mise-en-scène of circumscribed, sustained fieldwork relationships endures. The para-site experiments described here, which develop those relationships as performances for the sake of doing mutual concept work that structures ethnographic writing, remain central to what it means to "do anthropology" amid assemblages, within infrastructures, and in alignment with the paraethnographic practices and thinking of subjects.

The first event that represents such an experiment occurred on November 4, 2006. Jesse Cheng, an advanced graduate student, studied a movement among activist lawyers to mitigate the death penalty in capital cases. A practicing lawyer himself, Cheng worked with them and in other directions that their activities suggested in order to study the operations of the death penalty through the paraethnographic, descriptive-analytic work that the mitigation lawyers produce in their advocacy.

He conducted his own investigation through the forms of their investigation. This space is analogous to the classic "native point of view" but without a compass in traditional ethnographic practices to do this kind of research that requires collaborative conceptual work. This work needs a context, a space, a set of expectations and norms better than the opportunistic conversations that occur in just "hanging out." The para-site experiment is intended to be a surrogate for these needs of contemporary research that are certainly anticipated in practice but are still without norms and forms of method. It encourages addressing issues of design before a concept of design has reinvented the expectations of pedagogy in anthropological training. Undoubtedly, the para-site will take different shapes and participations between the field and the conference room in other dissertation projects. But in all cases it is a response to the imperative to materialize collaborative forms in contemporary ethnographic research.

The Ad Copy for Cheng's Para-Site
Methods of Humanization: Death Penalty Mitigation and Ethnography as Antidiscipline
Saturday, November 4, 9:00 a.m. to 4:00 p.m.
Invited participants: Judy Clarke, Scharlette Holdman,[2] Denise Le-Boeuf, Mark Olive, Russell Stetler, Jacqueline Walsh, Benjamin Wolff, George Woods
The Center for Ethnography is pleased to welcome eight of the nation's leading capital defense advocates to begin a dialogue with academic ethnographers at UCI. By setting the knowledge practices of engaged academics and advocates side by side, this event represents an attempt to

coarticulate the imaginary of the "human" as a potential point of convergence for knowledges.

Workshop Proposal by Jesse Cheng
To the extent that successful field collaborations are founded on a sense of shared engagement—the notion that anthropological ethnographer and collaborating informant are all in something together—there's always something tenuous about the spirit of collaborative goodwill. It seems the relationship can break down in so many ways—for example, if you feel I'm not doing enough to uphold my end of the bargain, or if you suspect I'll bastardize the knowledge that you entrusted me with, or if you think I'll leave you hanging once I have what I need, or if we both do everything that we promised and discover that our knowledges are irrelevant to each other. Whenever we experience a sharpened sense of just how irreconcilably unlike our agendas are—a difference that encompasses conflicts in knowledge's uses, modes, forms, and manners of representation and distribution—the conditions are set for breakdown. This concern has profoundly informed the evolving contours of my project. As I have put myself side by side with my collaborating informants, I have wondered how to go about reconfiguring this sense of "us anthropologists" and "your mitigation practitioners" and the divide between "what we do" and "what they do," what is same and what is different.

My engagement with works by yourself, Doug Holmes [Holmes and Marcus 2005], Bert Westbrook, and Chris Kelty [2009] has attracted me to the notion of the "imaginary"—an account of the contemporary, and possibilities for the sorts of counternarratives that can respond to it—as a posited point of convergence between various sorts of fugitive knowledge. What intrigues me is not the fact that anthropology and mitigation share the same imaginary (they do not) nor the fact that their respective sets of imaginaries may overlap in certain places (they might, but so what?), nor the notion that we imagine ourselves to have similarly oriented imaginaries (we are joined by an idea about an idea?), nor the idea that the squishiness of unarticulated imaginaries allows us to get along because we assume that we are doing similarly good things (we are all too cynical for that). I'm interested in another convergence. On the one hand, some intellectually curious, reflexive practitioners of mitigation desire to have their imaginaries articulated; on the other, some anthropologists muse about how the discipline can generate its own knowledge by staging imaginaries, and their concomitant possibilities for fugitive knowledge, within an ethnographic frame. As I've continued thinking along these lines, I've envisioned a dissertation that takes the form of a critical coarticulation of mitigation's imaginaries. I would make explicit mitigation's knowledge practices as their implications fan out into a broader epistemological horizon, but I would also use anthropology's critical edge to point out the limits of these knowledge practices along every step of the way. As such, the dissertation would stand as an artifact of anthropological knowledge—an ethnographic staging of a kind that has never been done before (I think . . .)—but also as an artifact of the field, a deliberate polemic to elicit responses and set the conditions for further collaborations.[3]

What Happened on November 4, 2006?
The morning opened in a typical UCI classroom with an illustrated lecture presentation by Professor Leo Chavez of the UCI Department of Anthropology, who gave a narrative account of how he collected and used materials from his own long-term ethnographic field research on the undocumented Mexican migrant population of Orange County, California. The visiting mitigation lawyers who composed most of the audience posed many questions. These questions went to technical matters of presentation and, frankly, issues of representation of experience as facts and for what kinds of audiences—these were the sorts of issues to which they were sensitive in their own work. Then we broke for lunch. For the rest of the day, no one made a presentation or came to the front of the room. Rather, those seated in the rows engaged in three hours of extraordinarily valuable crosstalk/conversation. This time was the "lateral," "adjacent," "para-site" part of the event, in my view. It is when the differences between ethnographic inquiry and mitigation inquiry were articulated at various levels. With the accent on the work of mitigation lawyering, what ethnography is was a framing concern, but what was made explicit, in a way that no other venue offered, was what sort of concept thinking was at stake. The session was not recorded (this might have been a lapse or mistake), but several of us were busy with old-fashioned notes. This is the sort of intense "shoptalk" though which para-site experiments unfold. It was an exhilarating discussion that spilled over into the social event we had that evening. Months later, I could see content and outlines of the afternoon session in the brilliant dissertation that Jesse produced (Cheng 2007).

The following is the reaction that I sent to Jesse Cheng after his event. It deals with how a form for epistemic collaboration in contemporary fieldwork might be located and clarified through a para-site event, and how such a para-site needs a "third"—a common object or a specific community of reception to address (here, high-minded debates about the death penalty)—as a basis for the complicit solidarity on which collaboration might be created in contemporary contexts of research, full of causes and activist motivations:

Jesse,

> That was a great first para-site effort. . . . Just a couple of personal observations: For me, the key to exploring "reflexive knowledge" ethnographically among expertises and "projects" of various sorts in the world, like death penalty mitigation, is to locate/discover where and how it is constituted para-ethnographically, so to speak—to find a "form" amidst practices of your subjects and counterparts in ethnographic research. In our session, this moment materialized after lunch, when Russ (one of the mitigation experts) revealed in response to my question that all of the elaborate research that such experts do in arguing the penalty phase of cases is built into the advocacy process as a "front-loaded" phenomenon in a situation of anticipation. And then at the end, Bill [Maurer, an anthropologist at UCI attending the event] crucially associated this "space" of legal research and representation with the formulation of the nature of contemporary ethnography itself as anticipatory. So, this is a space of both "fact-finding" and the imaginary, depending upon the development of reflexive knowledge. The question remains of what the role of the ethnographer/fieldworker is in this "found" space of para-ethnography. To describe it? to analyze it? to partner with it? to encourage the development of it? to pass it on, represent it elsewhere by some sort of mediation? . . .
>
> And this gets to some of the remarks of the final discussion of the event about what the stakes for anthropology are in research like this— for its own disciplinary project—and not part of helping to strategize, where the anthropologist participant might be perceived by the mitigation experts in the role of consultant (this is your "participant observation" role, your "blending in" identity in this kind of research). What is in this research for anthropologists themselves when they, in their own disciplinary discussions, have not really created a context to receive it as part of a significant problem that they have defined? Well, my current

solution to this problem of anthropologists themselves making something of topics that they themselves have not developed is that work in anthropology like yours has to be designed with a "third" primary area of reception for ethnography in mind—that is, neither the community of anthropologists who are not prepared to discuss such work deeply, nor the subjects themselves who have their own purposes and interests in developing your work with you. So what is this "third" arena of reception in which your work should have impact?—that is a key problem and integral responsibility of conducting ethnographic research today. It is as much a problem of ethnographic analysis as describing the work of your subjects—the mitigation lawyers—itself. It could blur into anthropology as activism, but I consider it first and foremost a theoretical and analytic problem of ethnography itself.

In your case, I evoked high-minded, often high literati discourse on capital punishment that usually has no subtle knowledge of ethnographic objects/subjects (with the reflexive knowledge work that goes on in fieldwork), but cumulatively is really important in influencing broad public change in social thought about issues such as capital punishment. I think that if your work is to have effect, it has a real contribution to make at this level of high literati policy debate, and it is an explicit task of design in your project to consider this realm of reception—as itself another, "third" site for ethnographic understanding. Here the methods and craft of mitigation defense, explained alongside and in dialogue with ethnographic craft—the work of the para-site—would be the "takeaway" that could enter the more abstract issue-oriented policy debates. The "ethnographic" stories of mitigation pleas would leaven and bring powerful details—themselves frontloaded—to the larger debates about the death penalty wherever they occur in contemporary media.

So, ethnography in its production is inherently dialogic where the key partners to dialogue are often not just the local communities of court process, but scale up to the larger policy projects of ethnographic critique [that] should incorporate a deeply understood (itself ethnographic in nature?) dimension of intended reception outside the scene and interests of fieldwork itself.... In this mode, the ethnographer sees the function of his work as mediation in a very specific politics or topology of knowledge that incorporates anticipated reception.

G.

Postscript

"The critique of the human sciences has had since the mid-1980s a peculiar fate, a fate that is burdened in one species of its knowledge by questions which as prescribed by its very nature it cannot ignore, but which as transcending its limitations it also cannot answer. Among these questions is the degree to which the language of critique itself has entered into those very discourses it was intended to transform."—T. David Brent, former acquisitions editor for anthropology at the University of Chicago Press, in a playful paraphrase of the first sentence of Immanuel Kant's *Critique of Pure Reason*.

Classic anthropological ethnography, especially in its development in the apprentice project/dissertation form, was designed to provide answers, or at least data, for questions that anthropology had for it. Nowadays, anthropology itself does not pose these questions. Other domains of discussion and analysis do—some academic or interdisciplinary in the conventional sense, others not—and it is a contemporary burden of projects of anthropological research—and especially apprentice ones— to identify these question-asking domains—also, domains of reception for particular projects of research—as part of learning the techniques of research itself. So, particular policy or development program arenas with many players—NGOs, governments, international organizations, indigenous and social movements—define the terms of anthropological research more powerfully than does any discipline-derived paradigm or center of debate. The very parties who are the primary audiences of such research are also its subjects. Thus, ethnography in its most classic inclination to make "subjects" of all of its interlocutors must develop the methodological practice today of making colleagues, fellow experts, and their frames of analytic discourse ethnographic subjects themselves in designing the multi-sited terrains of its research projects. Much ethnography shifts today from the study of culture or cultures to the study of knowledge-making processes, broadly conceived and diversely located, and in which its own expertise participates.

In this development, the function of the research project is not simply descriptive-analytic, to provide a contribution to an archive or debate that has been constructed by the discipline—it hasn't. At best, contemporary anthropology provides a license and an authority to engage, not just to be a reception itself to some observed site of social action. Ethnographic research out of anthropology thus becomes a mediation in some sense; it takes on agency. It is an experiment and a potential intervention that depends on the response of its subjects for any critical effect it might have. It sutures communities and contexts together in addressing those communities, in presenting its results in constructed contexts of collaboration as a key issue in the increasingly broad design of research beyond mere fieldwork.

Indeed, students are pursuing questions that fieldwork itself in its conventional Malinowskian aesthetics (intensive participant observation in communities of usually subaltern subjects) can't answer. And it is in the process of apprentice research—in dissertation making—that an anthropologist is most subject to these aesthetics and regulative ideals of research practice as they are imposed, not by the rules of method, but by the psychodynamics of professional culture. Here the process on its own is not at all stuck, but in transition. What is missing is an articulation of these changes.

At present, as a halfway measure, what prevails is a renewed experimental ethos for the conduct of ethnographic research which makes a virtue of the contingencies deep within its traditional aesthetics, and which works very well for the exceptional talents of those who enter anthropological careers by embracing this experimental ethos. In producing standard work, however, the experimental ethos serves far less well—it produces more often rhetorically driven repetitive versions of singular arguments and insights. A fuller account is needed of what kinds of questions contemporary ethnography answers, with and in relation to whom, and what results it might be expected to produce on the basis of what data. These are the sort of crucial second-order issues that arise in preparing, during, and in the wake of para-site experiments as proposed here.

AFTER THE 2000S: THE PARA-SITE IN THE MULTIMODAL

At one time the only experimental exception to narrative ethnography and its assumption to have been produced through participant observation fieldwork by a lone ethnographer, as a semiautonomous alternative in degree-qualifying research, was ethnographic film and, to a lesser degree, performative/theater anthropology. Now, with technological affordances, *multimodal*, presuming variable skilled working collaborations, has become a trend watchword related to research practices (for example, the long-standing visual anthropology section of the American Anthropological Association recently changed its name accordingly; see, for example,

Dattatreyan and Marrero-Guillamón 2019). In my view, the impulses of the working through of epistemic partnerships in the early 2000s, the attractiveness of design collaboration that led to modest para-site, lateral, adjacent, or "third space" experiments in fieldwork projects, now exist richly and more openly in a wave of the "multimodal" with the rapid growth in technological affordances. The current mood is marked by the formation of many similar ancillary centers or labs, like the one at UCI, established alongside the long-standing and enduring models of traditional professional training in many anthropology departments today. They represent entangled new objects of study and new means and methods that involve different configurations of working collaborations.

Still, within, and lateral to, the traditional Malinowskian/Boasian practice, the para-site protocol evoked and described in this chapter remains a modest experiment in mutual concept work that both unifies and divides anthropologists and their subjects in the development of all contemporary rite-de-passage fieldwork projects. It is the kernel of experiment that can be organized with minimal resources. Once analytics is shared between ethnographer and subjects as epistemic partners, the only way to enrich similarity and disentangle difference in those concepts is to perform them. This is what early para-site projects at the Center for Ethnography permitted.

PROTOCOL

- Identify a specific conceptual tension, puzzle, curiosity, or topic that you want to explore in a way that is not overdetermined by the existing literature or your own knowledge. Make notes from field notes and other data sources about where and how the conceptual tension, puzzle, curiosity, or topic (the intended subject of the para-site) arises in fieldwork.
- Identify a small group of your interlocutors with whom you feel you can have reflexive and conceptual discussions about the relation between that conceptual tension and the problem/event/process that is the focus of your research. Determine carefully who else, outside fieldwork, you want to attend the event (e.g., fellow students, faculty, experts).
- Invite them to be part of the para-site by letting them know the purpose of the event and what roles you intend them to play. Construct a scenario that might work to develop the conversations you are hoping for.

- Select a location appropriate for an open and frank discussion. The event can be held in private or with an audience—it depends on the nature of your project.
- Depending on your interlocutors and topic, you can organize the event as a roundtable for which you prepare questions, or you can use participatory design and collective decision-making methods, or you can just leave it as a conversation. Importantly, this is not a focus group, and it is not an extractive exercise. It is a moment of conceptual exchange, a space where a collective analytic will be generated. Knowing your subject, what is typical meeting/conference culture?
- Record and document, in whatever way is appropriate for your setting, the angles that emerge from the discussion.
- Take those conceptual angles as collective insights that need to be explored further throughout the ethnographic encounters and materials you are working with.
- In thinking about the use of ordinary spaces such as conference or seminar rooms as places for para-site events, I have found the arts of theatrical design in anticipation of performance (standing for the contexts of fieldwork here) to be particularly inspiring. Many methodological works might inspire specific applications in para-sites. For example, see *Dramatic Events: How to Run a Successful Workshop* by Richard Hahlo and Peter Reynolds (2000), *Creative Worlds: How to Make Immersive Theater* by Jason Warren (2017), *Codesigning Space: a Primer* by TILT Collective (2013), and *Ethnography by Design: Scenographic Experiments in Fieldwork* by Luke Cantarella, Christine Hegel, and George E. Marcus (2019).
- Write the "concept work" done collaboratively in your para-site into explicit analytics and a narrative strategy for your project. In Jesse's case, "front-loading" as a stance of anticipation has become a rich and enduring mine of thinking and research in his career of mitigation practice and teaching/research after (see Cheng 2010, 2017a, 2017b).

NOTES

1. I consulted and discussed this paper about our 2006 para-site experiment at the UCI Center for Ethnography with Jesse Cheng. After several years as a lawyer specializing in mitigation defense, Jesse has become a professor of social and cultural studies at Marquette University.

2. The name Scharlette Holdman among the mitigation practitioners deserves special mention. She died on July 12, 2017, at the age of seventy. She was a leading figure in the legal practice of death penalty mitigation. She did not hold a law degree, but rather a doctorate in anthropology from the University of Hawai'i. She fought the Supreme Court's 1976 ruling that reestablished the death penalty. She organized, inspired, and led an elite group of lawyers who defined mitigation law and practice. Her clients included Ted Kaczynski (the Unabomber) and Khalid Shaikh Mohammed, among many other infamous figures. To the extent that mitigation specialization has similarities to ethnographic research—especially its holism and the way it conceives of clients as contextualized subjects—it owes much to her. She was a watchful rather than active participant in our November 4 para-site, though she had much to say about it during the social gathering following the daylong event. As an unusual anthropological career, Holdman's was interesting to me. It seemed exemplary of where a number of contemporary careers were headed, if the students concerned were lucky! That is, anthropological thinking for many would not be embedded again in another project like that of professional rite de passage but would be highly relevant to other kinds of professional and activist contexts in which the analytics and concept work required by a fieldwork project would be crucial. Para-site events within the frame of conventional training in fieldwork projects seemed both to enhance the apprentice project at hand and to teach the students how to use anthropological thinking decoupled from it but in immersions with other kinds and situations of expert thinking—such as mitigation defense in legal practice, as in the career of Scharlette Holdman.

3. See Cheng (2007) for the full dissertation; and Cheng (2010, 2017a, 2017b) for publications resulting from his dissertation.

Juxtaposition

Differences That Matter

As ethnographers we continually make differences, relations between a "here" and a "there," a "this" and "that." And as we compare and contrast, we also decide to keep some things stable rather than others. How do we decide which differences matter? In this chapter I discuss an analytic technique for engaging with this question, which I have coined "juxtaposition." As I will elaborate, this technique was my strategy for dealing with a challenge all anthropologists face: determining how to relate to the dominant stories in our field, and how to avoid strengthening them while still recognizing their power.

Strictly speaking, juxtaposition is a literary device whereby one places things close together for the purpose of yielding contrasting effects. In my reworking of it, juxtaposition concerns the process of foregrounding and then contrasting particular elements in a messy and complex field. In my attempt to "reverse engineer" the craft of this technique, I will draw on my research on eating and health as they get problematized in the context of the reported "obesity epidemic" in the Netherlands (Vogel 2016).

CRAFTING THE LITERATURE

"Obesity" is a knowledge-dense field populated with numerous credentialed and noncredentialed experts. This begs the question of how to relate to all the literature written on this topic, and how to use "theory" to understand one's field. Many of my choices in this were predicated on my biography and theoretical cultivation (Timmermans and Tavory 2012).

Instead of, say, political economy or cultural health beliefs, my training and interest brought me to critical work inspired by feminist and poststructuralist theory. I read authors who, when writing on overweight, emphasize the disciplining, moralizing, and calculating character of nutritional recommendations, diets, and related bodily techniques. In their critical reading, these techniques aim at making bodies docile, their desires tamed. Moreover, these techniques call upon people to take control of their health as individuals. Some of these authors locate this normative injunction in a "lifestyle politics": part of being a good citizen now entails regulating one's weight by making so-called healthy choices and engaging in good behavior.

One possible way of analyzing my fieldwork is to point out how this, too, was happening in the Netherlands. Indeed, overweight people currently find themselves cast as part of an urgent societal problem. Statistics suggest that in the Netherlands overweight is a true "epidemic." In response to this main public health concern, food labels and pyramids implore people to "choose consciously," diet books promise swift weight loss if only their rules are observed, parents are warned to watch their children's weight.

That what I "saw" happening concerned me shows that the literature sensitizes you to what may be at stake in your field—to what matters. But what next? Whereas some social scientists unilaterally condemn everything infected by the "antiobesity discourse," my ethnographic encounters made me hesitant to follow this path. Early on I was struck by how reflexive my informants, who deal with the complex problems around overweight on an everyday basis, were about the dilemmas they encountered in their work. I soon began to recognize how their work entailed constantly navigating various concerns around health and well-being. Instead of leaving all critical engagement to the researcher, it was important to me to take seriously these ethical engagements. I thus felt uncomfortable talking about my informants, about presenting them as little cogs in a larger, powerful machine. Importantly, professionals often contrasted their approach to healthy eating with alternatives. For instance, some dieticians would promote ways of eating that stress nourishment and conviviality in direct response to the harmful effects of the commercial weight-loss diets they decried. These differences mattered greatly to them. How could I then lump all these approaches together as if they were, in the end, part of the same disciplining apparatus?

The technique of juxtaposition helped me overcome this challenge. Instead of merely repeating the biopolitics argument, it became a fruitful coherence to contrast my own material with. I distinguished some of the characteristic features of the biopolitics argument around the obesity epidemic: the desired practice is bodily discipline, individual willpower is mobilized to achieve this, and control is the encouraged mode of relating to oneself and one's body. Then, I articulated my research questions in response to these elements: Toward which desired practices is care directed, and how? Who/what is mobilized in the changes deemed necessary? What kinds of ways of relating to oneself, one's body, other people, food, and one's surroundings do these eating and exercise practices foreground?

The research variously elucidates how people relate to their bodies—how they control, listen to, enjoy, care for, and try to change their bodies; how they are taught to do so; and why. I did not focus on a dominant thread but aimed to learn from differences emerging between practices. It was another academic literature, sometimes termed *material semiotics*, that inspired me to explore such multiplicity.[1] In my doctoral dissertation and the resulting journal articles, then, I ended up articulating alternatives to the calls for bodily discipline critiqued in the literature I read. By contrasting different forms of care that come to matter in these practices, I hoped to explore anew how people may craft themselves as bodies and persons through eating and exercise when weight is a concern. My normative commitment was to help invent and foster better ways of living in situations where overweight is a concern—and to question what this "better" may be.

Although my approach ended up being very different from those applied by other researchers in the critical biopolitics literature, we shared an "enemy": real enough, but also a necessary simplification, good to think against. Rather than adding up my knowledge to an emergent whole, finding a "niche" that had not yet been explored, or applying a "theoretical framework," I related to the literature by oscillating between similarity and difference. This meant variously making orderings in terms of theoretical concerns, normative engagement, methods, and fields. In the process, I was fluidly positioned, and positioned myself, in collectives arranged by such orderings—social scientists, feminists, anthropologists, or STS researchers. Moreover, I was not just writing for an academic readership. I hoped my research might help "us" (researchers and practitioners) to rethink the problem of overweight and how it can be targeted. As I was attentive to my informants' concerns, they became part of my audience. Positioning myself in this collective pushed me to think of knowing differently, to wonder how my knowledge might make a difference.

Let me start by describing my fieldwork in some detail. The way we organize our methods, after all, invites particular forms of analysis and not others. In this sense methods are part of our analytical practice. Rather than around a place or community, my fieldwork was organized around the object of and concern with obesity. Many colleagues who took my fieldwork to represent the "Dutch case" were curious to explore the extent to which this case differs from how the problem of obesity emerges in other countries. I always had a hard time explicating the "Dutchness" of my material. Geographical specificities tend to present themselves when one travels elsewhere, but the Netherlands is the place where I had grown up and where I lived at the time of my doctoral research. In my ethnography, I was sensitive to, and actively crafted, strangeness in other ways, inviting different juxtapositions. To tell unfamiliar stories about familiar practices, I made differences within them.

In the field I focused on the techniques of healthy eating and living that were offered in health advice, taught by professionals, or developed by people seeking to lose weight. Such techniques, I stressed, are not just interventions on the body, but reconfigure the lives of the people involved. They shape the practicalities of daily life: of grocery shopping, of cooking and eating, of pleasure and pain, of being a family. But they do so in different ways. I was interested in whether and how these differences mattered.

Instead of conducting long-term participant observation in one clinic or research center, moving around and shifting between several sites allowed me to learn more. My fieldwork explored techniques as diverse as dietary recommendations, exercise, meditation, tasting, diet shakes, and surgery. I observed and attended meetings, joined in trainings, and sat in on consultations. My way of working foregrounded care practices themselves—and the people, bodies, techniques, and knowledges figuring within them—as exemplary social sites in which the problem of obesity emerges and is handled, both practically and ethically. To learn more about how care practices differed from other settings in which obesity is a concern—for instance, in how they stage the body, produce knowledge, or address people who are overweight—I also visited research facilities, including a department of human nutrition and a psychology laboratory studying self-regulation. I went to scientific conferences, observed public health interventions, and kept track of discussions of obesity in the media.

My notes are detailed and oriented to practicalities: "The dietician picks up a file displaying a table and shows it to Mrs. Jansen. The table lists food products and their caloric content: whole wheat bread, half-skimmed milk, an apple. The bottom of the table states the added total of calories: 1,995 calories. 'This week we will work with this menu. Where do you go for groceries?'" And so on. During interviews, I asked professionals (dieticians, doctors, psychologists, and physiotherapists) what they do and why. Likewise, when I interviewed people about their attempts to lose weight or become healthier, my questions focused on bodily practices—what the informants say they do to make themselves healthy, slim, or satisfied, or to understand their body's workings, often relating to concrete situations that happened recently. Thus organizing my fieldwork in ways that foreground the specificity and creativity of care practices drew my attention to food, bodies, and techniques rather than to beliefs or experiences.[2]

A professor in an ethnographic methods class once told me that the social scientist's job is to tell the stories of the people they study. He did not like my papers very much. Although what people say and feel matters greatly to me, focusing on the techniques that circulated in clinical care for overweight people allowed me to attend to how living with overweight (as a bodily state and a concern) not only is something that people do but also is, to an important extent, done to them. Techniques foreground particular ways of knowing and acting on bodies and food. They depict bodies, behavior, or food products as good or bad, and they call upon people to evaluate themselves and their habits in such terms. From these techniques, could we learn something about what is at stake in living with overweight? Through juxtaposition, I hoped to maximize the possibility for surprising insights around this question.

ORDERING MATERIAL

Fieldwork had spurred certain interests in me—things I found surprising, incomprehensible, disturbing, or, rather, great and promising. A crucial step, however, was to turn the field notes and transcripts into materials to work with. I started by isolating fragments of interview transcriptions or notes of observations. In the end, I had files of material, including documents and images such as flyers, scientific articles, programs, and websites that I had obtained both through my informants and my own searches. There have been many moments during my PhD fieldwork research when I was anxious about not having "enough" material, feeling as though I had only scratched the surface of the field's complexity. As soon as I started analyzing in detail, however, I felt overwhelmed by the sheer volume of observations, quotes, and images.

What did I look for when examining my material? As I mentioned, instead of seeking generality or an overall picture, I foregrounded differences. It was not particularly hard to show that the scheme of discipline and control identified by my colleagues is not totalizing, that cracks exist. Practices are messy and manifold, and there are always elements that resist order. My aim, however, was not just to describe or understand my field of study; I also wished to make an intervention, both theoretically and practically. I wanted to offer alternatives—to position the logic of control as one among several ways of approaching eating and health. By articulating other modes of ordering practices, I hoped to contribute to making the story of control less powerful.

In my analysis I thus focused on what characterized possible deviations from the scheme. Instead of discipline and appeals to willpower, I teased out the endless tinkering involved in adapting routines or allusions to bodily desires. At some point, I went through my material seeking how professionals taught their patients/clients how to handle their bodily cravings and desires. I collected a document full of relevant quotes and descriptions. I ordered them under four subheadings:

- "'Sensitizing' through 'learning tastes,'" which collected descriptions of techniques whereby people were taught to try foods they did not like (usually vegetables) over and over so they would learn to appreciate them;
- "Enjoy," which designated moments when clients were asked not to fight, but instead give in to, their desires and thereby calm themselves;
- "Skills to prepare tasty food," which focused on teaching cooking skills such as using herbs that would cut the need for more salt or make vegetables more appealing; and last,
- "'Reconditioning' the body," which described a technique for dealing with "powerful stimuli" such as the smell of fries in the street: expose yourself to something really tempting, then pause until the urge to eat it dissolves.

ARTICULATING WORLDS ENACTED

The elements in the list above provided an entrance into exploring how various modes of care become thinkable and "doable" through the alignment of social and material elements, including people, bodies, food, techniques, professionals, and activities. These elements are ordered in relation to each other and take shape in these very relations. I approached practices of living with overweight as a specific staging or "enactment" of the world. That is, I analyzed them as theater performances in which particular versions of food, bodies, and subjects (the entities that had my interest) play their part. Modes of care in which nutrients or calories are prominent, for instance, stage overweight as a problem of eating too much of the wrong food and taking too little exercise. But as the above descriptions exemplify, care practices mobilize more than just calories and exercise; psychological techniques and labels, cooking and exercise skills, coaching techniques, meditation, tasting exercises, and surgery all shape the realities enacted in care practices, staging other mind-body-life configurations. This staging is not simply a way of knowing or imagining obesity; it comprises actual world-making. Although the theater metaphor suggests a (more real) backstage, care practices reveal the ongoing, mundane work of putting realities into being. But how were these worlds populated? What was going on in them?

Articulating these worlds asked me to actively forego what I (thought I) knew bodies, food, and subjects to be, and instead to wonder, What are these entities here? The *here* in this question, which designates a situation or a practice I observed, provides an anchor in a conceptual space from where my analysis unfolds. By virtue of their juxtaposition, *here* is different from *there*. The contrast greatly enriched the elements under consideration. Take the body. The four headings order different kinds of therapeutic techniques, but also different versions of what bodily desires are, and they foreground different possibilities of changing those desires. The last subheading contained only one quote, but I felt it was different from the others. Upon reflection, I realized that in the contrasting scheme I had set up, the difference "matters" because in proposing to "do" something different with desires, this technique also "does" bodies differently: the "enjoy" examples stage a body with a sensitive internal feedback system that is disturbed by attempts to control it, whereas the attempts at "reconditioning the body" present a body as organized by patterns and processes that can be reprogrammed so that one can better adapt to one's surroundings.

The articulation of these different bodies required listening to what my informants said, but also to how in practices certain things are staged as possible and not others. Documents, graphs, diaries, and other tools used by professionals were helpful in exploring how eating, bodies, subjects, and food were configured. These sources helped me tease out the kinds of techniques that were included, what realities they created and how bodies and subjects figured in them. I thus noticed, for instance, that in juxtaposing the techniques I organized under the headings, I could also juxtapose the practical consequences of the different knowledge repertoires that served as their inspiration—respectively, neurophysiology, mindfulness, cooking traditions, and cognitive behaviorism. Whereas the literature usually spoke of "the" biomedical approach to overweight, my analysis revealed the rich, diverse, and often contradictory knowledges circulating in health care practices.

Equally revealing was another question I posed to my materials: What is not here? In any practice concerned with obesity, certain contexts are mobilized—family, foodscape, psychological dimensions, socioeconomic inequality or poverty, weight stigma, and beauty ideals—and others are left out. Instead of assuming they all somehow matter, it was revealing to me to explore what was foregrounded in one setting and backgrounded in another. While food production and preparation are often absent from nutritional advice, food activists put these issues front stage. The analysis required me to forego my own assumptions about the problem of overweight, but my increasing knowledge of the field also provided me with powerful analytical tools. What patients who were deemed "morbidly obese" shared about their numerous failed attempts at weight loss, for instance, made me look differently at the promises of swift weight loss incorporated in dieting techniques.

Juxtaposition also allowed me to highlight how different forms of care present possibilities and problems; in other words, it implies various notions of good and bad. For instance, my field notes detail sixty-year-old Sandra visiting a dietician. She admits that when she went for dinner, at the encouragement of her husband she "sinned" and ordered an apple pie. In a responsibilizing logic, both the apple pie and Sandra are bad, and restraint is the assumed good. Instead of scolding Sandra, however, the dietician here "asks whether she at least enjoyed it: 'If you do take something, make sure to take pleasure from it, too.'" The apple pie is still staged as bad, but "good" things other than health are at play, which makes Sandra taking the pie less bad: enjoyment, spending quality time with family. In this example, moreover, the content of the nutritional advice (which enacts foods as either healthy or unhealthy) is at odds with the forgiving, lenient style with which is delivered. In my analysis, I kept enquiring to what style of normativity these goods/bads come—moralizing, forgiving, encouraging, or matter-of-factly pragmatic—and what frictions or tensions I could identify.

These inquiries into entities staged, their goods/bads, and their frictions provided me with the terms to further describe the different elements that I juxtaposed. As a result, the techniques I studied emerged as much more than just alternative ways of intervening in the same problem. In the act of juxtaposition, contrasting logics about healthy eating and living, in which different things were at stake, came to the fore. What story to tell with this material, however, does not automatically follow from the exercises and questions I laid out in the previous section. Writing an argument is in itself performing a world. If in the previous section I outlined the props and players, the next step is to make them play a scene, tell a story. The question is not only which elements to put on stage and what to contrast, but also how to juxtapose them in ways that make for an interesting argument in relation to the literature. To go with the example of bodily techniques discussed above; in a paper contrasting, say, how diverse overweight care stages bodily desires, the knowledge embedded in "skills" is equally other to that in "reconditioning" as to the nutritional facts infusing a "control" approach (see figure 4.1).

I realized, however, that the four subheadings mentioned above also have something in common when contrasted with the dominant scheme. Part of this dominant scheme is the idea that our bodies are evolutionarily hardwired to greedily seek out ever more food. Indeed, my informants who counted calories experienced bodies as insatiable, only (sometimes) controlled by rules and determination. The material I organized, however, performs bodily cravings as something that can be tamed, developed, negotiated with, and sensitized. Desire, in other words, does not emerge as natural and wild, but as cultivated. In the paper my supervisor and coauthor Annemarie Mol and I ended up writing with this material, we interrogated the often assumed opposition between "health" and "pleasure" (Vogel and Mol 2014). We argued that this opposition is indeed embedded in a controlling approach to appetite (one must resist the cookie!)—but not in the

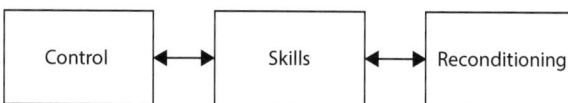

FIGURE 4.1

other approaches to desires. This plotline, then, emerged by positioning the four headings as subordinate to the more dominant juxtaposition of control versus cultivation of desire (see figure 4.2).

I compare these two modes of juxtaposition here to illustrate that how elements are arranged and contrasted in writing makes a difference to the argument they help make. Before and while writing all my articles and chapters, I make a few of these outlines, each time indicating what material (a quote, a description) will illustrate them best. They act as a storyboard, directing me and my material as I write.

DIFFERENCES WORTH MAKING

The technique of juxtaposition helped me elucidate "what matters" in my field and to discern what is at stake politically and normatively for my informants. Importantly, however, it also allowed and required me to actively interrogate and put to the test my own critical sensibilities toward my material. This became particularly clear to me when Annemarie Mol and I, in the spirit of innovating the academic seminar format, brought "the field" to the academic collegial space where we analyze and write. We invited one of our informants to give a mini-workshop on mindful eating. This

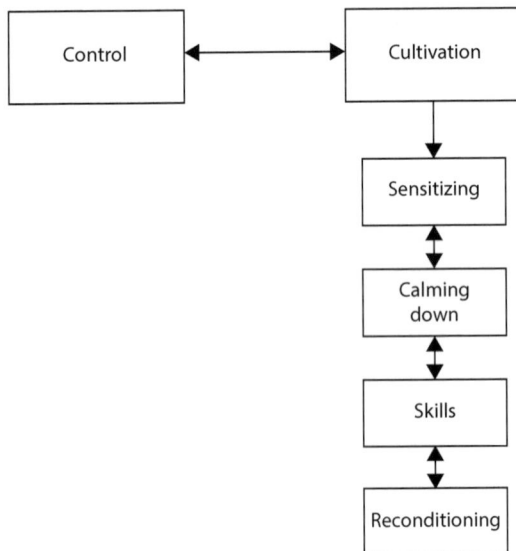

FIGURE 4.2

coach, whose professional motto was "count pleasure, not calories," figured prominently in the draft paper we presented that day. Mirroring the plotline presented in figure 4.2, in this paper we questioned the contrast between health and pleasure by exploring how professionals encourage enjoyment, thus cultivating a body that can feel when it has had "enough." We believed that this approach made a refreshing break from the refrain of restriction dominant in discourses on healthy eating. The difference between these two approaches was important to our informants—and to us. The style with which we discussed what we coined "alternative practices" in this first draft consequently came closer to praise than to modest witnessing or critique.

Our colleagues, however, did not share our enthusiasm. Some remained simply disinterested, but others outright resisted its normativity. Who was this coach to "tell them" to "enjoy" their food? All this was expressed with the coach present. Things became quite awkward indeed! At that moment I was very discouraged: Was I not critical enough of my informants? Did we not see what my colleagues could sense in less than fifteen minutes: that this was a hopelessly middle-class, moralizing way of relating to food and life?

Later, I began to see this moment, and other moments when colleagues critiqued my work, as the productive and sometimes challenging exchange between my fieldwork, where I allowed myself to be "in/af-fected" (cf. Zuiderent-Jerak 2015) by my informants' concerns and passions, and the discussions I had with colleagues and the critical social scientific work I read. While the latter kept alerting me to the political and social stakes of calls for bodily discipline and individual responsibility, the realities enacted and the concerns addressed in care practices allowed me to explore alternatives to the moralizing discourses these social scientists critiqued. From the resistance of my colleagues I learned to add caveats and hesitations in my texts and in the process of fieldwork. More than rhetorical, this shaping has analytical value: rearticulations further situated the difference these practices presented—In what ways do they make a difference? What is at stake?—thus sharpening my argument.

IN CLOSING

Juxtaposition was part of each step of my research: in relating to the literature, when making a field, in articulating worlds enacted, and when writing an argument. Note the active verbs: the elements I contrasted are not out there for us to "find" or "recognize"; they are products of the analysis. Working through juxtaposition is thus not only about doing justice to the material. It is about offering a description that is also a re-scription, that changes how we can see, engage with, and care for the practices we study. Describing always means intervening. This is, after all, ethnography's critical potential.

Somehow, the differences we as ethnographers deem worth making emerge in what Marilyn Strathern (1999) called a "complex relational space" between the field of observation and forms of writing—or, put simply, between field and desk. Once again seated at my desk, I have suggested that the messy and haphazard practices of observing, reading, and writing through which I bridged this space somehow share a common analytical technique. I hope this redescription will be an inspiration—or provide a productive point of contrast—in your own analytical journey.

PROTOCOL

- Articulate a dominant narrative in the literature, be it in terms of argument, concern, or enemy.
- Dissect some of the elements that are central to this narrative (e.g., bodies, foods, subjects, techniques).
- Articulate your research questions in such a way that they interrogate how these elements emerge in your field.
- Set up your fieldwork in a way that gives the phenomenon under study the greatest chance to exhibit rich, complicated versions of itself. Within practical limits, this might mean going to various places, engaging with various groups, experimenting with different methods, or focusing on different techniques and knowledge repertoires.
- In your field notes and transcripts, focus on small descriptions, quotes, or observations that diverge from the dominant story. Arrange similar ones together. Think of what word(s) would characterize them, and code them accordingly. The material ordered together may be bigger fields (care practices, epidemiology) or may consist of a single quote. There is not one "right" way in which it should be shuffled together. Focus on what is revealed through juxtaposing the bits of material under the different headings. If you are undecided which differences matter, start with the ones your informants care about.

- Take two or more of the resulting categories and focus on the elements articulated in point 2. While going back and forth between the different materials, articulate: What is entity X here and there? What is not here but is there? Consider what other striking differences emerge between them, for instance in terms of the goods and bads, the style of normativity, and the tensions or frictions that emerge.
- Make a few storyboards with the headings you articulated. Practice with different modes of juxtaposing. Articulate the difference it will make to the story they help tell as you compare and contrast the worlds articulated in point 5 with the literature. How does your story complicate, enrich, and interfere with the dominant narrative?
- Share your analysis with others. If you receive criticism, take a deep breath and then use it to sharpen your articulation of which and how differences matter.

NOTES

1. See the work of Annemarie Mol (2002), Ingunn Moser (2005), and Jeannette Pols (2003).

2. For similar analytical approaches contrasting techniques in health care practices see Skeide (2019) and Driessen and Ibáñez Martín 2020). For more details on the theoretical implications of attending to practicalities, see Annemarie Mol's (2002) discussion on "praxiography."

PART II

PHYSICAL OBJECTS

....

CHAPTER 5

ENDRE DÁNYI, LUCY SUCHMAN, AND LAURA WATTS

Relocating Innovation
Postcards from Three Edges

This chapter is based on a research project titled "Relocating Innovation: Places and Material Practices of Future Making" that we undertook between 2008 and 2010 (Suchman, Dányi, and Watts 2008). We were working across three diverse, seemingly incomparable field sites: a nascent renewable energy industry in the islands of Orkney, Scotland; the Hungarian Parliament in Budapest; and the Xerox Palo Alto Research Center in the Silicon Valley region of California. We knew that our project was held together through our shared interest in questioning narratives of innovation based in geographies of center and periphery. But how could we produce generative connections between our ethnographic research materials, which seemed so disconnected? How could we compare, and what should we compare, when comparison is not random juxtaposition but thoughtful work that must cut strategically in order to produce conversations and openings across continents and time zones (Niewöhner and Scheffer 2010; Jensen et al. 2011; Deville, Guggenheim, and Hrdličkova 2016)? One answer for us was a collaboration technique that involved making, sharing, and comparing ethnographic postcards.[1]

Our chapter offers a demonstration and discussion of three of those postcards exchanged between our "edgy" future-making field sites. We draw on archaeologist Michael Shanks's notion of katachresis, a forcible juxtaposition designed to produce frictions (2004, 152), suggested to us as an empirical strategy during a project workshop. In what follows we show how to make postcards from moments with "ethnographic effect," how to use those postcards to create katachresis across field sites, and how postcards helped us both to think differently about field sites and to re-specify what we could mean by innovation and future-making.

The idea of making postcards came early on, while we were preparing for a workshop with the Anthropology Program at the Massachusetts Institute of Technology (MIT) in 2009. The aim was to engage workshop participants in thinking about how our field sites could generate interesting, unexpected connections. During our research we had sailed away, over the curve of the Earth, at different times and to different parts of the planet. Perhaps it was that sense of distance and difference, not just geographical but also experiential, that inspired us. On Laura's shelf was an old, much-loved book, *Postcards from the Planets* (Drew 1992). In its beautiful pages, a future tourist had sent back to Earth a series of postcards from the planets in the solar system. The postcards rendered each planet as a human experience, one the reader could imagine and inhabit—a mixture of both evidence and somewhat florid interpretation. In a similar way, we thought we could send postcards from our distant field sites to make them more accessible for ourselves and for each other, and to make them travel. More prosaically, because at that point we had not visited each other's field sites, the postcards would share both our experiences of places unknown to the others, and specific empirical evidence from those places. Postcards could render moments from our ethnographic field sites and make pieces of places that could travel.[2]

In practical terms, the internet (a blogging platform, to be more precise) was our initial postal service; we each "posted" an image and a related paragraph.[3] We were sporadic, with the upcoming workshop providing impetus. But it was still a conversation, a blog thread, where one person made a postcard or two, and another responded with their postcards. Now, almost a decade later, we have returned to reflect on this process. Let us remember: How did we make each postcard? How did we cut out a field site fragment, as an image and some text?

From Silicon Valley: The project takes me back to materials collected over a twenty-year period, roughly from 1980 to 2000. The materials exist primarily as paper files, items kept on the hunch that something interesting might be said about them later, in some future when I would have the time to engage them. The call to make postcards suggests a particular pass through the files, a hunt most obviously for photographs but also other visual images, or fragments of text that might be framed as an image. Most of these are images generated from within the everyday life of my field site rather than from my own photography. Among the former are multiple instances of a particular genre, a variety of modes of mapping one's work in a way that indicates a history of productive labor and a promise of future returns on investment. Among these I'm struck by one titled "Flow of PARC Contributions" (figures 5.1 and 5.2).[4]

In a trope reminiscent of the "waterfall model" of product development but rendered pastoral, the image pictures a torrent flowing from the upper left corner of the frame, falling as a broad cascade that dominates the view. Two clearly unnatural elements mark the picture's iconography. The first is a reversal of time, as the future recedes upstream. The second is a structural fixing of the cascade's flow, as time stops in a freeze frame of the year 1993, and the waters divide into four distinct streams labeled "Leverage," "Process," "Product," and "Intellectual Property." Onto each stream is affixed a label that in turn translates activity into an enumerable entity (Verran 2010), a project. Time is mapped to a space of intervals between a present moment and a projected future. If maps have politics, this map is a technology of accountability to a narrative of product(ivity). Not having a place on the map indicates the uncertainty of one's own future. The fact that our own research group barely shows up is a portent of troubles to come. As our themes developed (of which more below), this postcard became an example of the theme "Place and Landscape."

From Budapest: My postcards included several images of the Hungarian Parliament as a monument, a tourist attraction, a complex organization, a theater-like arena for political debates, and a backdrop of mass demonstrations. I also had a few images of politicians and one related to Hungary's socialist past. The image on one of my postcards is a photo that I took in the so-called Statue Park—a private collection of dozens of socialist statues that were removed from public squares and almost destroyed after 1989 (figures 5.3 and 5.4).

The postcard shows the negative image of a socialist scene in one statue: the march of soldiers in uniform, rifles in hand, moving from left to right under the guidance of the Red Star. The soldiers, who used to be metal figures, have been removed, and the Red Star is completely missing. All that is left is a star-shaped hole in the concrete.

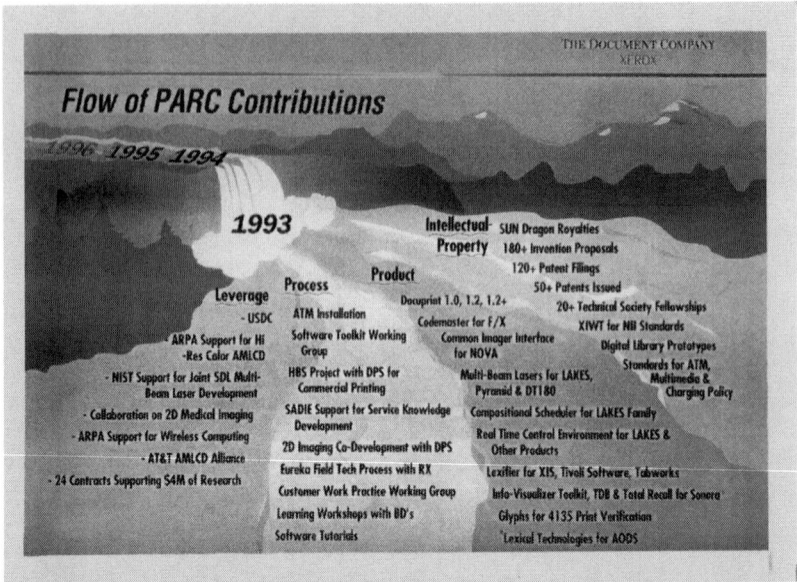

Flow of PARC Contributions

THE DOCUMENT COMPANY
XEROX

1996 1995 1994

1993

Intellectual Property
SUN Dragon Royalties
180+ Invention Proposals
120+ Patent Filings
50+ Patents Issued
20+ Technical Society Fellowships
XIWT for NII Standards
Digital Library Prototypes
Standards for ATM, Multimedia & Charging Policy

Product

Docuprint 1.0, 1.2, 1.2+
Codemaster for F/X
Common Imager Interface for NOVA
Multi-Beam Lasers for LAKES, Pyramid & DT180
Compositional Scheduler for LAKES Family
Real Time Control Environment for LAKES & Other Products
Lexifier for XIS, Tivoli Software, Tabworks
Info-Visualizer Toolkit, TDB & Total Recall for Sonora
Glyphs for 4135 Print Verification
Lexical Technologies for AODS

Leverage
- USDC
- ARPA Support for Hi-Res Color AMLCD
- NIST Support for Joint SDL Multi-Beam Laser Development
- Collaboration on 2D Medical Imaging
- ARPA Support for Wireless Computing
- AT&T AMLCD Alliance
- 24 Contracts Supporting $4M of Research

Process
ATM Installation
Software Toolkit Working Group
HBS Project with DPS for Commercial Printing
SADIE Support for Service Knowledge Development
2D Imaging Co-Development with DPS
Eureka Field Tech Process with RX
Customer Work Practice Working Group
Learning Workshops with BD's
Software Tutorials

theme: **Place & Landscape**

This 'landscape' invokes the 'cascade' of valuable contributions from the research center (located here in the upper remote margins of the scene) to the sponsoring corporation. Space maps time, as a receding future provides the headwaters, the source of continuous innovation in the present. At the same time, research is fixed and held in place by this representation if, indeed, it is visible enough to appear.

Waterfall of innovation
Representation of PARC contributions to Xerox, c.1993.

FIGURES 5.1 AND 5.2 "Waterfall of Innovation," courtesy of PARC, a Xerox company.

theme: **Newness**

'Annus Mirabilis' –this is how 1989 is usually remembered, the miraculous year
when state socialism collapsed in Central and Eastern Europe. However, the
same year marks the disappearance of yet another dreamworld of modernity,
that of a unified, homogeneous West. 'Against the often-repeated story of the
West's winning the Cold War and capitalism's historical triumph over socialism,'
Susan Buck-Morss argues that 'the historical experiment of socialism was so
deeply rooted in the Western modernizing tradition that its defeat cannot but
place the whole Western narrative into question.' Susan Buck-Morss: Dreamworld
and Catastrophe: The Passing of Mass Utopia in East and West, 2002, Cambridge,
Mass.: MIT Press, p. xii.

Disappearing dreamworlds
Buda Volunteers Regiment Memorial, Statue Park, Budapest.

FIGURES 5.3 AND 5.4 "Disappearing Dreamworlds."

These are traces of iconoclasm, or iconoclash, to use Bruno Latour and Peter Weibel's (2002) term. For the statue park is a record, not only of attempts to destroy the icons of the past, but also of the grotesque effect generated by the relocation of those icons. Stalin's gigantic boots overshadow the stone figures of Marx and Engels, who stare at Lenin addressing a group of peasants. Socialism is easy to ridicule—it stands for a future that has somehow expired or lost its credibility. The back side of the postcard is a reflection on exactly this sentiment. It is a quote by Susan Buck-Morss (2002), who has suggested that 1989 marked the end not only of the East but also of the West. Socialism was a "convenient other" to capitalism, the latter of which was gradually exported to Central and Eastern Europe as the only viable future—see the oft-cited fantasy about the end of history (Fukuyama 1992). This postcard became an example of the theme "Newness."

From Orkney: At the time, I was just beginning what would become a decade of extended fieldwork (Watts 2019), taking field notes each day and keeping a photo record. But there were always moments—little stories told, pieces of places—that snagged and caught my attention, a glow suffusing particular parts of my memory and notes (these were inseparable). The requirement to make postcards was akin to wielding a craft knife: it made me cut out those glowing moments and turn them into bounded pieces of a story. Sometimes the words led directly from my field notes, and then I found a photograph as accompaniment. Sometimes the place led the story, and I began with a photograph and then sought to find the words for the postcard. Sometimes it all came together as a tangle, and I had to unravel and cut out the precise words and the precise photograph. The story, the moment, never existed before. Looking back, I feel ambivalent about the solidification and smoothing work that the postcards, as a method, did to my ethnography. I cannot evade or ever lose those stories. They rattle around like ball bearings whenever I reflect on my field site in retrospect. Making stories always has consequences.

This postcard began with a quote that I do remember—from a conversation with a colleague and collaborator over tea and a sandwich in Orkney (figures 5.5 and 5.6).

He talked about how the islands had held an international conference for renewable energy back in 2002, one of the first such conferences in the world, and how this history of taking a leading role in innovation was never remembered in metropolitan political centers—hence this postcard became an example of the theme "(Non)histories." I also knew how the is-

There is an archaeology of the future here on Orkney. It's place where futures happen first, but then cannot be moved, and are abandoned at the edge. Long forgotten state-funded future for a UK wind energy industry rot as concrete platforms in the ground, a derelict visitor's centre. When futures cannot move, they get re-invented as new elsewhere. Who remembers when Orkney is first? All remember when London is first. "We see problems and feedback quickly... we can move quickly, but when it [finally] happens in a in a big metropolitan city, with its money and location, you cannot compete..." explains a local academic.

Future Archaeologies
Remnants of the UK's first large-scale wind turbine, installed in 1986.

FIGURES 5.5 AND 5.6 "Future Archaeologies."

lands had been the test site for the UK's burgeoning wind energy industry in the early 1980s. I had visited the remains of that wind energy test site, taking a photograph of the great concrete base, still there on the hilltop. This entangled evidence was smoothed into some text for the postcard, to make an empirical point, and my photo of the concrete archaeology of the long-gone wind turbine was attached. I labeled the photograph "Future Archaeologies," a concept that I had been exploring in a previous project (Watts 2012b, 2014a). There are no neat edges between projects; ideas overflow, previous thoughts helping to shape others. I posted this all to the blog.

Returning to this postcard now, its story may roll around with hard edges, but it remains pertinent. Interestingly, the conversations with the other two postcards now make me retell this story in new ways. It is not as hardened as I had perhaps imagined—although this should not be surprising, given that stories are rehearsed, performed, and that within those moments there is always the potential for accounts to be made otherwise. We can always read against the grain, for example. Making a postcard is only the first part of the method. Reading a postcard is the next move, with its own located-ness and politics. We are as implicated in our reading as in our making. "One story is not as good as another," as Donna Haraway (1989, 331) puts it, reflecting on the politics reproduced by our choice of stories. Similarly, one reading is not as good as another.

THEMATIZING THE POSTCARDS

But there are more steps to the method. We did not end with the online versions, as they were blog posts and not postcards as we had intended—the interactions are very different between these technologies. We took the posts and turned them into physical form, printed as draft postcards on paper. In total, we made thirty-five postcards, around ten postcards each (though we weren't counting). Turning them into physical form was a crucial step because it meant we could spend some time working with them on a large table, sorting them, discussing the connections, exploring them as a set. Out of this first workshop we finalized groups of themes.

The themes ran across our project, and some we had already begun discussing during the project proposal. But they were ongoing conversations, and the postcards enabled us to enrich our critique and discussion of them, to explore what they might say, how our field sites informed and deepened these themes and gave them shape. Most postcards could fit under several themes, and our discussions focused less on choosing a theme than on the insights we could gain from reading the postcards together under different themes. In short, the point of the workshop was not to solve the problem of fitting a postcard to the best theme, but to open up the themes by using the postcards as evidence to explore our comparisons and construct our arguments. Our list of themes developed into these five: Place and Landscape, (Non)histories, Newness, Distributed-Centered Subjects/ Objects (with thanks to Mialet [2012]), and Centers/Peripheries. Once the themes were made and agreed between us (although the list could have

FIGURE 5.7 Postcards.

gone on), we made the final sets of postcards, printed on stiff card stock. Each set was enclosed and packaged in a DVD case (figure 5.7).

Design skills and attention to detail were required in order to construct the aesthetic we wanted (the font, the layout). Each postcard image included its short description (placed beside it in the blog postings) on the back, following the typical format of postcards. We did not include the conceit of an address, because that was not important for us (though it might be for others). Having this collection of cards was akin to having our project in a box. It helped allow our project to travel as a whole, beyond just the three of us. We then took the postcards to the workshop with colleagues and students at MIT. There we asked them to help us reread and reflect further on the postcards. One participant, Chris Witmore, was particularly helpful: he suggested that the method we had been effectively following was a form of "katachresis"—how Michael Shanks (2004) referred to the forceful (artificial?) juxtaposition of things and places that don't normally go together.

READING THE POSTCARDS AS KATACHRESIS

Lucy's image of the eternal flow of innovation shows what was supposed to come after the end of the Cold War—the end of history, not only in Central and Eastern Europe but also everywhere else. We associate this image with the kind of neoliberal program that has generated so much frustration in the former East, to the extent that today, for most people there, Vladimir Putin's Russia and Viktor Orbán's Hungary seem more attractive than any future with well-functioning parliaments.

Laura's image of a hill in Orkney shows, in the foreground, a concrete spot that marks the absence of a large wind turbine erected there in 1986. The turbine was subsequently disassembled and removed, for back then the UK government did not consider wind energy to be a viable source of energy. Just how wrong this assessment was is clearly demonstrated by the row of newer wind turbines (manufactured in Denmark) in the background. The concrete spot reminds us of various attempts—socialist and capitalist alike—to fix the future: to make it, in all senses, concrete. Is Laura's image the counterpoint of Lucy's? A sign of hope? Some kind of socialist version of capitalism? If so, it is also a counterpoint to Endre's postcard, as it suggests something other than nostalgia, other than a return to a past that never was.

Reading the "Waterfall of Innovation" against "Future Archaeologies" and "Disappearing Dreamworlds" indexes the folding of futures into pasts (a katachresis of futures, perhaps). The landscape of "Future Archaeologies" is one of futures produced through wind, rather than water as in the "Waterfall of Innovation." But, like the water upstream, the future recedes here into the line of turbines, subsequently raised. The lost opportunity of the abandoned prototype is underscored by the line of now commercially available working wind turbines, not invented here. The "miraculous year" of collapse inverts the trope of future productivity to one of creative destruction, the necessity of ending to make space for beginning. Then, the flatness of the cement pad, all that remains of the first wind turbine, echoes that of the absences in "Disappearing Dreamworlds." But the ending, it turns out, as we march from left to right, is not just of the past of socialism but also its constitutive outside, the future of capitalism. That future flows uphill in PARC's contributions to the profit margins of its corporate parent, immersed in the intensifying competition and consolidation of the tech industry to come.

All three postcards are about absences: the absence of past innovations. The great experiment that was socialism in Central and Eastern Europe came to an end in the late 1980s. Around the same time, the great experiment that was wind energy in the UK also came to an end. Both ended as a result of shifts in national and international politics. Both left monumental, concrete residues in the landscape. The image from Xerox's PARC does not show, but is haunted by, its history as the place credited with inventing the personal computer. The image can be thought of as the residue of that former time of innovation and experiment. Innovation does have an afterlife: it does not end but has ongoing consequences. It haunts places and people, long into the future, by its absence as much as its presence.

In all three cases you could wonder whether they are failed projects by some measure. Did socialism fail in Hungary? Did wind energy fail in the UK? Did Xerox's PARC fail? The quick answer in all three cases might, in retrospect, be yes. Hungary is a democracy. The UK does not have a wind turbine manufacturing industry. PARC is no longer a research organization within Xerox. But look closer. Hungary has a complicated relationship with democracy and its socialist past—it is not quite an unmarked, same-same European country. The photograph from Orkney shows a line of wind turbines on the hilltop, so wind energy *is* being generated—in fact, the islands now produce more than 100% of their electricity from renewable energy, largely from their wind turbines. PARC is still around, and still doing much of its research for Xerox, which remains a large customer. The afterlife of innovation continues, and the story shifts.

Finally, as we look at these three postcards now, we see monuments to innovation being made. This is most obvious in the Statue Park memorial, which is a monument to socialism itself. The absent wind turbine seems monumental from its concrete infrastructure on the Orkney hilltop. The PARC slide shows a waterfall of innovation, a geological feature, also intended to endure. All three marks of innovation inscribe a permanence. Despite much discourse about speed and change in innovation, it seems that, in these cases, innovation holds still, is memorialized; its monuments remain as an afterlife.

POSTSCRIPT: AFTERLIFE OF A PROJECT

But ethnographic research also has an afterlife. What we have briefly shown here is the afterlife of a method of collaboration that does not presuppose the production of a singular account as its outcome, but rather each of the accounts that are generated are enriched by the opportunity to think these multiple projects, times, and places together.[5] The connecting circuit of our research and collaboration was a shared analytic commitment to contingency, the openness of our endeavor, which did not need closure and categorization. Postcards as a medium for katachresis—for thought-generating juxtaposition across disparate locations—helped us to think together, to find the resonance among our research sites while also articulating their differences. Our method of writing, sending, and rereading postcards was a practical way of communicating across the three empirical cases, supporting the creation of connecting themes informed by the incomparability of their specific enactments.

PROTOCOL

- Convene a collaboration of two or more researchers with an interest in reading across multiple research sites as katachresis.
- Develop an initial set of analytic themes. (This step is optional.)
- Have each collaborator assemble a corpus of heterogeneous materials and inspect it for provocative/generative instances, either visual or textual. A short commentary, along the format of the front and back of a postcard, should accompany each example.

- Post examples generated in above step on a shared website, in a postcard format (i.e., showing "front" and "back" side by side).
- Print some or all postcards on paper (for ease of juxtaposition).
- Reprint some or all postcards on high-quality card stock and package them in an appropriate box. (This step is optional.)
- Hold a workshop to develop themes and readings across postcards.
- Write, either together or separately.
- Repeat the Protocol, informed by each last round, for as long as it seems generative to do so.

ACKNOWLEDGMENTS

The authors are grateful to the Leverhulme Trust for providing financial support for the project (grant F/00 185/U); to the participants in the MIT workshop held May 20, 2009; and to all those who generously took part in our "OrkneyLab: The Futures" workshop (Stromness, Orkney, September 22, 2009), which deeply informed the making and readings of our project stories.

NOTES

1. Postcards as a mechanism for comparing data have also been explored through the data visualization project "Dear Data" (Posavec and Lupi 2016). For recent invitations to write postcards as a form of ethnographic method, see Gugganig (2017); Gugganig and Schor (2020).

2. "Pieces of places" is how archaeologist Richard Bradley (2000) has described the technology of Neolithic stone axes, which are manufactured in dramatic mountain locations and then travel, a material-semiotic device (akin to a postcard, in our thinking) that allows those mountain places to travel with them.

3. The full set of postcards is available for download through "Relocating innovation: places and material practices of future-making," available at http://sand14.com/archive/relocatinginnovation/download/.

4. PARC is the acronym for Xerox's Palo Alto Research Center, founded in 1970 to stake out the corporation's claim to the future of computing. For further accounts of the twenty-year residence during which these materials were collected, see Suchman (2011, 2013).

5. The outcomes of our research have been published as a PhD thesis, journal articles, a book, and several poems. See Dányi 2012, 2013, 2015, 2017, 2018; Suchman 2011, 2013; Watts 2012a, 2014b, 2019.

CHAPTER 6

TRINE MYGIND KORSBY AND ANTHONY STAVRIANAKIS

Object Exchange

ORIENTATION

Collaboration has been a long-standing concern in anthropological research. As a practice in anthropology, it frequently solicits attention in terms of the relations between fieldworkers and those with whom they are working: the stakes, debts, power relations, and ends of the anthropological inquiry. Certainly since the 1960s, if not before, collaboration as a theme and practice, if not as a specific concept, has revealed the ethical and, more commonly, the purported political parameters of the practice of fieldwork engagements (Brettell 1996; Lassiter 2005a, 2005b; Holmes and Marcus 2008). Collaboration has also figured as an object of anthropological study (for the Boas-Hunt collaboration, see Jacknis 1985) or, simultaneously, as an object and practice of participant observation (Stavrianakis 2015). In this short text we return to a specific methodological concern with collaboration in which we build on Paul Rabinow's endeavors at the University of California (UC) Berkeley, over the course of more than a decade, to invent multiple forms of collaborative practice, and we draw on our prior work with him to invent collaborative techniques.

We describe a simple but somewhat surprising exercise in conducting collaborative thinking between anthropologists about objects drawn from fieldwork. By using *object* we follow Rabinow's reflections on the term in *Anthropos Today* (2003, 48) and in particular his later reflection on the term in the sense of the American pragmatist philosopher John Dewey: "The name *objects* will be reserved for subject-matter so far as it has been produced and ordered in settled form by means of inquiry; proleptically, objects are the *objectives* of inquiry" (Dewey 1938, 119; emphasis in original). An object, in Dewey's sense, is precisely not a thing, and it cannot be reduced to either its material or its ideal aspects. An object is a product of inquiry and is therefore not to be considered in contraposition to a subject, but rather as the correlate of what happens through the practice of inquiry. Objects include "things" but are taken up and considered "as objects" within the movement of inquiry. The conceptual power of Dewey's orientation to objects is what Dewey scholar Tom Burke has called the emphasis on "operational perspectivity": "whether some given thing is the subject matter of, or an object within, a given inquiry is relative to the perspective of the inquiry" (1998, 154) (cf. Rabinow and Stavrianakis 2016, 2019).

As we embarked on this exercise of object exchange, experimenting with new forms of collaboration in the university space was not new to us. In 2005, in his office at UC Berkeley, Rabinow created the "Labinar," a venue for collaborative thinking among professors and graduate students that we have both participated in. This work has since ramified into many different forms of thinking together, between, and among the Labinar's participants (Rabinow 2011; Korsby and Stavrianakis 2016). One of the reasons Rabinow initially created the Labinar was a growing fatigue with the individualization and the nefarious power relations of the university space. The core aim of the Labinar was to experiment with participation, thinking, and friendship. The ethical endeavor was to keep the possibilities of "joyous science" alive in the contemporary university. This current exercise in object exchange is thus one of a series of exercises based on a longing for collaborative thinking within the university to be indexed to an ethos of flourishing (Rabinow 2011; Rabinow and Stavrianakis 2014).

We had previously forged collaborative thinking about common objects of inquiry on the basis of either collaborative fieldwork (e.g., in synthetic biology; see Rabinow and Bennett 2012; Rabinow and Stavrianakis 2013) or unfamiliar objects, which could act as "testing grounds" for concepts and questions (Korsby and Stavrianakis 2016). A more recent undertaking is based on a challenge to forge a zone of "interconnected problems" by bringing together objects drawn from individual inquiries. On the basis of inquiry into the fields of assisted suicide, transnational pimping, and modernist art practice, we sought to develop interconnected problems around craft, style, and manners of living (*bios*). In that particular exercise, the objects we worked through were very concrete "things" such as a bottle of pink nail polish from Korsby's fieldwork among Romanian sex workers;

three images, whose significance pertained to bodily position, drawn from a documentary film about a situation of assisted suicide in Stavrianakis' fieldwork; and two paintings by Paul Klee, which Rabinow was working on (Stavrianakis, Rabinow, and Korsby 2018).

Against this background, we started discussing what could be achieved analytically if we moved to a new approach of allowing an element drawn from fieldwork to be handed over to, and worked through by, another person. As such, what is at stake in this exercise, which we describe in the following pages, is allowing an element of one's own inquiry to become an object through exchange with a collaborator.

EXERCISE

The question we started asking each other was, What would happen if one allowed oneself to give over something from one's own fieldwork to another person, letting that person work conceptually and analytically, as well as affectively, with it? We imposed no a priori limitations as to what it could be, only that it be an element from fieldwork—possibly in the form of a material object, a crafted field note, a video or image—as we had previously experimented with. We decided that we had no need to agree on a prior method as to how the other person should work with the proleptic object once it was handed over; the only guideline was that once it had been handed over, we would try to make it our own in some way before returning it. Minimally, this guideline meant that we would have a certain commitment to engaging with it as an object of inquiry, to endeavor to "incorporate" it, so as to work it through, to give it back transformed. The reciprocal task and challenge is to reincorporate the transformed object.

Interestingly, without having agreed beforehand, we both chose to hand over things from fieldwork that were ethically challenging and that we thought had a yet-to-be-understood potential: the kind of condensed objects from fieldwork that one simply cannot ignore but doesn't necessarily know what to do with. The wish to collaborate, to invent a new exercise in our ongoing work of collaboration, provided the occasion to take up, by giving over, elements from fieldwork that were blocking us.

We asked a sincere but not innocent question: What might happen if, instead of controlling what is drawn out of fieldwork as artifacts of field experience, in order to then reflect on the conceptual and intellectual stakes of the interconnection of those artifacts, we simply let the other person re-objectify our experience, and thus our object of inquiry? The question was not innocent to the degree that it is sincere: it interconnects the question of how one does fieldwork to that of what one seeks to know, to who one is, as the kind of person who does this kind of fieldwork and seeks to know these kinds of things. As Dewey wrote, objects and objectives of inquiry are linked.

But what does the process of "holding" a field object from another person's research entail? Is it a matter of a psychodynamic relation in which the anthropologists are searching for a "holding environment" (Winnicott 1986) in which the capacity for their own interpretation of their own material and experience can flourish? We could deny this psychological transaction but that wouldn't mean it wasn't there. Perhaps more importantly, regardless of the presence of psychological exchange, in practice what mattered from the point of view of the exercise as a technique of collaborative inquiry was what, if anything, we learned. Furthermore, it mattered how and why these objects were exchanged rather than others, what any of this tells us about our practice, and the determinations we can draw out of these specific field inquiries.

Having now introduced the trajectory of how we ended up engaging in this collaborative exercise of exchanging objects, we offer below an instantiation of the movements of the exchange and the analyses that followed. We briefly reflect on the moments of both disquiet and relief that emerged. We also suggest that seeing another person's relation to one's own field object could be a useful tool in transforming one's own relation to the object in question and thus in developing one's analysis and concept work. Systematic attention to such a mode of intersubjectivity in thinking about objects of inquiry and its consequences is not, we think, the same as the regular academic practice of commenting on other people's analyses and papers. In the following pages we endeavor to specify what we mean by such a "transformed relation."

MOVEMENTS

Very briefly stated, our two projects are (1) a field inquiry about the political and affective economy and relations between Romanian pimps and sex workers, and (2) a field inquiry into assisted suicide in Switzerland. Interestingly, without having agreed upon this beforehand, we had both selected field objects in the form of written objects: an excerpt from an interview and a "rule" written down during fieldwork, respectively. We each sent our object to the other.

Object A, Korsby: Interview with Andrei, Experienced Pimp
The feeling in you, in your chest, is like a volcano coming out. This is the feeling when you do something bad. When you are evil to someone, like when I kicked someone's ass and I was afraid that I had killed him, that was the feeling. When I was beating Diana, I had that feeling of being sorry in my chest, because you are hurting and beating a girl. It is a different feeling when you are hurting a girl. Everything is shutting down in you. When you do something good, you feel it in your whole body, also in your head, then there is sun, you can think in another way. It is like you take everything out, then you are not swallowed [*înghiți*]. It is like you threw up everything that was bad in you and changed everything in your body, even your movements, your whole body.

Object B, Stavrianakis: "Fieldwork Rule #1"
"Do not accompany anyone in their voluntary assisted death who is not also accompanied by a relative or friend." I made this rule after an encounter in the field with a woman in her forties, Madame Borg, who suffered from multiple sclerosis. She asked me, in my capacity as anthropological inquirer, to be the one to accompany her to Basel to her voluntary assisted death. During our meeting it became clear that she had difficulty both expressing her plan and her wish to her daughter and talking about it with her boyfriend. In fact the boyfriend, who was reluctant to discuss the issue with her, broke up with her after her meeting with me, which he had been aware of. I suspect he did this because her meeting with me clarified for him that she was seriously considering and making plans for an accompanied suicide. She then made a request to an association in Switzerland. After discussing the situation with several people—and not least after experiencing the intense reaction of my wife (also an anthropologist), who deemed it unethical to take the position of a kinsperson or friend—I decided to make this rule. I explained the rule to Madame Borg, saying that I could accompany her only if a family member or friend were also with her. She then informed me that she had decided that her daughter still needed her, and thus for now would not be seeking assistance with suicide.

Korsby

The object I sent to Anthony was an excerpt of one of my many interviews with pimps and people convicted of human trafficking, which had been challenging in my work with my fieldwork data. My challenges did not stem from a lack of analytical ideas, but rather from the reactions I got from audiences at conferences and workshops, as well as reactions from colleagues, friends, and family, when presenting these excerpts. I was curious about the lives, thoughts, and actions of a group of people whom we rarely hear about, not only because of their lifestyle, which makes them difficult to access, but also because their voices are seldom invited into conversations about sex work, human trafficking, and (transnational) criminal activities. Despite my own curiosity, I could not disregard the strong moral responses of both private and professional audiences (cf. Borneman 2012) who questioned the legitimacy of even hearing the voices of "the bad guys" and my personal role and ethics in interacting with this group of people. These moral responses were so consistent and strong that I could not ignore them.

I kept meeting this moral blockage: besides how I as a young woman gained access to the field, it was all people wanted to talk about. I felt stuck. I did not know how to take a quote like the one by Andrei (above) and present it in a way that did not mainly elicit people's personal moral responses, which I experienced as radically blocking the way for an actual conversation about the moral worlds, bodies, and kinship relations of pimps in eastern Romania. It was a relief to hand over the object to someone I trusted.

As I sent off the object to Anthony, however, my annoyance with the overpersonalization and moralizing I had experienced from various audiences was now replaced with a reflection on what Anthony might think of me—as a person, a friend, an anthropologist—when working with this object. Whereas I had never considered this before when presenting my work to larger audiences, I now looked at the object again and wondered whether Anthony would somehow judge me for having lived and taken part in this environment for extended periods of time during fieldwork. It seemed as if the fact that I had handed the object over to him in this way— that it was his to hold onto for several weeks, during which I would not work on that part of my material—and had not just asked for his response at a workshop or after reading through a section of my analysis, personalized the exchange for me to a new extent.

Stavrianakis

The object I sent to Trine is not an excerpt from my encounter with Madame Borg, on a day in April 2015 in a village outside of Strasbourg, a day on which a steady affect of composed attentiveness, I'd like to think, gave way slowly to a creeping disquiet and a slightly sickening feeling of having gotten into a situation that was quickly moving beyond my control, a feeling stemming in large part from the clear fact that my request to meet individuals who were in the process of requesting assistance with suicide was being taken up as an offer of just such assistance—in other words, the feeling of a mistake. Rather, the object I sent to Trine was the outcome, the working over and working through, of two conversations: one with a Swiss anthropologist, with whom I am collaborating in this project, whose response to my narration of the event was to ask me whether I would be prepared to take the role of a "first-order" accompanier; and the response of another anthropologist, my wife, whose cutting intervention, which I took utterly seriously, was that I "could not" take the position of Madame Borg's daughter (the closest kinsperson). I understood her point not in the sense of a moral outrage—that is, "you mustn't"—but more literally: that it would be impossible to take that position, and that if I were to try to occupy that "place" I would be blinding myself to something essential about the process of requesting and fulfilling this kind of death.

I think I sent this object to Trine because I wanted to test my own working through of this experience against hers, in particular because she is a person who I know has been in very difficult field situations in a terrain in which the management of position and proximity is likely to have been a key challenge.

HOLDING THE OBJECT

Korsby

For me this object opens up questions about the range of concepts of accompaniment and participation. Could Anthony have accompanied Madame Borg to Basel without accompanying her to her voluntary assisted death? When on the journey would he have become the direct accompanier? Or, put more sharply: When does accompanying someone start and end? Is he already accompanying his informants in their assisted voluntary deaths—participating in the event—through his conversations and meetings with them leading up to the actual event? Are we already active participants in an event by the way the event is "primed" through our dialogues and interactions with our informants? As Anthony writes, after Madame Borg's meeting with Anthony, it became clear to Madame Borg's partner that she was seriously planning to move ahead with the plan.

Initially I wondered why he had sent me this particular object, because it was a decision (rule) already made—How would I be able to add to it or push it further? But now I think that his object might tell us interesting things about fieldwork methodologies and crucial events in the lives of our informants. The questions are basic ones: Where does an event start and end? Is it the actual event (in this case, death) that is the most defining marker, rather than all the surrounding elements leading up to the event? When is an event solely for our informants, and when does it become our event too? Being invited intimately into the event pushed Anthony to reject it and to create a rule in order to not find himself in that situation again. A rule puts complex actions and emotions into some kind of system. But it also pushes us to ask what a rule is in the first place: How is it made, for whom, and why? Rules are structures we can lean on to find solutions and ways out, so we can move forward. In that way they support us, but they also narrow our field of vision if we follow them blindly. How has the rule worked since he created it? Has it been productive for him methodologically, preventing unwanted situations? How have other informants responded to the rule? The fact that he numbered the rule points to an expectation that there would be more rules to come. Why?

I agree that Anthony could never stand in for Madame Borg's daughter; that would be impossible because he is not her kin. His role, and leeway, would take very different forms from the daughter's in relation to Madame Borg's planned death. He would not hold her, caress her, and talk to her in the same way. And perhaps that was exactly what Madame Borg wanted: someone by her side, who knows her and the process, but who is not a close family member.

The object points to a classic ethical dilemma—one I also encountered in the field—which concerns the researcher's level of involvement. One day during fieldwork I told an informant (a Romanian pimp) how uncomfortable I felt about hearing a conversation between two other interlocutors about planned criminal activity. He said: "You are a very strange person. You come here and ask my friends and me all these questions about what we do and how we do it. And then I arrange it, so you meet these guys, and then you hear what they are up to. And then you complain?"

I had to agree with him that it seemed strange that I asked for insight and participation but then did not want it when it was given to me. I did not want it to this degree and in this way. I acknowledge that my case and Anthony's are highly different, but both cases touch upon our own uneasiness with the world of our informants and how we are actively dragged into that world. I wonder whether our uneasiness arises because of the asymmetry in ends between our informants and ourselves.

Stavrianakis

I think this object shows two forms of violence, the significations of such forms for the relation of a subject to himself and to others, and the challenge of grasping these significations and forms of violence in an anthropological mode. I found Trine's object very challenging to receive: to the degree that I received it as violent, and the sending of it as an act of violence, was the degree to which it resisted analysis. I wondered why she sent it to me, thinking that perhaps it was just as resistant to analysis for her as for me, and that my challenge was to not hide my experience of the violence of the object but to present it through an understanding of that violence.

I suggest that the first example primes attention to an economy of violence in which the concern is when and how to include force within power relations, and to what extent. This claim is speculative, of course, insofar as another plausible observation might be that the use of violence Andrei first describes, of almost killing a man, has no signification. If that is the case, I don't know how Trine, or any other anthropologist, could use the object to further inquiry. By contrast, we might be permitted to make several interpretations of Andrei's "fear" that he used too much force, not least by asking on what scale—that is, relative to what—this level of force was deemed excessive. For example, it could be relative to political relations with other criminal organizations, in which excessive force, killing, would provoke a counterforce beyond that which he is willing and able to manage. Or, that within his own economy, he was excessive relative to his aims; it was too costly, to put it in those terms. As Trine has underscored for me many times in discussions, the pimps are aware that physical violence is not the most economical manner of managing people. The first example points to his not having been careful or economical enough.

The second example "is different," as Andrei says himself. "It's different when you are hurting a girl." Despite what pimps have told Trine—that using violence on women who work for them indexes loss of control, a poor economy—nevertheless it seems to me that something else beyond the question of the correct economy enters the scene when discussing violence against women.

Andrei, I think, gives us good reason to think that this violence is of a different form. He can give a rival gangster a "good enough" beating in order to secure his economic position, but it doesn't seem to be the same with women: "when you are hurting a girl" (present progressive tense), "everything is shutting down in you." Very simply, it seems to me, violence against women, for Andrei, introduces and draws out a signifying split in his subject, which he can only approach negatively as "not doing good," unlike beating a man, which he could name as "doing bad" and "being evil" for a reason (though such a reason remains unnamed). Andrei gives me reason to think that these two forms of violence are distinct: He beat the man, and was concerned about him. He hurt the woman, but his guilt is only about himself: "everything is shutting down in you." Negatively contrasted, doing good is the opposite of hurting a woman, which in turn is not isomorphic with beating a man; it is when you are not being "swallowed." The violence that comes with shutting down is thus attached to the feeling of being swallowed (not hurting = not being swallowed / hurting = being swallowed). I read Andrei's account of hurting Diana as basically narcissistic (it was about him); I wondered whether "shutting down," in Andrei's narrative, being swallowed, is not (only) the consequence of violence but (also) the cause: fear of being annihilated, swallowed, is externalized, projected, and then identified with. But of course, Trine's role is not to provide therapy for Andrei. So what is happening in terms of "knowing" in the scene of encounter: is the challenge to find a mood through which to grasp or hold the evil that has been contained? The inquiry set out to understand the practice of men in transnational pimping relative to the women they work with. As Trine has pointed out (Korsby 2015, 2017), several key lessons from the inquiry are that these men are heavily dependent on the women who work for them; the men's position is much more fragile when they go abroad than the positions of the women, who demonstrate capacities to adapt that the men don't have; and that the relations between the men and the women also include love.

It seems that within this configuration an anthropological account of pimping that could include not only the observation of but also an account of the use of violence against women might ask how configurations of love and violence, economic excess and affective (psychic) deficiency, can be observed together without remobilizing, or mirroring, the kind of splits and separations through which they are presented—if that is possible.

Korsby

Until reading Anthony's analysis of my field object, my focus in this quote had been on the difference between doing "good" and doing "bad": I had been analyzing Andrei's description of the way the body is perceived compartmentally when doing "bad" (felt in the chest) versus feeling the entire body when doing "good." When doing "bad" the experience is condensed and intensified (like a "volcano coming out"), which creates energy and momentum, versus the surrender of the body to the "good" acts, which take over the entire body and change how the body feels and moves. Instead, Anthony points to the narcissistic shift from the external to the internal in Andrei's experience of being violent toward men and women—an element that I had more or less seen as simply an accentuation of Andrei's own evaluation of the severity of violence against a woman versus a man. Even though I am not sure that this is a matter of narcissism but rather of a visceral, bodily experience of the energy and power of a particular kind of violence, this perspective gives me new paths through which to think about my informants' sense of the relationship between self and other during the act of violence.

Stavrianakis

Receiving Trine's working through of my object was a confirmation of the impossible position of standing in for another in the position of the loved one; at the same time, I read her as asking, Why not occupy that impossible position? Trine says, like the Romanian pimp, "You ask to accompany these people in the search for an assisted death, and when they agree you say that you don't want to do it." I think it's not a matter of "level" of involvement, but of what can be seen and learned depending on how one is placed. On the one hand, it's true that Madame Borg probably would have liked a stranger to take her away and deliver her from her suffering; but this is a fantasy. On the other hand, from this object exchange, I am aware that to participate in voluntary death means that a form of collusion is necessarily at play, which no rule can purify.

DISPLACEMENT OF UNDERSTANDING

When comparing the analyses we offered to each other, we see that this exercise provided a slight displacement of our understanding of our own objects. However, no matter its modesty, the process was nevertheless a displacement—a movement—that unblocked our analytical processes by redirecting the perspective. Seeing the field object through the eyes of another opened up a point of view that we did not have previously, and being aware of that view transformed our own view on the blocked objects in question.

- Identify a field object (for example, a thing, a picture, a smell, an excerpt from field notes or interviews) that you consider potentially important for your analysis but that you have not been able to fully analyze or grasp—an object that calls for your attention but that you find yourself blocked from working with or thinking through.
- Hand over the object to a trusted colleague, and receive their object in return. Let go completely of your own object, and engage fully with your colleague's object.
- Hold the other person's object: work with it, analyze it, think through it. Such holding may spark memories of past conversations with this colleague, things they have told you about fieldwork, which may be important in your possible analysis. Write down your analysis and document your experiences of having handed over your object to a person you trust for a set period of time.
- Return the object and receive yours, including the new analysis.
- Have a conversation with your colleague about the analysis you made and the one you received. What are the resonances and dissonances? Identify what you gained in your analysis by allowing a new perspective on your object.

CHAPTER 7

RACHEL DOUGLAS-JONES

Drawing as Analysis

Thinking in Images, Writing in Words

When did you last draw something by hand? A map of how to get some-where? A picture in a letter? A diagram? In this chapter I am concerned with the capacity of images to bring forward and assist ethnographic analysis. My argument is that during analysis, shifting medium can be genera-tive. But I also want to suggest that, no matter how bad you think you are at drawing, your artistic abilities are simply not what is in question here. The task is one of honing the visual dimension of your conceptual imagination, the challenge that of how one might go about drawing an idea, a relation, an ethnographic problem. How can we use images to work with the incho-ate? This text describes the practice of thinking with drawn images as a means of analyzing ethnographic material, with a view to providing insight into how spatial, diagrammatic, and visually materialized thought can sup-port analysis and critique.

Ours is not the business of reporting found facts. As we make our fields, they make us, tuning our interests, speaking to our curiosities and concerns (Simpson 2006). Immersing ourselves in the things we learn to see, whether in the field or at our desk, brings us ethnographic knots and problems, puz-zles and jigsaws. These become the kernels of our chapters and articles, their hearts or frames, precisely because they arrest us, challenge us in some way. Sometimes their interestingness lies in their mundanity, sometimes in their strangeness; at other times, it is the sense of unease we are left with, that something is not yet quite understood on its own terms. But how do you draw an idea, a relation, a problem?

Analyses are tricksters, appearing in one form and then another, often patterned across years but indiscernible in a given moment. The drawing I describe here is a step on the way toward analysis as newfound understanding, a mode of being with material in a way that acts as a companion and scaffolds space for thought. I was brought to image making during my own writing process while assisting on a project called "Writing Across Boundaries" at Durham University, originally co-convened by Bob Simpson and Robin Humphrey (Newcastle). Thinking earnestly and intently about writing alongside and through commissioned essays from senior social scientists, I became haunted by the rather devastating sentence that opens Roy Wagner's "Depersonalizing the Digression": "The findings, speculations, arguments, and conclusions of an anthropologist are no better than their ability to write them down, in clear, distinct and acute prose or prosody" (2010, 1). He continues, compounding the issue: "One thinks no better than one can write, and for the simple reason that one's audience, one hopes, is not exclusively in one's own head" (1). But often, we need some help getting from these first thoughts to prose on the page. Over the intervening years I have worked with, against, and around Wagner's comment that one thinks no better than one can write, because writing is a form of thought.

My examples here seek to expand the tools at hand for thinking, so as to help those thoughts into dialogue with audiences outside of one's own mind. In analytical work decisions have to be made about what we will make, how we will give our accounts in a way that challenges and unsettles the known or the given; is the author a "neophyte un-learner" for whom perpetual openness is the doing of analysis? (Kapferer 2017). It is in this work that drawing—by which I mean making lines, shapes, boxes, visual associations—is a useful way of linking ideas and organizing thoughts, of living with openness and guiding the reshaping of arguments. It is a technique that, as educators, we often draw on in the classroom, at a whiteboard or blackboard, or even when making slides.

The techniques I describe below simply require paper of varying sizes and a pencil (for the hesitant at heart). Colors are enjoyable but not required. With a few circles, squares, and notes within them, images can be used as part of an analysis of empirical material. I am interested in images for their potential to synthesize and objectify (Pink 2006, 8)—but I am less interested in knowledge remaining in that "objectified" state. Although diagrams and drawings as method fascinate me, they are not the end point I have in mind.

In anthropology, drawing has been extensively used to convey research analyses. Long used in fieldwork, the diagram in its explanatory and descriptive mode has documented social life—houses, villages, markets, and kinship trees—conveying complex ideas through moves such as abstraction, simplification, and detail. Condensers of meaning, diagrams seem to offer at a single glance something pages of words might fail to convey. Perhaps in response to the resurgence of the visual in broader analysis, anthropological and otherwise (Taussig 2011; McCosker and Wilkin 2014; Kennedy et al. 2016), a range of projects are again attending to the place of the image. Three such examples have recently come to my attention.

First, Elizabeth A. Hodson's 2016 exhibition called *Drawing the Anthropological Imagination* included marks on a surface, diagrams, maps, and visual notetaking. Curating the work of a range of anthropologists, Hodson (2016) aimed to explore "the importance of aesthetic forms for observing momentary sensations and securing fleeting ideas," studying "how these impressions and recordings develop beyond the field" both for exposition and speculation. She reveals the persuasiveness in the beauty of a well-drawn image, whether schematic or representational. In contrast with Hodson's interest in the aesthetic, Tristan Partridge's review of anthropological diagrams (2014) takes a thematic approach: the particularly diagrammed domains of kinship and exchange. Replete with examples, Partridge's text demonstrates how diagrams have been central to theoretical debate, from Evans-Pritchard's visual trees of Nuer clans and lineages (despite Nuer figuring being differently organized) to the place of linearity. His opening epigraph, quoting Massumi (2011, 99), addresses the diagram as "the activity of formation appearing stilled," a formulation that prefigures his later attention to the danger that diagrams "freeze" the flow of time, halt a world in motion, reify shifting relational states. Time, too, is a component in drawing in the field. A similar attention to the temporality of images appeared in my final example, when Engelmann, Humphrey, and Lynteris convened their conference "Diagrammatic: Beyond Inscription?" (2016). As they sought to explore the "dialectic of inscription and erasure as an inherent and generative trait of diagrammatic practices," they foregrounded the way diagrams operate at the "threshold of vision and the unseen," a provocative formulation for my purposes here.

Hodson, Partridge, and Engelmann et al. all are predominantly interested in the images that emerge from analysis rather than those that constitute it. I am interested in drawings as analytical tools, part of a process often unseen. I therefore borrow from these techniques with a different aim in mind: rather than explaining ethnographic material or generalizing, the images of this essay work as a means of making visual traces of ideas that are more felt than thought, that emerge from conceptual proximities, observed elisions, conflicts, gaps, and erasures. In what follows, I explore the generativity of visual nondeterminacy, the relationship between the drawer and drawing, and the potentialities in drawing as a praxis of translation.

THREE EXAMPLES

To write this contribution, I had to dig into boxes for old notebooks I had used while drafting my doctoral thesis. I first drew in order to think, in order to write. My preferred notebooks at the time were very large, with the forgiving expansiveness of blank pages. The three types of drawings I discuss come from the spiral-bound pages of a notebook dated March 2012, making them early efforts. My research, which had taken place over the previous two years, was a multisite study of a regional nongovernmental organization (NGO) in Asia-Pacific that was working to build capacity in ethical review. My observations came from conferences, audits, training sessions, conversations, and ethics-committee meetings. By March 2012 I was spending my days waiting around in a set of Welsh law courts, having been called up for jury service. With regard to my research, I had just arrived at what felt like a crucial wrangle with chapter 4 of my thesis. I could not take a laptop into the court's waiting room, so to give myself a sense that I could continue to think through the chapter as I waited to be called as a juror, I took one of these very large sketchpads through the metal scanners to the waiting room, and I kept my planning and thinking work going with a pencil and paper. After my jury service I returned to my desk and kept drawing. While I have in the years since marginally refined the drawing practices I developed to work with this material, they remain much as they were at the time. Ethnographic work is perpetually open, and the work of analysis moves between openness and momentary fixity: what will hold steady, what produces something that feels like insight.

Although Wagner hopes that one's audience is not exclusively in one's own head, getting ideas out of one's head—particularly in the often solitary spaces carved out for writing—is quite the challenge. Yet it is also part of the analytic process to take moments of being overwhelmed by one's material and move in and out of them. The first technique is the "everything" route: throwing down ideas, events, moments, places, words, author names. It requires a large sheet of paper and a willingness to cover it entirely. As Fortun (2009, 173) requests a "laundry list" from her students as they begin to formulate their question-asking in always provisional starting points, this exercise asks, What is the shape of this material? What does it span? Where are the poles? What belongs together? What seems to belong together but is actually a recurrent version of the "same" thing? This is a way of beginning to see how you see.

Giving yourself a single, uninterrupted hour, without reference to notes or computer, internet or field books, throw down the scope of your thoughts. Not everything you carry in your mind related to your project is going to make it onto this sheet of paper.[1] But things will rise to the surface: That moment someone made a comment you didn't understand. That article that changed the way you thought about how you might approach or frame something. A line from an interview. A single word. A theme you've been thinking of. A place you visited that you want to describe. A look. A discussion you had with Fred while on the bus. Don't try to specify too much; rely on your own shorthand to remind you what "apple talk" means (Fred was eating an apple at the time of the discussion you think was important). As you come up with things, try to group them together. You might choose to organize into "writing" objects—chapters, sections, paragraphs; you might work thematically. This process of writing is not intended to be exhaustive but, rather, exploratory. At the end of an hour you will have made visible to yourself materials that you want to assemble. You may have put some alongside one another or discovered that some could belong in several places. You also will have provided yourself with a snapshot of your current view on a particular slice through the material you have. And the snapshot can then become part of the dialogue of analytical work.

For example, one thing that became clear to me in doing this exercise myself was the challenge I would have in describing the NGO I had worked with: How "big" was it? I had drawn its name in large letters at the center

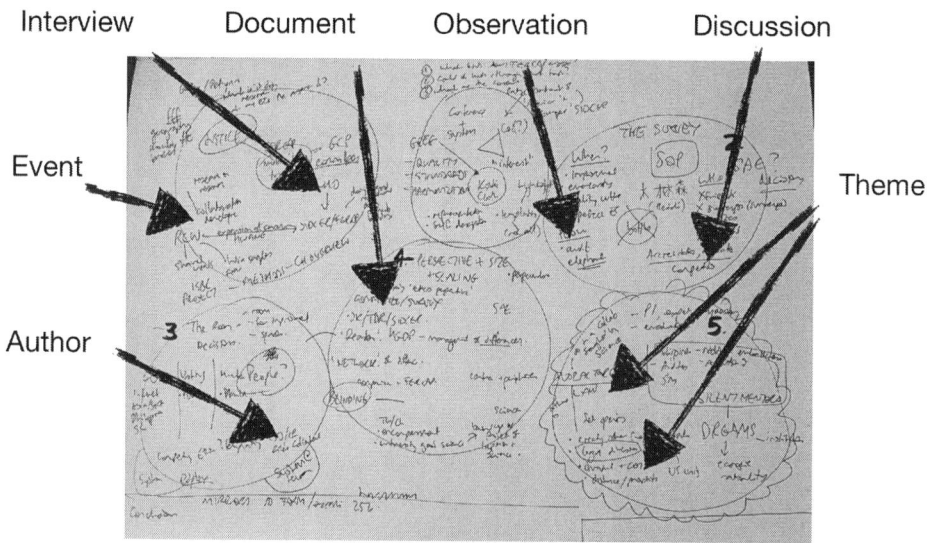

FIGURE 7.1 Collecting thoughts, assembling analysis.

of several stories, but at the time it had little standing in the international literature. More interestingly, I realized it was "made small" by other actors who dismissed its work. Through making choices about how large or small to make the NGO's activities, this "making things visible" exercise became a form of relating to size as a problem in my field. In *Reassembling the Social*, Bruno Latour asks us: "Does it not make perfect sense to say that Europe is bigger than France, which is bigger than Paris, that is bigger than rue Danton, and which is bigger than my flat? Or to say that the twentieth century provides the frame 'in which' the Second World War has 'taken place'?" (2005, 185). It does, Latour, it does. This is the everyday work of contextualization, and it is also often what feels comfortable in making this kind of organization. We lean toward the nation as "larger," a somehow explanatory force. But this blinds us to the everyday work of scale making being done in our material. "The big picture is just that: a picture" (Callon and Callon 1981). What kind of picture have you drawn? More importantly, whose? Making semitacit assumptions visible (such as the "size" of our actors) makes them more tangible, arguably much more so than organizing a Microsoft Word document to carry and contain them. An organization can be "drawn large" (e.g., the World Health Organization) far more easily than this weight can be conveyed in writing, and as such, this exercise allows for the drawing of a "proportional field" (after Corsín Jiménez 2010) in which we attend to the given weight and size of actors in their accounts as much as in our own.

Fortun (2009, 183) reminds us that ethnography is not about everything. As an exercise that aims at having your project before you such that you can survey its contents, drawing offers the opportunity for a moment of selection and, with the resulting physical piece of paper, a chance to take hold of its character. It is a tool for all that it will include and all that you will forget, the initial scoping of exclusions, its politics of representation, and its many possible routes forward.

INDETERMINACIES: SEPARATING AND DISTINGUISHING

Above I have described a technique for exploiting something of the "all at once" character of images on paper. I now move to the image as a focused technique for thought. Much analytical work depends on carefully distinguishing, selecting, weighing what belongs together and what should not be elided. Here I want to argue for the generativity of visually sorting out ideas and its potential to help clarify—particularly in the case of making distinctions. The diagrams described in the "Diagrammatic" conference occupy "a liminal space between representation and prescription," existing in this "dialectic of inscription and erasure" (Engelmann, Humphrey, and Lynteris 2016). It is a lesson that revelatory moments of analysis are frequently not the end point but another step toward a good description, a precise conceptualization, another turn in the lengthy processes of analysis.

For example, while researching the professional background of one of the conference speakers I'd seen present, I found a set of slides from an earlier conference that discussed the concept of "duty-based ethics." Although these slides referenced Kant, I knew that the way "duty" was being taken up among my Asia-Pacific interlocutors bore little resemblance to Kant—it was being interpreted and put to work in quite a different way. I also knew I hadn't thought very deeply about ideas of duty. To bring these ideas together while thinking about their separateness, I drew a circle with a line through the middle, putting choice on one side and obligation on the other. Did knowing more about ethics oblige my interlocutors to act in a new capacity in their workplaces? How did the invocation of a Kantian duty-based ethics appeal to those at the conference? How did it play out within professional settings?

Using the space of a sheet of paper, ask yourself what binaries seem to organize this topic or field within the literature—more interestingly,

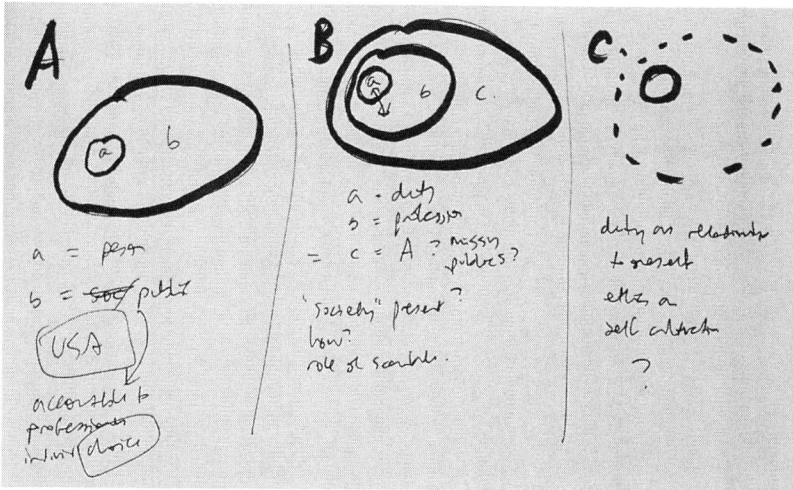

FIGURE 7.2 Diagramming duty.

within the field itself. Set them at opposite ends; a spectrum isn't necessary unless you feel one is already being drawn up. Before allowing the polarization to settle, now ask what doesn't fit those oppositions. What is pulling in another direction entirely? As above, once the drawing is laid out, there are questions to be asked of it. Whose are these contrasts? How are they produced? What are the "motivated oppositions" (Strathern 1980, 181) within them? What is presumed given in this setting?

These questions are necessary because diagrams can mislead us, reveal us in our assumptions. In *The Gender of the Gift* (1988), Strathern considers a diagram drawn a decade earlier by Godfrey Leenhardt to depict New Caledonian personage. Leenhardt argues that, "[w]e cannot use a dot marked 'self' (ego), but must make a number of lines to mark relationships" (Leenhardt 1979, 153, cited in Strathern 1988, 270). He is left with a diagram that centers the self, the personality, and the ego: a "star shaped configuration carries the one and same presumption: living within, guided by, driving, functioning as, or knowing these structures of relationships must be the individual subject" (Strathern 1988, 269). Strathern's critique draws together Leenhardt's diagram and his "discursive observations" (Strathern 1988, 268–69) to observe that the diagram has led Leenhardt astray: it does not allow for the subtleties of his notes, recorded elsewhere in his ethnography, to lead him to a different conclusion from the one prefigured and underpinning his diagram's imagination.

Although an image's capacity for simplified summary can be uncritical, it can also take us to sites from which new critiques can be formed. From this exploratory point of view, starting with text in order to generate text is frustratingly linear. Learning how to order ideas, the stages at which they need to appear in a narrative, is difficult, and in today's working conditions it is regularly subordinated to the continuous scrolling up and down a laptop screen.[2] Something else is required. In this third technique, the visual becomes a summary of a different kind. Still analytic, these drawings offer a more structured opportunity to organize materials. As much a form of composition as analysis, in the creation of an ethnographically driven argument the two are deeply intertwined. The order and tone of our stories changes how our analyses proceed when they are shaped into linear unfolding.

Let us take an example I was working with. It is a form of archaeology because in this case the image itself is merely a tool for clarifying an idea or thought. It has no place in the final text, as a diagram would, and may not even be the form the analysis eventually takes. The problem was a chapter. I had the cluster of things belonging to the problem, so to each topic I gave a section and boxed it off. I organized the layers of text according to what needed to go in what sections, which paragraphs. Visually planning my dis-

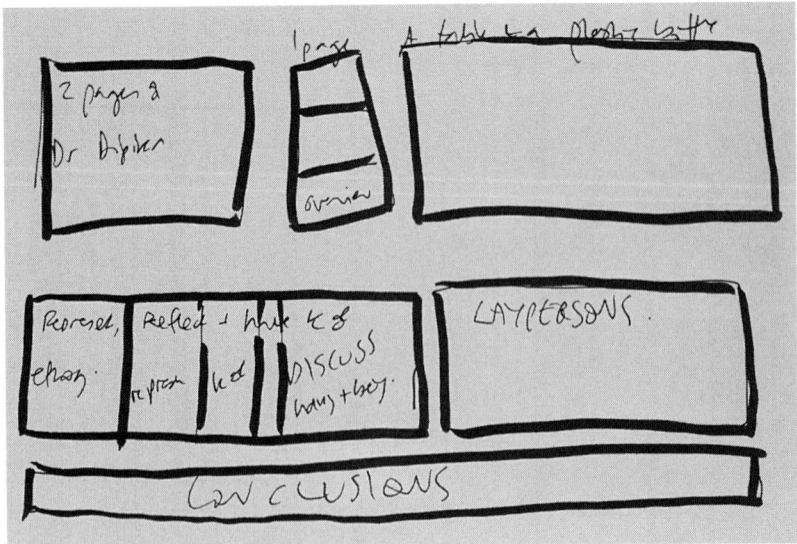

FIGURE 7.3 Finding density.

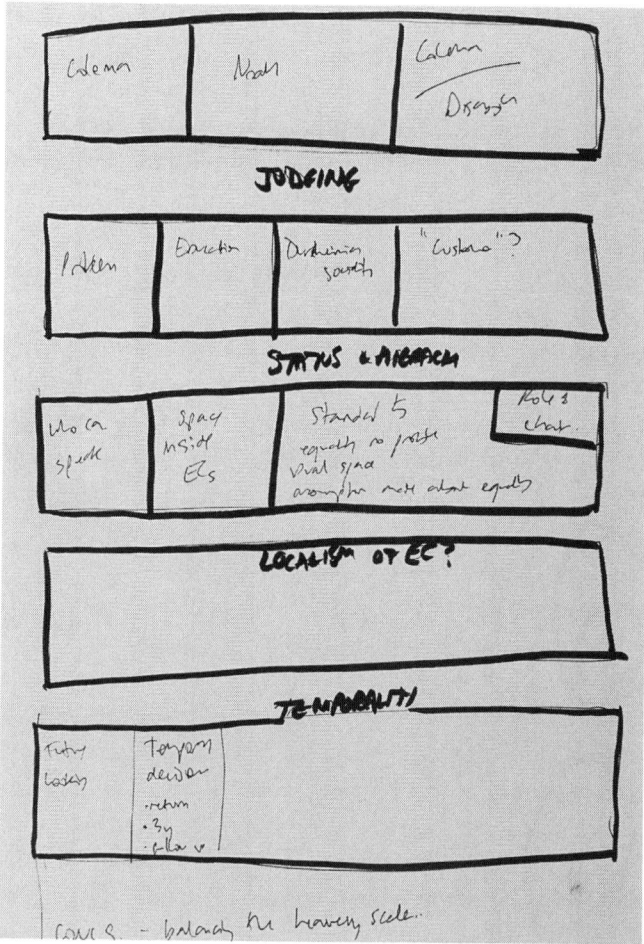

FIGURE 7.4 Finding gaps.

cussion and analysis of the practices of ethics review committees led me to a problem I was otherwise not aware of: although I had plenty of stories and ideas to put in my sections on how committees handled their sense of making judgments of colleagues, I had very little sense of what belonged in my section called "localism." By making a drawing of the chapter, I realized that while I thought it was important and belonged there, I had yet to articulate to myself the character of the connection between hierarchy and localism, localism and judging. I also realized that while I had given the grouping of thoughts a name ("localism"), I had not yet assembled what it would contain.

Composing our ethnographic moments, our stories and insights, is the relational work that brings an argument together. Image-based analysis exists prior to a clearly articulated argument; it exists at the level of a sense that these stories speak to one another. Although drawing did not tell me what those relations between localism and my other sections might be, the exercise pointed to a gap in my explicit understanding of what they were, or why I was drawn to discuss these topics together. An image of what you are combining is an exercise easily undertaken, quickly sketched, straightforwardly organized, if one is willing to face aporias. Once laid out, a drawn ordering can help produce statements that articulate your choices as particular and deliberate, and whether or not those statements themselves remain in the final text, they can act as the momentary grounding necessary to step again into the unknown.

CONCLUSION

One does not need to be a fine artist to draw on image-making to aid analysis. Spatial, diagrammatic, and visually materialized thought can support analysis and critique in the ways I have outlined here and doubtless many more. In her contribution to the Writing Across Boundaries series, Marilyn Strathern writes that, when starting new projects, "[a]n air of unreality hangs over my beginning efforts, though if I am lucky that can temporarily clear by my hanging the argument on someone's else words (you know how real other people's words appear, solid and sensible things as they are!), just as I began this piece" (2009, n.p.). In suggesting you "draw" out ideas emerging from your ethnography and the nascent conceptual space of analytical work, I am proposing a shift of medium, a form of work that steps around the screen and keyboard and takes place with simpler instruments. On these images we can "hang our arguments" built with tools well suited to making material the problems, concepts, and moments that occupy our ethnographic everyday. Analysis, when read in published form, appears in its synthesized completeness. The uncertainty bound up in arriving at a configuration of thought is concealed because the author has moved themselves beyond their earlier drafts. Large sheets of paper offer a chance to make material connections between as-yet unclear ideas, bringing the practical profane into sight. I maintain that writing is a form of thought; that when we write, we work at the edges of what we know. That is understandably a daunting place. If a drawing, diagram, or outline tacked to a desk or office wall can provide a sense of company, a sense of being already in the material, this may be enough to provide an analytical space wherein we can put our descriptions to work.

- At any time during your fieldwork or writing period, switch mode from words to images.
- Use the blank page to spatialize and organize your thoughts. Don't think "art"; think about affinities, shapes, circles, proximities. Depending on what you want to achieve, you might throw everything that comes to mind onto a piece of paper and start to link things together. Or you might make a separation between things you perceive as distinct but don't yet have reasons for.
- Be in dialogue with the image you have made: reflect critically on what you have put together, what assumptions your organization of field moments or terms reveals. How could this be thought otherwise?
- Move on from your drawing. Part of the purpose of drawing as analysis is to move you forward through realizations and toward the eventual textual format your work will probably take.
- Let time pass.
- Revisit the images you have made: Are there things in them that you have forgotten or that have become natural? Things that no longer make sense? Seeing disjunctures is part of analytic work—seize it!

NOTES

1. A chapter or an article are equally suited brackets to this practice.
2. Multiple monitors help but still have their limitations.

Diagrams

Making Multispecies Temporalities Visible

The combination of multispecies ethnography and feminist theories of assemblage and entanglement opens up powerful tools for social analysis. On one level, it illuminates the centrality of relations between humans and nonhumans to the making of culture, place, and history. On a more radical level, its attention to relationality as that which precedes and enacts subjects is a provocation to reimagine the dynamics of difference and belonging. "Subjects, objects, kinds, races, species, genres, and genders are products of their relating," writes Donna Haraway (2003, 7), pushing for close attention to histories and practices of significant otherness. To study modes of relating—that is, relationality as a plurality of verbs—involves becoming attuned to the temporalities of how things hold (Gan and Tsing 2018). Relationality depends on timing. But how exactly does one study timing? For the intrepid fieldworker, this comes with a few challenges. For example, how does one follow closely what happens when different species gather in and out of place, in and out of one's time frame of study? Seasonal animal migrations and asynchronous flowering are cases in point. How does one track presences and absences, latencies or anomalies across assemblages that may cohere through other-than-human rhythms and scales, as is the case perhaps with disappearing wetlands? Importantly, how does one decenter modern systems for reckoning with time (e.g., Gregorian calendars, digital clocks, historical timelines) as just a few among many ways that we make, socialize, and write about continuity and change?

In this chapter I look at diagrams. Diagrams are playful ways of engaging with multispecies temporalities. They offer a handy graphical language that operates between notetaking, representation, and abstraction. While in the field I might jot down keywords or sketch a curious object to help me recall or transcribe details at a later time. Diagrams, in contrast, are always in play, never just a fragment or memory aid, never a finished story or complete statement. I begin to work ethnographically by drawing diagrams. They allow me to work and rework how I consider processes and connections, appearing in my field notebooks and in the margins or on the back sides of writing drafts. They open up a provisional space where empirical and theoretical engagements might start to come together or work in tension. Diagrams are great to think with.

In what follows I present diagrams that I encountered early in my research and then some examples of my own. Perhaps because it is generally assumed that diagrams function best as illustrations of a closed cycle, a fixed system, or a network of kinship, the use of diagrams remains underexplored as a mode of attunement to open-ended and indeterminate processes that involve humans and nonhumans. I close with a protocol that I use in my teaching to play with the possibilities of diagrammatic experiments.

ARROWS AND CIRCLES

I study a flowering grass that most readers here know as rice. As with many multispecies ethnographers, I draw from multisited fieldwork and a wide range of historical, ethnographic, scientific, and philosophical literature. Natural history observation, animal tracking, and ecological surveys work alongside interviews with rice breeders, molecular biologists, farmers, and technicians, which also work alongside close readings of cartographic, ethnographic, and visual representations. The "field" is not given or known in advance; it is not a bounded territory or holistic object awaiting discovery (Gupta and Ferguson 1997). I encountered one kind of rice, which led me to the next and so on. Paying attention to the ways in which a flowering grass is enacted (e.g., as crop, data, taste) brings into focus multiple kinds of coordination (Mol 2012) and more-than-human assemblages (Tsing 2015). Early in my research, I was struck by two kinds of diagrams and how they indexed different relationalities: the first is from crop production manuals (figure 8.1), and the second is from an ethnographic atlas (figure 8.3).

Figure 8.1 is a composite of illustrations used in rice production manuals to describe the life cycle of rice as a crop. Many of these images were first formalized by the International Rice Research Institute (IRRI) founded by the Rockefeller and Ford Foundations in the early 1960s and based in the Philippines. From the start, IRRI scientists and agronomists have been tasked with building a "food-secure future" by developing varieties that can produce higher yields on an accelerated timeline. Diagrams are essential to visualizing that task. Crop diagrams always begin with a lone seed that undergoes three growth phases—vegetative, reproductive, and ripening. One point in time matters: harvest.

Figure 8.1 eliminates how and with whom the plant grows. Stripped of all companions, each stage is significant only as a lead-up to the production of grains. Materialities that have coevolved over centuries are excluded; instead we see a succession of ahistorical intervals. The plant's sole purpose is to produce grains as quickly, predictably, and uniformly as possible. The temporal orientation is toward yield or future harvest. At the bottom of figure 8.1, a straight arrow moving toward harvest appears along a horizontal axis. The arrow of time appears as a universal measure, a fixed track of days against which different rates and stages of growth may be compared. I use the term *one-point temporality* to describe this unilinear logic (see figure 8.2). It is a riff on the term *one-point perspective* used by art historians to describe an aesthetic technique from early Renaissance Europe. Oil painters introduced an illusion of deep space by

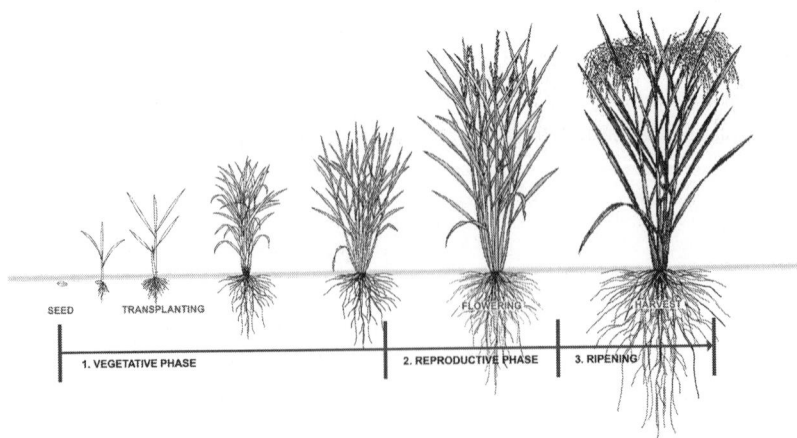

FIGURE 8.1 Scientists describe three growth phases: during the vegetative phase, seeds germinate and then develop leaves and roots; during the reproductive phase, panicles and flowering heads develop and pollination occurs; in the final phase, grains fill, ripening for harvest. Source: Elaine Gan, composite of IRRI rice production images, 2016.

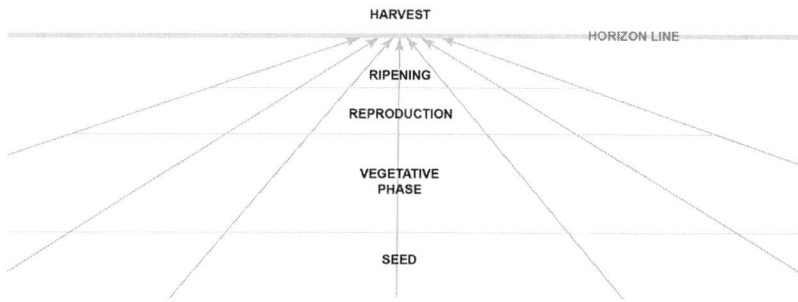

FIGURE 8.2 Rice agriculture is organized around "one-point temporality"—a future of bountiful harvest that depends on isolating rice from the temporalities of other species.

positioning their subjects along lines that converged in a central vanishing point on a horizon line.[1] Rice scientists deploy a similar technique when they orient the life and assemblages of a plant around the single vanishing point of harvest.

For a modern crop to grow as illustrated and as scheduled, a technoscientific assemblage that includes chemical fertilizers and pesticides, irrigation networks, credit and loans, and state policies has to be in place, while assemblages of animals, plants, microbes, and others have to be ignored or eradicated. The logic of one-point temporality makes attending to co-constitutions or contradictions between and within these assemblages irrelevant because it is only the productivity of lone autopoietic seeds that matters. High-yielding rice varieties that were at the center of a green revolution throughout Southeast Asia in the 1960s emerged from the logic of one-point temporality—with disastrous consequences because no plant ever grows alone (Gan 2017).

Figure 8.3 offers something different. Whereas figure 8.1 hinges on a single arrow of time, figure 8.3 orients us toward multiple nested cycles. An agricultural year in the Ifugao mountain provinces of northwestern Philippines is an interplay of seasonal activities and synchronized events. In his *Ethnographic Atlas of Ifugao*, anthropologist Harold Conklin (1980) diagrams a year as a succession of events that are intricately coordinated around the ecology and annual cultivation of pond-field rice, the most highly valued crop among thousands of plants in Ifugao life. While crop production manuals focus on one end goal, namely harvest for sale, the Ifugao calendar focuses on the coordination and timing of many activities. Each figuration sees and attends to rice as a particular kind of being:

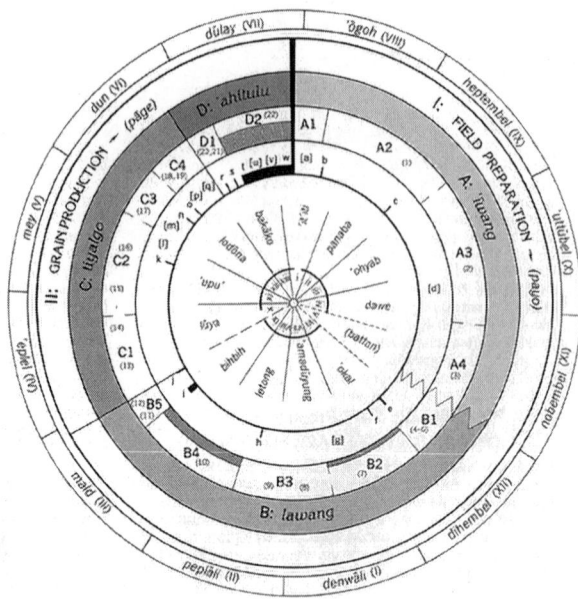

FIGURE 8.3 Harold Conklin represented an Ifugao calendar year as a set of nested activities. Source: Harold Conklin, *Ethnographic Atlas of Ifugao* (1980), 64.

the first rice is a means to an end and the second is a rhythm enacted collectively.

Conklin's diagram has two main rings: the outermost ring represents the twelve months of the Gregorian calendar; within it is the Ifugao agricultural year, which varies in response to seasonal fluctuations and socioecological changes. The year is divided into two general "phases" of field preparation and grain production (I, II), which are subdivided into four "seasons" (A–D), subdivided into "periods" (A1–D2), subdivided further into agricultural and ritual "events" (a–w), and finally a thirteen-month lunar cycle in the innermost ring. "Battan" is a provisional fifth month and indexes a variable interval when Ifugao maintain coordinations by adjusting to environmental phenomena. While the twelve Gregorian months in the outer ring are seen as fixed, the thirteen Ifugao months on the inner rings are variable—responsive, let's say.

I met Conklin's diagrams almost a decade ago now, and they have changed the way I think with relationality and how I use diagrams to respond to relationalities otherwise. I became interested in searching for interplays, coordinations, and encounters between rhythms, recursions, and historical trajectories.

Figure 8.1 and figure 8.3 make use of arrows and circles to represent time. Attending to multispecies relations challenges us to think with more expansive practices of figuration. Other lines are possible: curvy and warped lines; bold, directional lines; dashed, virtual lines; erased, inadequate, alienated lines. I have found it extremely generative to think with feminist scholar Karen Barad's agential realist account of "intra-active spacetimemattering" (2007) in which entanglement folds and refolds worlds all the way through. As a philosopher-physicist, Barad uses diagrams to explicate dynamics that enact agential cuts through which beings/becomings or ontoepistemologies materialize. Barad aims to render spacetimemattering between two points—shown in figure 8.4 as points α and ß—as an infinite set of all possible geographies/histories/temporalities, or what they call "iterative reconfigurings." Here, there is no single relation of causality between the two points, no preordained arrow or circle of time between a past/source α and a future/destination ß, no α and ß that preexist our attentions in the field or at the writing desk. This diagram suggests a way of reconceptualizing the one-point temporality that organizes crop agriculture in figure 8.1 and the recursive cycles of Ifugao life in figure 8.3. Taking point α as seed and point ß as harvested grain, the lines aim to express relentlessly indeterminate yet agential intra-action. Everything

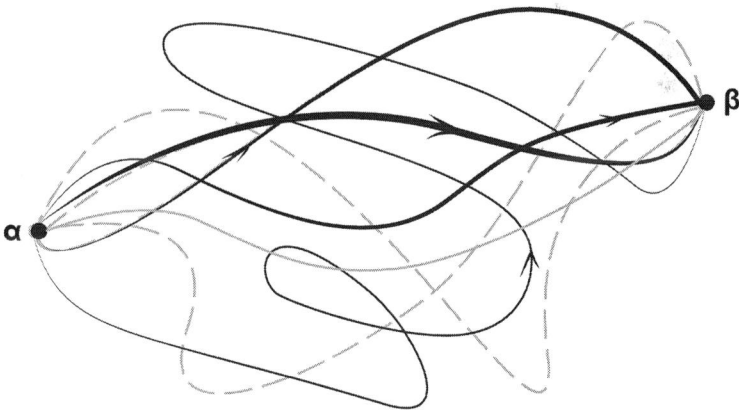

FIGURE 8.4 Karen Barad's (2018) diagram of quantum entanglement visualizes an infinite plurality of paths (hauntological sedimentations of virtual, possible, and actual) that configures and is reconfigured by any past/source point α and a future/destination point ß. Source: Karen Barad and Elaine Gan, 2017.

in Barad's diagram is in process of mattering, of configuring and being reconfigured.

This does not mean that we now ought to add as many points and lines as possible. Multiplicity for multiplicity's sake is a fallacy of data science, a field in which the harvest of more and more information can be mistaken as the best solution to all kinds of problems. Barad's diagram makes me slow down and reconsider how relationality comes in and out of being— when, how, for whom.[2] Sketching and drawing diagrams, for me, opens up an exploratory space to connect with iterative reconfigurings, to be made and unmade in the process of slowing down.

THREE DIAGRAMS OF MULTISPECIES TEMPORALITIES

What follows are three diagrams that have helped me think through more-than-human dynamics. Each plays with graphical notations to express entangled processes—and specifically, temporal patterns. None of them aim for a full accounting of a field or dictate universal rules for drawing diagrams. At most, they are more coherent versions of working sketches in my notebooks, and I share them here as thinking-making aids. Each does try to offer a specific way of making visible the timing of more-than-human relations. The first, represented in figure 8.5, considers phenology or seasonal timing in a farm in Laos. I retain the one-point perspective seen in figure 8.1 but open it to rice companions that appear seasonally. At each stage, different species gather in a rice paddy; some become dominant while others go dormant. In the second diagram, represented in figure 8.6, I show how multiple oscillations may be expressed together, expanding on Conklin's diagram in figure 8.3. Oscillation offers a way of thinking about cycles and periodic motion in order to express events that recur over very brief or very long timescales. Seasonal fluctuations are one among many oscillations through which continuity is made or broken. My third diagram, represented in figure 8.8, considers disruption and emergence, or changes to periodicity that are best understood through assemblages rather than single species. With the ongoing construction of dams along the Mekong River, for example, some assemblages collapse while others flourish. The diagram offers a way of seeing how relations come in and out of being, intra-actively.

Diagram of Phenology

I arrived at a farming cooperative in Luang Prabang on the first day of the Lao New Year in 2017. It was April, the end of a long hot dry season and the beginning of a new rice season. On my way to the farm, revelers lined the streets, gleefully flinging water to welcome the coming rains. In my sketch (figure 8.5), rain appears at the upper right corner. Rain softens the hardened soil in the paddies, turning clay into mud. At the farm, knee-deep and barefoot in mud, a Hmong farmer teaches me how to use a wooden plough hitched to a pink water buffalo. The mud is slippery and the movement rhythmic, requiring interspecies synchrony—and very strong legs and glutes. Together, we turn the soil, pulling nutrients to the surface. In the meantime, seeds are selected from the previous year's crop and germinate in flooded seedbeds. Seedlings are then transplanted into paddies.

Figure 8.5 is a representation of multiple pond fields; it mixes figuration and abstraction in order to focus on phenology, or events that coordinate with seasonal rhythms. The farm plants more than thirty kinds of rice that grow over different durations: three months, four months, or six months. This allows farmers to spread out harvests, the most labor-intensive and time-sensitive phase. *Khao na pi*, or floating rice, is the most reliable but also has the longest growing time of six months. Between the wet and dry seasons, multiple interspecies coordinations unfold and must be negotiated. Different species become significant at different phases; farmers know to look out for seasonal activity patterns. After the rains, water buffaloes are key to breaking the soil and preparing the paddies. Like water buffaloes, ducks are a boon to farmers; they are a constant presence, eating weeds and fertilizing pond fields. Other species arrive as rice grows, competing against farmers for food: fast-reproducing golden apple snails favor young rice plants and arrive early, reproducing rapidly at night; grasshoppers feed on leaves as plants mature, but when caught, they become delicacies for farmers; flocks of gregarious munia fly in as grains start to ripen, and children try to trap them for sale at the local market; field rats are active at night and become easier for farmers to catch when rains force them out of hiding and they run for higher ground. Water, too, is part of the mix. Irrigation and drainage are essential; too much or too little at the wrong time can kill crops.

By focusing on phenology, I can approach assemblages as not just groups of species that gather in one slice of time, but as shifting relations and activity patterns that materialize in different seasons and with different temporal rhythms. The one-point temporality represented in figures 8.1 and 8.2 opens

VEGETATIVE
PHASE

PINK
snail eggs.
invasive
species.

REPRODUCTION

RIPENING GRAIN

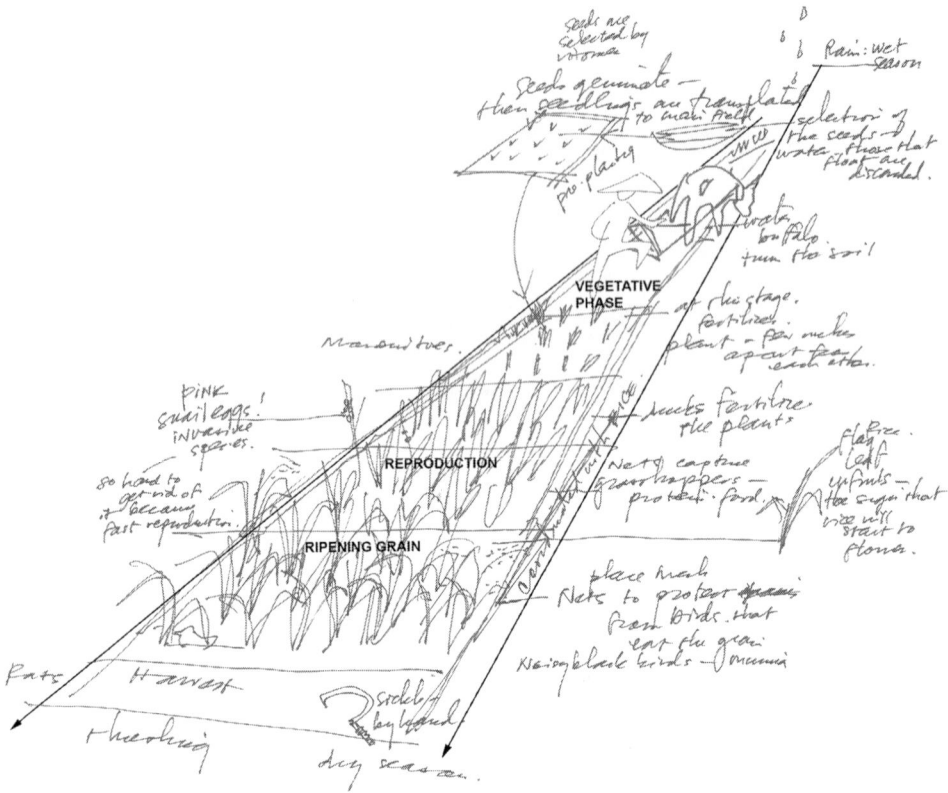

FIGURE 8.5 Working sketch of seasonal multispecies life in a farming village in Luang Prabang, Laos. Source: Elaine Gan, 2017.

into a manifold of coordinations that are constantly made and remade through differential timing.

Diagram of Oscillations

Oscillation is a recurring movement between two states (figure 8.6). I can look at the movement between wet and dry seasons in figure 8.5 as one kind of oscillation that interacts with many other oscillations. Figure 8.6 superimposes oscillations that occur over long and short intervals of time: diurnal rhythms that are synchronized to day and night cycles; lunar cycles from new to full moon that occur every twenty-nine days, approximately; wet and dry seasons that constitute an annual cycle; and the multiyear fluctuations between the El Niño (warming) and La Niña (cooling) phases in wind and sea temperatures across the eastern Pacific Ocean.

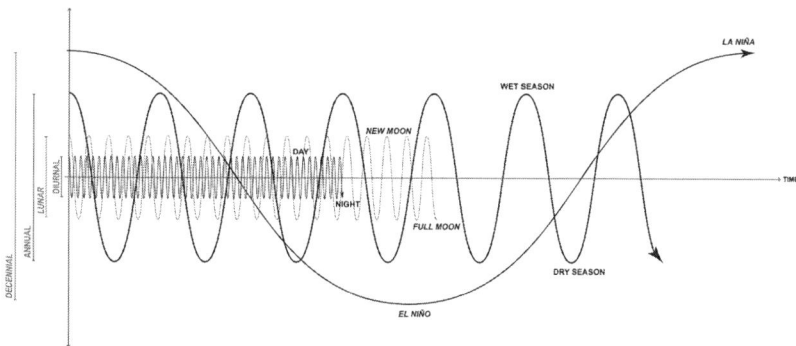

FIGURE 8.6 Diagram to show relationships between multiple oscillations that occur over different intervals. Source: Elaine Gan, 2018.

Expanding on Conklin's diagram in figure 8.3, I can contextualize seasonal events within a broader interplay of oscillations, and expanding on Barad's diagram in figure 8.4, I try to articulate a plurality of entangled paths as oscillations.

Notice that each cycle in figure 8.6 appears as a sustained oscillation (figure 8.7A), a movement back and forth that goes on infinitely without variation. Different oscillatory modes exist in the real world. Some oscillations decay over time; energy dissipates, either as a result of friction or other kinds of resistance. Others become unstable or divergent as energy builds.

A damped oscillation (figure 8.7B) is an oscillation that becomes smaller and smaller in magnitude. Seasonal migrations of species may be visualized as a sustained oscillation that has evolved over long timescales. Mekong giant catfish (*Pangasianodon gigas*) travel from the South China Sea and up the Mekong River; when their migratory routes are blocked by dams and overfishing, the pattern of their movement weakens. Their gradual disappearance may be visualized as a damped oscillation. In contrast, divergent or unstable oscillations (figure 8.7C) occur when energy builds and increases exponentially. There is no expected bounceback to the original periodicity. When non-native species such as water hyacinths (*Eichhornia crassipes*) clog waterways, the effects are nonlinear. Water hyacinths are particularly detrimental to phytoplankton that release oxygen into the water and sustain several aquatic webs. The spread of water hyacinths over time may be visualized as a divergent oscillation.

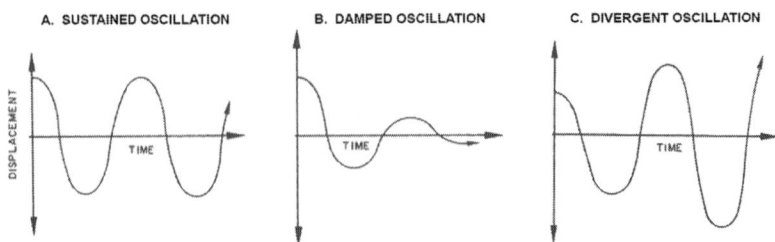

A. SUSTAINED OSCILLATION   B. DAMPED OSCILLATION   C. DIVERGENT OSCILLATION

FIGURE 8.7 Diagrams of various oscillatory modes effected by disturbance. Source: Elaine Gan, 2018.

Disruption and Emergence

A disruption changes a process, a trajectory, an assemblage. Damped and divergent oscillations, described in the previous section, may be causes or effects of disruptions. When we think of disruption we tend to associate it with collapse or breakdown. Seeing disruption through the lens of only one species or object—as is the case, for example, with the extinction of a species or the construction of a dam—can be dangerously misleading because disruption also conditions emergence, and emergence in turn conditions disruption. Disruption and emergence shift coordinations across multiple scales, conditioning the flourishing of some assemblages and the demise of others.

In figure 8.8, my subject is not a single species or thing, but the transformations or iterative reconfigurings of Mekong assemblages. The Mekong rises in the Himalayas and descends southward through Yunnan Province in China, then through Myanmar (Burma), Thailand, Laos, Cambodia, and Vietnam, where it meets the South China Sea. From April to September, summer monsoon winds blow eastward across the Indian Ocean, bringing rain. Rainfall intensifies into storms and floods in June and July. From October to March, winds reverse direction and blow westward to the Arabian Sea. Rainfall eases and the weather becomes dry. The oscillation between wet and dry seasons has enabled particular assemblages to flourish over millennia. In figure 8.8, assemblage 1 indicates freshwater fish and plant species, as well as fishers and farmers who participate in their lifeways by learning the timing and routes of animals and the plasticity of plants, for example.

Disruptions alter the assemblage, shifting dominant relations. In the eighteenth century, migrating Vietnamese displaced lowland Khmer and Cham and brought wet rice farming south to the delta, which has become

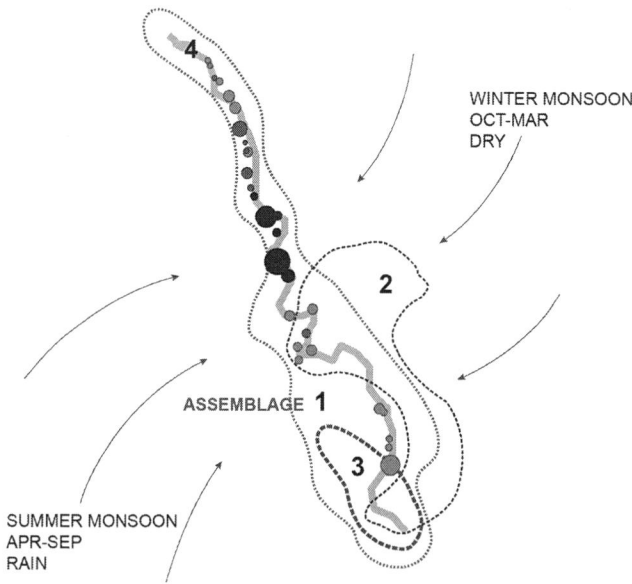

FIGURE 8.8 Working diagram to understand assemblages in flux. Source: Elaine Gan, 2018.

one of the largest rice-exporting regions (shift to assemblage 2). In the twentieth century, U.S. military campaigns sprayed 21 million gallons of chemicals on Vietnam, Laos, and Cambodia. These chemicals persist and make their way to Tonlé Sap Lake, where twenty-first-century fisheries supply international markets (shift to assemblage 3). Meanwhile, construction of hydropower dams in the Upper and Lower Mekong accelerates. Water hyacinths proliferate, clogging dams and waterways, enabling other agential nonhumans such as disease-carrying mosquitoes and snails to thrive (shift to assemblage 4).

SUMMARY

Drawing diagrams is a slow art and science that mediates between field-work, analysis, and writing. It is an iterative, provisional, playful practice for working ethnographically; I believe it is vital to decentering human exceptionalism and rethinking *anthropos* as multispecies relationality. In this chapter I have shared some examples of diagrams that make visible just a few of the many temporalities of more-than-human relations, and that call attention to differential timing that makes particular relations matter. Figure 8.1 illustrates a logic of one-point temporality that pervades industrial agriculture; this logic has violently led to the degradation and contamination of landscapes and must be dislodged. Conklin's diagram (figure 8.3) and Barad's diagram (figure 8.4) offer far richer engagements with multispecies life. Diagramming can refine our attention to temporalities such as seasonality (figure 8.5), oscillation (figure 8.6), and disruption/emergence (figure 8.8), and to other rhythms and figurations we live by. Diagrams animate wonderful possibilities for writing relationality otherwise.

PROTOCOL

- Pick a field site that is near you or easy to visit. It may be a public park, a wildlife refuge, a pond, a farm, or even a garbage dump.
- Invite a group of colleagues to go on a series of walks together over two to four seasons. Visit the site regularly at different times of day/night, in different weather conditions. Keep field notebooks for sketches, observations, and maps during each visit.
- After the first visit, select one nonhuman species to focus on. Follow something that intrigues you; follow something you love.

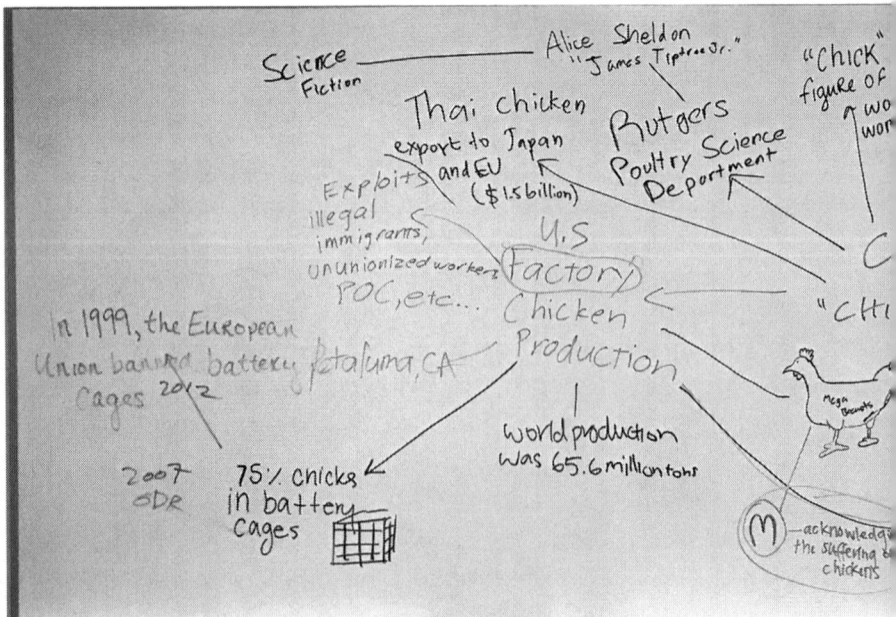

FIGURE 8.9

During the next few visits, learn about its companions and its activity patterns. How did they get there? Figure 8.9 offers one way of collectively mapping a web of relations on a whiteboard. A long scroll of paper would work well too and can be used to collect and keep track of the group's field observations over time.

- Look at the physical forms and arrangements of species and things. Look up, down, and underground. Take up different points of view by letting your senses guide you; perhaps you pick up an un/familiar scent or notice a bird call. Where is the wind blowing, and what might it be taking with it? Allow that to decide your next step.

- Supplement your field observations and discussions with readings from a wide range of sources (e.g., biology, geography, anthropology, history, environmental studies, documentary films, literature). Focus on relations, not individuals.

- Can you begin to identify an assemblage, or at least three species and things that are significant in one way or another to your selected species? How does the quartet interact to re/configure relations? Diagram the interactions as simple seasonal events. Which are more or less dominant in different seasons? Why?

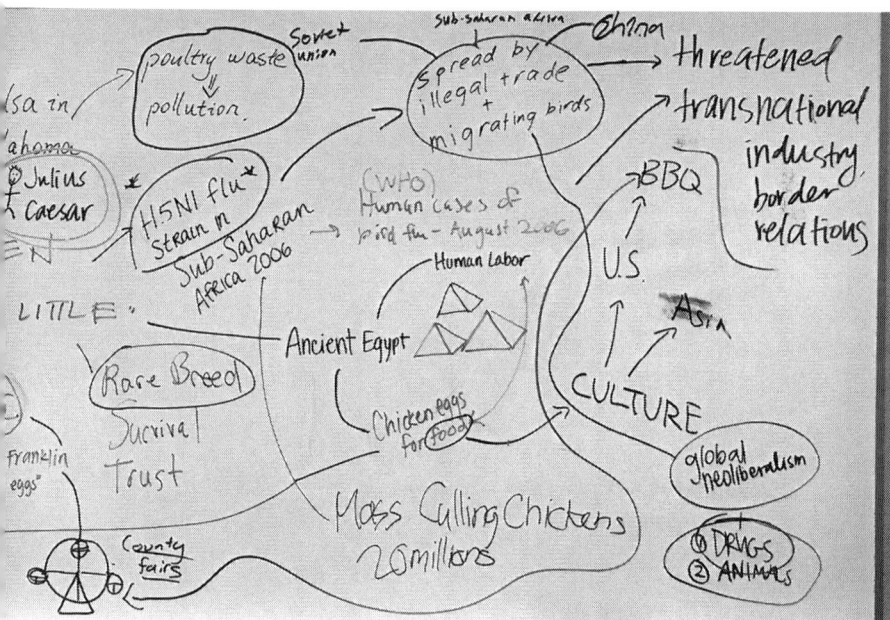

- Do you notice subtle/not-so-subtle signs of change, encounter, de/composition that may be keeping the assemblage together or reconfiguring it over different scales and rhythms of time? Does the assemblage become meaningful in new ways when you pay close attention to those signs?
- Can you express relations without resorting to arrows or circles? Diagram your assemblage in six different ways, using the various figures included in this chapter as aids. Play, mix, repeat.

ACKNOWLEDGMENTS

Hearty thanks to Andrea Ballestero and Brit Ross Winthereik for the kind invitation and encouragement to articulate how diagrams work, to Karen Barad and Anna Tsing for many scribblings on post-its and notebooks that led to this chapter, and to Fritzie de Mata and Colin Hoag for close and thoughtful readings of early drafts.

Diagrams in Action (figure 8.9): Eighteen undergraduate students at University of Southern California read Donna Haraway's chapter on "Chicken" from *When Species Meet*, then collaboratively sketched this diagram to visualize as many historical trajectories and interactions as they could find in Haraway's text. The class exercise prepared students for fieldwork along the Los Angeles River where they followed the protocol to study multispecies assemblages.

NOTES

1. For one of the best examples of one-point perspective in the Renaissance, see *The School of Athens* by Raphael (1511).

2. Philosopher Isabelle Stengers's proposal for "slow science" also calls for modes of attunement and engagement that are immersed in the materialities of worlds, letting them guide methods and inquiries rather than making them serve modernist schemes of classification and extraction (2018).

PART III

INFRASTRUCTURAL PLAY

CHAPTER 9

ALBERTO CORSÍN JIMÉNEZ

Ethnographic Drafts and Wild Archives

It took us almost a year to write the letter. It was a good letter, though. I do not mean to say that it was well written, which I suppose it was, nor that it was a letter with goodness in it, a bearer of promises and good intentions, which, frankly, given how long it took us to write, some were now a little skeptical about. Rather, it was a good letter because it felt good to have it with us, a reminder of the good work we had done together. The letter worked as a companion-device of sorts, providing a record of our perseverance and resolution, as well as an archive of our hesitations and grievances. The draft of the letter had accompanied our thinking and our drinking, our meetings and our exchanges, online and offline, in person, in writing, and in absentia, for almost a year. In this guise, the draft helped us inscribe and enlist our emotions and expectations as we described and essayed our reasons and motivations for writing it. The draft had offered us a venue for sounding out the horizon of our mutual complicities while trying out different styles of authorship, different registers of amicability, different expressions for our volition and commitment. The draft, then, as material vector and social relation.

The letter in question was addressed to the director general of culture at Madrid's municipality and was composed by a loose federation of urban activists who operated in Madrid from 2012 to 2015 under the name of La Mesa (The Table). The collective first convened in October 2012 in response to an open call by the municipal government to submit proposals and generate discussions for the city's next Strategic Plan for Culture. A group took the opportunity to gather to discuss the establishment of a permanent roundtable (hence, La Mesa) to talk publicly about the requirements and obligations citizens would incur if they were to assume the competency and responsibility for managing public spaces. "What would public space look like," the group set out to inquire, "if we were to problematize the 'public' as a sociotechnical assemblage?" The letter was addressed to the municipality as an invitation to join the activists in this exercise in problematization (an invitation that was eventually accepted).

La Mesa was part and parcel of a wider ecology of *cultura libre* (free culture) activists among whom I conducted fieldwork in Madrid between 2009 and 2017. The free culture movement first emerged in the late 1990s in the US as a response to corporate efforts to expand intellectual property legislation to digital cultural works in the internet age (Postigo 2012). Inspired by the philosophy of free and open-source software, the movement contributed crucial legal and technical innovations to the cultural economy of the digital era, including, for example, the stock of Creative Commons licenses and Wikipedia. In the Spanish context, however, the movement quickly outgrew its digital circumscription and assumed the contours of a very specific urban ecology. Spearheaded by autonomous activists, hackers, and curators at public art institutions, the notion of free culture became the centerpiece of a number of experiments and designs for the "liberation," as activists would put it, of the material politics of the city, such as initiatives for managing "copyleft" squatted social centers (Durán and Moore 2015) and for open-sourcing urban infrastructures and equipment (Corsín Jiménez 2014).

In this spirit, the "culture of 'free culture'" in Madrid was characterized by a number of practices aimed at opening up the black boxes of the city's infrastructures and material politics. Three practices in particular were of concern to activists. First, activists were determined to document exhaustively every aspect—technical, juridical, pedagogical, organizational—of their doings. To this end they used collaborative technologies such as wikis, PiratePad, or Google Docs (La Mesa's choice for the choral composition of its letter) for keeping notes, taking minutes, or drafting proposals. Such technologies allowed them to keep the nature of their descriptions in suspension, by holding them open to ongoing re-descriptions, but also by bifurcating them, such as when a group decided to fork a description to produce their own version. Just as importantly, these technologies also allowed activists to experiment with documentary practices, using montages of drawings, video, text, photographs, or all of these to produce different renditions or accounts of the issues at hand. Second, it was imperative for activists that all these files remain available for download, distribution, and modification, and to this effect they were adamant defenders and users of free intellectual property licenses. Last, activists were equally obstinate in using open-source repositories (such as GitHub) for archiving and storing all files, to the point of developing their own digital archives and databases if needed.

In a very practical sense these various archives, documents, images, and licenses circulated as drafts for one another. This is how people spoke of them: *borradores*, "drafts." Anything could be a draft—a text, a drawing, a photograph, an email thread, a module of source code—so long as it was made available for reuse and re-description through the use of free licenses, open-source archives, and radical pedagogies. They were objects that perpetually drafted (into) other objects through an ongoing motion of solicitude, exegesis, and transformation.

In this chapter I take inspiration from free-culture activism and invite you to think about the role that drafts play as carrying-figures of description, sociality, and analysis all at once. Of course, drafts may not play this role in your work. Notwithstanding, I believe the questions that thinking with drafts illuminate are at the heart of how we operate as anthropologists. Let me explain why.

As my opening vignette illustrates, during the year that it took for La Mesa to write to the director general of culture, we were not so much drafting a letter as designing and inhabiting an ecology of drafts, at once a habitat and a heuristic for our work. Every description was followed by a re-description—an annotation, a remark, a drawing, a deletion, a hesitation—whose traces were legible and important to the group and in this capacity re-inscribed the group's ongoing process of analysis and reflection. Analyses were not only produced in drafts, of course: people mused over this or that predicament over drinks or in other spaces of confidence and complicity, or would insinuate and body forth intimations of analysis through other gestures and hints, or would just go ahead and publish their opinions in blogs or Facebook posts. But drafts were carriers of analysis also, and in this material form refunctioned the wheres and whens of how and by whom analysis is made visible. We can think of drafts in this guise as a triplex of sorts: a mode of relation that does triple duty as a mode of narration, a mode of encounter, and a mode of enquiry.

This carrying capacity of drafts to describe, engage, and elucidate is what drew me to them as devices of anthropological description more broadly: as material and social forms that express the traces that ethnographic analysis leaves as it moves between descriptions and re-descriptions. Ethnography moves in drafts, in huffs and puffs that are temporarily and tentatively inscribed in notebooks, sketches, or Evernote; in documents and illustrations that are often drawn and written with others, that circulate as invitations for commentary or modification, at different times and in different spaces, and that in this guise outline and accompany the ongoingness of social process. Such movements and displacements invite us to think carefully about the effects of ethnography—both its registers and its sites—as a form of "dynamic archiving" that is messy, "open-ended, multileveled, and transitive in authorings, genres, publics, commons, and internal relations" (Marcus 2012, 438). Ethnography, in other words, as a "wild archive" (Trüper 2013).

The figure of the draft I outline here is therefore not (just) a heuristic or analytic, nor a design or method. Neither is it a surrogate for "eFieldnotes," as Roger Sanjek (2016) has called the mediations inflected by digital tools on ethnographic recordkeeping. In its stead, I prefer to imagine drafts as infrastructures that foil how complicities alloy complexities and how complexities ally complicities—how ethnographic engagements re-describe themselves. The draft as a wild archive of ethnographic effects.

In the rest of this chapter I describe how my ethnographic practice has changed since I decided to get a hold on the effects that drafts were having on my work. Building on this, I offer some questions for reckoning with and making explicit the purchase that drafts may have in your work. This may not apply to all readers equally, of course. But I believe this list of questions has some merit in framing and pointing in rather unequivocal terms to the infrastructures and material distributions of rights, memory, authorship, and responsibility that subtend the organization of ethnography today. Finally, I conclude with a tentative protocol for working with drafts.

WILD ARCHIVES

The impact of the internet on the archival practices of anthropology was noted early on by Johannes Fabian (2002) and David Zeitlyn (2000), who were quick to point out the pressures subjected on the ethnographic genre under the advent of new digital technologies. For Fabian, the possibility of making ethnographic records available online (say, transcriptions of interviews, descriptions of rituals, etc.) refunctions the nature of the anthropological project. The perpetual presence of an ethnographic record in a digital archive, argues Fabian, places anthropological analysis under a constant pressure and vigilance, making it possible, "if not to get rid of our conceptual arsenal then at least to keep it in abeyance often and long enough to make what I call confrontation productive" (2008, 93). Such a confrontational edge turns analysis into a modest form of provisional and unstable "ethnographic commentary."

For Zeitlyn, on the other hand, digital archives enable scholars to design systems for taking care of future, perhaps subversive, reorientations of ethnographic materials. In particular, Zeitlyn thinks such "radical archives" may in time operate as "surrogates for anthropology": sites for problematizing the registers and demands shaping the "legal structures, privacy debates, or the models of openness" of cultural production today (2012, 474).

The archives used by free-culture activists, however, are not archives by any conventional sense of the term. Free-culture activists resort to digital technologies such as PiratePad, wikis, or GitHub to be used not just as repositories but also as writing machines and interlocutory venues. They are spaces of record as well as platforms for ongoing encounter, analysis, and interpretation. They are archives whose designs care not just for the records of description but also for the capacities for re-description (Corsín Jiménez 2015). In this guise they are spaces of messiness, erasure, recognition, contradiction, and response. Such archives are designed to help pose questions about the attribution and specification of rights, permits, roles, and responsibilities in the making and stewardship of cultural productions. These questions address fundamental issues of political ontology. For example, for almost two decades Kimberly Christen has collaborated with indigenous communities to design and develop community-based archival projects using indigenous local protocols and information-management models, including Mukurtu (a free and open-source content management system designed with the Warumungu people of the Northern Territory in Australia) and the Plateau People's Web Portal (a digital gateway to cultural materials curated by Native American nations). These platforms explicitly position communities as the owners or stewards of the archival materials and define cultural protocols for viewing, accessing, using, or circulating materials, such as "if a tribe has traditional access parameters around the viewing of sacred materials limited only to elders, or if some songs should only be heard in specific seasons, or if only initiated members of a specific clan should be allowed to view cultural objects" (Christen 2015, 5). These archival forms therefore function at once as libraries of representation, networks of invention, and exercises in cultural problematization.

What do such archives do to anthropological practice? What does it take for us to rethink our field sites and field notes as complex networks and infrastructures of re-descriptive effects across archives, media, and other compositional designs (Kelty 2009)?

Over the past ten years my free-culture interlocutors have invited me to join, contribute to, or edit hundreds of open collaborative projects, from simple notepads (text editors), spreadsheets, or wikis to much more ambitious and sophisticated urban databases or community-run archival projects. Over time some of the conversations or exchanges we have had about a project have grown in importance or size and merited forking into a new and separate project. Sometimes I participated in these forks, sometimes I observed from the sidelines. Every time a decision was made to create a new document or project, we had to make concomitant decisions regarding the granting of permissions to different users (to access, view, edit, etc.). Of course, these permissions are always culturally coded, responding to criteria such as expertise, experience, hierarchy, and so on. We also had to agree on the editorial roles and functions to be assumed by different people. For example, whether we would have specific roles for site administrators, content curators, managing editors, copy editors, and others. In truth, we generally gave everyone full rights to every document—a decision that every now and then some people abused, provoking serious and flaming polemics (which, of course, were not without their interest).

Many such documents were created in Google Drive, so in time I realized that the platform functioned as a wild archive for my own ethnography, and eventually I created a folder structure and index to organize all such materials. Of course, many of my folders and files nested within other people's folder classifications, which I may not have been aware of. Sometimes I candidly asked some of my closest friends in the field to give me a snapshot of their folder structure and hierarchy. These overlapping and nesting folder topologies quite literally drafted my field site as a relational field: a field of people I related to and a field of knowledge relations.

For a number of years now I have also complemented my use of hardback notebooks with Google Keep to track ideas that cross my mind when I am on the move. Google Keep was recently integrated with Google Docs, so I can now tag and search across both. Sometimes I come up with tags in a moment of lucidness or bedazzlement, and I then use those tags to reorganize the archive through search patterns. This ongoing shuffling and reshuffling of archives was also a prompt for my thinking of it as a system of drafts.

Now, I am not ingenuous about these reorganizations. I am aware they have consequences for the legacy of my ethnography as a memory, epistemic, and social form. For a start, I do not, of course, delegate all my ethnographic notetaking to digital archives. There are things that I keep to myself in personal notebooks. I am also fully aware that the mainstream technologies enabling such digital archival projects play a key part in the development of the stack megastructures of platform capitalism (Bratton 2016). Free-culture activists are specially sensitive to these issues, which is why they have long been advocating for the use of free software technologies whenever they can. Notwithstanding, from the point of view of the shaping of ethnography as a field of writing and analysis, the use of these wild archives helps me keep in view how the people I work with trace, move, and reshuffle their own itineraries, interests, and apprenticeships as archival projects and fields. For it goes without saying that these archival fields make no distinction between fieldwork and deskwork, nor do they delegate or separate the work of analysis from the work of description. The archives carry both at once (while exhausting neither).

During my fieldwork I also curated a blog with my ethnographic partner. We used the blog to publish and invite commentary on preliminary analyses and to publish preprint or open-access versions of our academic texts, or to summarize in Spanish arguments of texts that had been written in English. I also contributed to numerous debates and discussions in various digital forums (other people's blogs, email lists, Facebook threads, Google Hangouts, seminars, etc.). Keeping track of these various exchanges wasn't always easy, but it did raise my awareness of my field site as a meandering and unruly archival field with connections to places or people that were surprising and unexpected. It also gave me important insights into the circulation of academic knowledge within and outside academia, in English and Spanish.

Finally, my thinking about the wild archives of free-culture activism— and recursively, the wild archives of ethnography—led me to develop, in collaboration with my interlocutors, an open-source archive of free-culture urban practices (http://ciudad-escuela.org/) and to curate an exhibition and digital repository on such archiving practices (http://a-medias.org/). It also prompted me to cofound Libraria, an advocacy network that aims to catalyze demonstration projects in open-access publishing (http://libraria.cc/), because it truly makes very little sense to have some of the records of anthropology (our articles and monographs) behind paywalls and in proprietary archives that only a few have access to.

In light of the above, I offer here a list of questions that I believe can help us start problematizing our ethnographic sites and registers as drafts:

- What are the systems of inscription and the systems of description of your ethnographies? For example:
  - Where do you take notes? Do you use notebooks, text editors, mobile apps running on cloud-computing servers (e.g., Evernote, Google Drive)?
  - Who gets to read your field notes? Do you write them in collaboration with others? What technology do you use to such an end (Dropbox Paper, Google Docs, PiratePad)?
  - Do others get to edit your notes? If you work with others, do you follow writing and recording conventions or styles? Or do you perhaps have tacit conventions for commenting and annotating the writings of others?
  - What languages of description do you use: text, drawings, photography, etc.?
- Do you keep a (collective) blog about your fieldwork? Who interacts with the blog, and do such interactions make their way into later analyses?
- How do you manage your data and metadata? Do you use open research data repositories? For example:
  - Can you make your tapes, recordings, or files publicly available? What would it take for such recordings to be available? Where would they need to be stored and preserved, under whose stewardship and control? Under what formats and standards? Under what ethical precepts and guidelines?
  - Who is granted access to these systems (to read, edit, analyze, or redistribute)?
- Where do you publish your findings: in open-access journals or library repositories, with commercial publishers, in online magazines or blogs?
- What intellectual property licenses do you use to publish? Can others copy, edit, and redistribute your work?
- Do relations of acknowledgement, attribution, credit, or authorship get reshuffled as your work progresses from draft to draft?

These questions suggest that to think of ethnography as a draft entails thinking about its nature as an archive; as a memory practice, a circulatory economy, a system of distributed authorship; and as an infrastructure of rights, permits, and obligations. It involves tracing the material journey of ethnographic effects from our fieldwork notes to our evening reflections and back again; from the insights or intuitions annotated in a rush on the margins of our notebooks or in Evernote to the drafts we share with our interlocutors in the field, as well as the drafts they share with us; from fieldwork exchanges in a Facebook thread to the promises and the afterlives of open-access publishing—and reckoning throughout with their tensions, risks, and uncertainties.

In conclusion, to view ethnography as a draft is to recognize that ethnographic insights appear and disappear in huffs and puffs, in the material crisscrossing of archival traces and signatures. Who and what gets invited and enlisted into such journeys will help us get a better sense of the material accompaniment of our analyses, their circumscriptions and risks as well as their affordances—an intuition, a draft, of how complicities and complexities mutually alloy and ally other complicities and other complexities.

PROTOCOL

- Make your plan to design your field site into a space for curating and problematizing content with others—into an archival field.
- If you have worked with wikis before, create a new wiki upon arriving at the field site. If you have not, then just open a blog. A simple WordPress site will suffice. Do not use this blog as a personal diary or log.
- Identify materials to upload onto the wiki/blog (e.g., photographs, drawings, data sets, ethnographic descriptions), and ask your friends and interlocutors in the field to provide descriptors and tags for each item.
- Extend editorial rights to your interlocutors and invite them to upload their own materials, and to include descriptors and tags for each item.
- Sooner or later you will have to redesign the wiki/blog as you and your friends start classifying or creating hierarchies for content: for example, when someone decides to create a new "page" for specific types of objects or materials (e.g., for photographs of ritual objects, descriptions of festivities, etc.).
- When and if controversy arises over such classifications, invite your interlocutors to take the discussion to a dedicated "page" on the wiki/blog.
- In other words, relish the opportunity to design the archive together.

- If you are working with a wiki (less so if you are working with a WordPress site), you will be able to trace and track how people make changes to the structure and content of the site. Do not lose sight of what these moving drafts enable, what they distort or constrain. Ethnographic insight surfaces and hides somewhere along the material travels of such drafts.
- In sum, cherish the draft nature of your archives rather than the archive of your drafts.

Multimodal Sorting

The Flow of Images across Social Media
and Anthropological Analysis

MULTIMODAL SORTING

In this chapter, I discuss how to work with smartphones and social media, focusing on the images that informants make and share, and images that anthropologists make and collect. I argue that ethnographic insights may emerge through multimodal sorting of these (digital) materials alongside other fieldwork materials. Each fieldwork and each process of analysis is particular and differs from the next, yet certain steps and techniques can be discerned in the process. They emerge as techniques in retrospect, whereas I offer them in this chapter as prospective, in a template form to be appropriated and adapted.

In my work smartphones and social media have increasingly become objects of analysis, integral parts of the methodology, and "triggering devices" in the analytic process at the desk. The study I primarily draw on here is long-term ethnographic fieldwork and filmmaking, from 2010 to 2011 and 2014 to 2016 in the Danish capital of Copenhagen, with young women whose parents had fled or emigrated from countries in the Middle East[1] and had arrived in Denmark (see Waltorp 2013, 2015, 2016, 2017, 2018a, 2018b, 2020). A wide range of online media platforms and spaces made up part of this fieldwork, as did shorter trips with informants to the Islamic Republic of Iran and United Arab Emirates. I was interested in the affordances of a specific urban environment at a specific historical juncture of global flows of people, and the affordances of an object—the internet-enabled smartphone—in relation to the person using it, emplaced in this environment. In the hands of the young Muslim women in Copenhagen with whom I worked, the smartphone can be seen as a tangible relational device, as a technology of the imagination (Sneath, Holbraad, and Pedersen 2009), and as making up part of the environment in which they move.

The way people live with technological devices and digital infrastructures has changed dramatically since I carried out my first fieldwork in the South African township of Manenberg in 2005. In many places—like my Danish field site, and Manenberg, where I have done recurrent fieldwork since 2005 (the last in 2018)—social media have become ubiquitous. In my Danish field site, internet-enabled smartphones are ubiquitous as well. In their immediate situation, both recent graduates and the current generation of anthropologists need to reckon with this ubiquity (see also Dattatreyan and Marrero-Guillamón 2019). It invites an anthropological rethinking of how place, temporality, sociality, and personhood are being reconfigured and to what effect. These changes have reshaped the fieldwork devices I have made use of in subsequent projects and thus, by implication, the kinds of fieldwork material generated. How is this fieldwork material in multiple modalities to be sorted and analyzed? And how does this process engender the sought-after ethnographic effects? I discuss this below, after a brief overview of the structure of the chapter and some considerations of "the ethnographic effect" reconfigured with the pervasiveness of digital media and infrastructures.

HOW THE CHAPTER IS STRUCTURED

I begin this chapter with a general description of the various forms and formats of data material generated in the field, which I work with in analysis. I go on to describe the coevalness and iterative process that digital communication technologies afford, focusing on how feedback around still and moving images is part of a politics of inviting informants and other audiences into the analysis.[2] I describe the ongoing "multimodal sorting" and share the steps I take in a protocol form at the end of the chapter. It is an iterative, flexible, and "underdetermined" template I offer here. It is always in dialogue with a field in which the fieldworker makes up part of the assemblage interrogated—thus no two iterations can ever be the same.

Marilyn Strathern has pointed to how analysis ("writing") begins "in the field," and rather than thinking of two trajectories pertaining respectively to observation (out there) and analysis (at the desk), we might engage the fields together, she suggests (Strathern 1999, 5–7). Ethnographic writing creates a second field: writing an imaginative re-creation of some of the effects of fieldwork itself (1). The ethnographic moment works as an example of the relation that joins the understood (what is analyzed at the moment of observation) and the need to understand (what is observed at the moment of analysis): "Any ethnographic moment, which is a moment of insight, denotes a relation between immersement and movement" (6). This double field is separated by time, Strathern tells us, yet managed and inhabited at the same time. The "first" field and the imaginatively re-created field exist alongside each other. Social media make it possible in new ways to momentarily reenter the field when at the desk, as part of feedback in different registers, radically transforming the management and inhabitation of the double field. This holds new potential and new challenges. Strathern discusses "writing" specifically, yet her argument that "immersement yields what is often unlooked for" (3) still holds with multimodal forms of inscription and expression. (Audio)visual material is brimming with excess and with layers that only reveal themselves through revisiting over time. Part of the unlooked-for meaning is revealed through minute attention to the framing of the image or video: How did the person who shared the image frame it? How was it shared—through which platform? What kind of conversation was it a part of, and with whom? If and when all this material in various modalities is amassed, then how to access and release what it holds—what to do with it? What kind of data are they, and what status do they have?

The analytic approach or technique that I propose in this chapter is "multimodal sorting"—more fundamentally, to inhabit infrastructures for seeing, thinking, and knowing together, taking seriously the smartphone and social media as part of this. Things easily disappear from view: exactly how a knowledge-making process is entwined with specific digital technologies and platforms, and how these are also part of enabling the iterative formation of knowledge and continued feedback in specific ways, as I exemplify below. This intricate entwinement requires a sensitivity to framings and invites us to play with new framings as well—a process always also shaped by the technologies and software used. In analysis this concretely means visually sorting one's material in numerous ways, to ask different questions of it. A part of this analytic sorting process is the fact of a changed temporality that smartphones and social media introduce in terms of relations in/with/to the field. This coevalness potentially adds a

presence/present that cuts across analytic modalities and invites an iterative mode of anthropological analysis.

The material and historical layers of the exceedingly abstract communications and computing processes that we ordinarily take for granted are
part of a focus on the flow of images (Marks 2015, 2016) and how people
interface with digital technologies, smartphones, and social media. The internet is not a distributed network, and there is no "Cloud" in the air, but
rather an unevenly distributed digital-material network with fiber-optic
cables running in specific routes and centers in specific places (Hu 2015),
layered with power and ideologies (Massey 1994). The scope of this chapter does not allow for a discussion of the materiality of the digital realm
as a backdrop to working ethnographically with smartphones and social
media. Here I limit myself to describing the (back-and-forth) steps and
techniques that I tend to make use of when re- and defamiliarizing myself
with my ethnographic material. The processes of (visual) sorting, coding,
thematizing, juxtaposing, and finding patterns (analysis at the desk) add
layers to and challenge the tentative analysis an anthropologist forms consciously and unconsciously during fieldwork (analysis in the field). The
software invites different kinds of sorting of the (audio)visual material, as
I return to below.

HOW TO INCLUDE SOCIAL MEDIA IN FIELDWORK

I consider before any fieldwork the particular social media applications I
imagine I will use, but fundamentally I let my interaction with informants
lead the process. Many a failure on my part has been through wanting to
"document" in ways that were not "in tune" with informants. One initial
idea was having the women I worked with in my Copenhagen fieldwork
download a specific app to track their physical movement. Several of the
women subtly avoided this, others downright rejected the idea. Nevertheless, the failed idea offered insight around movement, monitoring, and
skillful navigation of sets of expectations of my informants. I soon understood how keeping a log of their physical movements would decrease this
room for maneuvering, including navigating expectations around where to
be, at what time, and in what company.

One of the most frequently used apps among informants was Snapchat
(see Waltorp 2016). This photo-messaging application allows users to take
so-called snaps—photos or short videos onto which they can add text
and drawings—and then send them to a controlled list of recipients im-

mediately or as a continually updated compilation of selected snaps called "MyStory" available to all contacts. The users of Snapchat "chat," so to speak, using "snapshots" from their lives. The snap is automatically deleted after a set time limit of up to ten seconds. As the snap is only seen once, the ephemeral feel is the framing (Waltorp 2020). As I became more familiar with my informants and spent more face-to-face time with them in their homes, I learned about the different ways they communicate through different social media platforms, sending snaps and using various other popular apps such as WhatsApp (which integrates text, photos, and sometimes film clips), Instagram, and Facebook. I was already active in some of these social media platforms, but I learned to use them differently—and that it is not a given what an app or platform is to whom. This is only possible to understand through trust, time, and immersing oneself in interactions though these platforms. My informants keep a close eye on who is allowed to see what, who to trust with what, and when: secrecy, (in)visibility, and timing are of the essence. Most of my informants text and call frequently and at all hours. Tango and Viber have taken over the platform that Skype previously occupied as the so-called most-preferred VoIP (voice over internet protocol). These apps are often used to communicate with siblings who have married and settled either in their parents' country of origin or neighboring countries.

In semipublic and intimate spaces both on- and offline, these young women act out and experiment with accepted, virtuous versions of themselves and try out behaviors and relations that would be gossiped about if they occurred in public, as they would be detrimental to a woman's reputation. The point is that social media use is emergent and cannot be dissociated from a larger social context of which it makes up part. The women I worked with carve out for themselves spaces in which they modify, censor, and reveal, depending on audience and context, within otherwise seemingly very "public" platforms. Operating with a profile under an alias is a widespread practice. On the "official" Facebook pages, where many people use their real names and pictures, content on the "walls" ranges from food, fashion and beauty, work or study, and children and family gatherings to new political developments and ongoing crises in the Middle East. Some informants share on Facebook their devotion to the Prophet Muhammad and his teachings. These displays have their own recognizable aesthetic with pictures and drawings, often quoting *ayat* (verses in the Qur'an).

Many social media posts communicate different layers of sentiments to discrete others: Depending on how intimately the audience knows the person posting these images and quotations, different readings are possible. In some instances family members are keeping a close watch on subtle messages being sent and posted on Facebook, responding to a practice that is already well in place (Waltorp 2015, 55–56)—surveillance and carving out spaces for oneself are two sides of the same coin. Mass media, especially Flow TV, also make up part of this mix as private discussions in the home become more public and shared through social media: scenes that people particularly liked or disliked in popular TV series and *mosalsalat* (Arab series) are shared on Facebook or linked to on YouTube, spurring debate on moral issues—such as sex before marriage, drinking in public places, (im)modest dress, and gender roles—that might otherwise be seen as very personal and controversial (Waltorp 2013). This practice has migrated to the Snapchat app; users take a snap of the TV screen while watching a broadcast of an episode of a TV series and write comments directly on the picture before sending it to recipients.

This short introduction to the field shows the ways in which social media use is inextricably entwined in social life (for a thorough introduction see Waltorp 2020). Every person engaging in social media via a smartphone is always already embodied, emplaced, and encultured somewhere, as is the fieldworker. Digital technologies and platforms contribute in various ways to interactions, both to what is communicated and how (see also Madianou and Miller 2012; Archambault 2013; Pink et al. 2016). These mediated interactions in turn are shaped by the face-to-face relations that oftentimes exist prior to and alongside the communications via media. I have discussed elsewhere reciprocity and mutuality as necessary in qualitative research in the private spaces in social media, as in all other anthropological fields: I do not subscribe to the idea that the data generated in social media should be treated in a way that fundamentally differs from those used for all other observations, encounters, and dialogues in fieldwork. Instead it should be analyzed alongside and as part of the flow across physical and digital realms. The app within which a text, piece of information, or image has been shared is one "frame" (see Bateson [1972] 2000), often part of the meaning. Other frames are delineated by the fieldworker, who might have been part of the situation that has been "snapped," "posted," "liked," or "tagged." We and our informants live in worlds saturated with media, and we all interface with imaginaries and cosmological ideas and notions. The religious, spiritual, or other cosmological ideas that we are slowly introduced to by informants and adapt to by spending time in an environment are part of what I term *the infrastructure of seeing, thinking, and knowing.* Separating these flows of embodied, (un)conscious knowledge and images from the digital circuits is an artificial divide. There is no way around participant observation in order to gain understanding of how these realms relate, how images flow across and are made meaningful to people. Below I go into more detail about how I organize and sort multimodal data material as part of analysis.

HOW TO ORGANIZE DATA MATERIAL GENERATED ACROSS THE PHYSICAL AND DIGITAL REALMS

As students in the humanities and social sciences, we are taught that analysis is a process of hypothesis, antithesis, and synthesis. But what do these concretely entail? The organizing and reorganizing of material generated via the smartphone and social media alongside various other modalities of notes are initial steps in my "analysis at the desk." For example, I have a "folder" for each person I work with, which holds subfolders for different modalities of material (see the list below). This framing allows me to consider the material alongside other material. One such subfolder gathers images according to who has sent/posted/snapped/tagged and shared them. Other folders gather the images according to which platform they were generated through. All of the images are also part of a different sorting and framing in iPhoto software, which arranges them according to metadata such as GPS location, time, events, and people in the images (identified with face-recognition software). The video footage from informants' smartphones, my own smartphone, and video cameras is also sorted and framed (temporally) in and by the editing software and by various "timelines," whereby I place materials alongside each other and rearrange them continually as themes emerge and prove to be more salient.

Below I list the kinds of materials that I usually end up with, and how they are roughly organized in research during—and after—fieldwork. The first step at the desk is to familiarize myself with the data material by looking at, flicking through, sorting, and coding it. I evaluate:

- Digital pictures and short smartphone videos sent through various social media platforms; these are sorted in my iPhoto library in folders according to person and to platform.
- Pictures taken during fieldwork, which are stored in my iPhoto library, in folders according to person and to platform; I eventually juxtapose and arrange these in InDesign.

- Video recordings that were recorded on a smartphone or a video camera and edited in Adobe Premier Pro or other editing software; these are logged and sorted in various folders.
- Handwritten and digital notes, including jottings and fuller written-up notes, appointments, prepared questions, questions that arise—in the moment, on the bus, in bed before going to sleep, upon waking up from the fieldwork dream—and require follow-up; I record these in a Moleskine notebook or in the notes app on my smartphone (notes in the latter are then exported to my computer).
- Kinship diagrams, Venn diagrams, life lines, sketches, etc.; I draw these in a Moleskine notebook, digitize them by taking and uploading a picture, and then formalize them using software.
- Digital notes (descriptive, tentative analytical thoughts, interpretations, questions to be pursued); these I store in chronological order in word diary software on my laptop.
- Transcriptions of interviews, extended field notes, etc., stored in Microsoft Word software on my laptop.
- Folders on my laptop for each informant, which include transcripts, kinship diagrams (made by hand—mostly collaboratively—and digitized via taking a picture or redoing the diagrams digitally), screenshots of various shared content in social media, and written notes.

In immersing myself in sorting various modalities of notes alongside each other in various framings (and concretely in folders and programs such as Adobe Premier Pro), I discern patterns and themes. This process unfolds alongside my reading of regional and thematic literature, and discussions with colleagues and informants.

HOW THE SMARTPHONE AND MULTIMODAL SORTING AFFORD A NEW OPTICS

Raw data do not exist independently of the researcher and her instruments (cf. Bateson [1972] 2000, xxv–xxvi). My body, with the prosthetic devices, visualization techniques, and other technology I make use of, configures a distinct infrastructure for seeing, thinking, and knowing. Donna Haraway introduced the idea of "apparatuses of visual production, including the prosthetic technologies interfaced with our biological eyes and brain" (1988, 589). Haraway was not speaking of smartphones in the 1980s when she offered her vision of the cyborg figure and possible affinities in/ through technology as alternatives to military visions and capitalist power, mapping how information technology linked people around the world into new chains of affiliation, exploitation, and solidarity (Haraway 1985). Yet I take a cue from her line of thinking that "vision requires instruments of vision; an optics is a politics of positioning" (Haraway 1988, 586) and propose that the smartphone and its image-making and -sharing technology afford knowing and sensing together in new ways. A new way of seeing and sensing changes the affordances perceived in the environment (Gibson [1979] 2015, 128–35): What we as anthropologists are able to see and know depends on how we interact with the field and with the people, entities, technologies, and infrastructures that we work with/through. This is attuning to the field, and reattuning though immersing oneself in analysis at the desk.

Jean Rouch, the pioneer of ethnographic film, denoted those intense moments when field, ethnographer, and the technological equipment of the video camera merged "ciné-trance" (1978), and Walter Benjamin argued that "Evidently a different nature opens itself to the camera than opens to the naked eye"(1968, 236). We often look without seeing, and the camera and images can help us. With the images made and shared with a smartphone, I am allowed to stay with the details and to revisit them. Working in different modalities beyond the verbal, stringing material together in collages or montages (Suhr and Willerslev 2013), is an analytical process that challenges one's "unconscious optics," in Benjamin's terminology, and helps us pay attention to what we do not "perceive" initially (Benjamin 1968, see Waltorp 2018b). In the process of perceiving our surroundings, the camera introduces us to unconscious optics. In analysis it acts as a guard against thinking that "general knowledge" of something makes us able to analyze it without paying attention to ethnographic details of each new situation, context, assemblage of elements and entities.

Seeking to synthetize—but also juxtapose—different kinds of data, framings during the analytical process, and one's own part in its creation, allows new layers of connections to be grasped. This might counteract premature analytical closures. This juxtaposing step in analysis at the desk bears resemblance to "de-familiarizing" (Marcus and Fischer [1986] 1999), an artistic technique originating in Russian Formalism's *ostranenie* and the *Verfremdung* of Brecht's theater (Brecht and Willett 1964). The technique works by presenting mundane or taken-for-granted things or phenomena to audiences in an unfamiliar or strange way in order to unsettle the habitual perception and thus enhance perception of the familiar (antithesis).[3] Slowly, and also in what sometimes feels like epiphanies, connections are grasped, patterns emerge—and then are challenged anew. These insights most often occur when we are deeply, systematically engaging with material (not necessarily knowing where it is taking us). Perhaps at the desk, maybe while washing the dishes, or possibly in dreams. The analytical frames and theories that we work from shape our way of seeing and slowly morph with the field. Figures 10.1–10.4 provide examples of collages (still images, juxtaposed) and montage (video footage edited together and juxtaposed in temporal sequences, which would have demanded a hyperlink to an uploaded video to share).

FIGURES 10.1 AND 10.2 *Left:* Collage of images made by informants with analogue disposable cameras, layered on top of each other in a way that helps draw nearer to the "feel" of the place. *Right:* Collage of images shared by informants via smartphone in the Snapchat and Instagram platforms. Notice the circle with seconds counting down on the snaps, the text across the image, and added emojis.

Step by step, jottings and headnotes become thematized, diagrams are double-checked and "formalized," and accounts are "written up" in a coherent form to be presented to informants, colleagues, or other audiences. The analysis of the digital photos and video material reaches a form that can be shared, eliciting feedback that informs the further analysis (see figure 10.5). A film cut or a draft paper or article is a tentative analysis to be presented, one that elicits feedback, new questions, and conversations with various audiences or publics. I have worked extensively with having informants give feedback on papers, either face-to-face, over the phone, or via FaceTime. In the endeavor to include feedback in our ongoing analysis, (moving) images, exhibition making, and the web have an

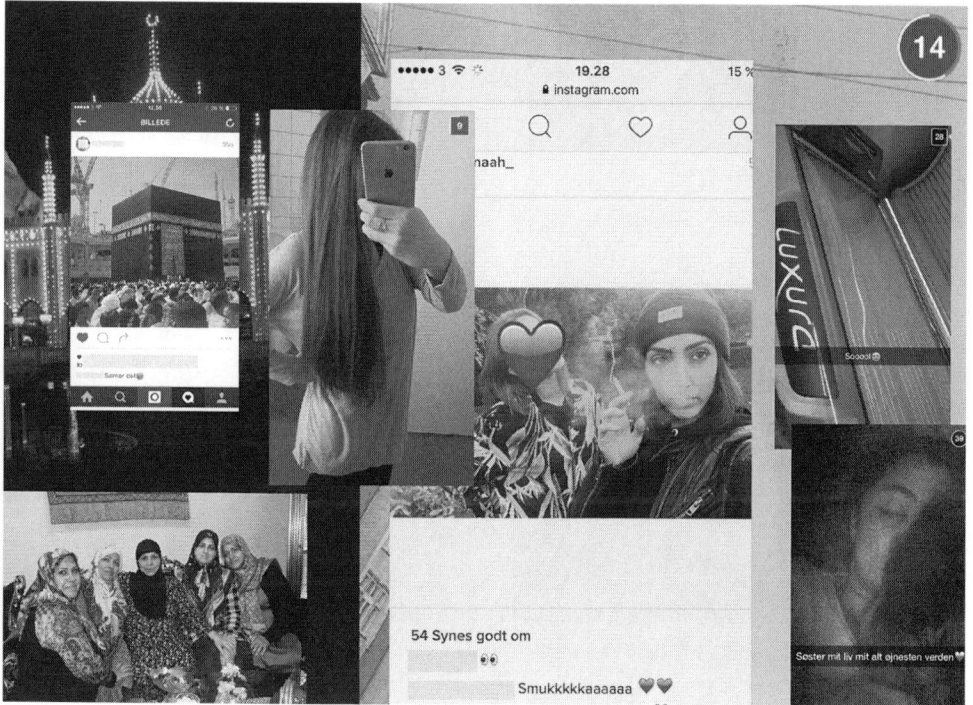

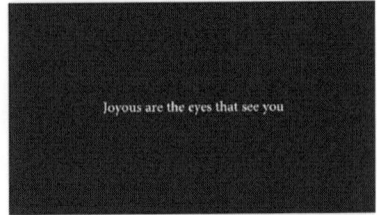

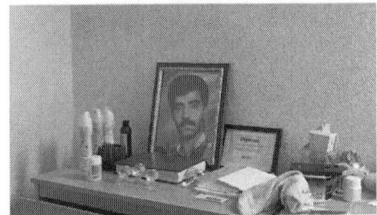

FIGURES 10.3 AND 10.4 Film stills from the experimental ethnographic film *Joyous Are the Eyes That See You*, filmed across Copenhagen, Tehran, Esfahan, and Dubai, with the smartphone as an integral part of both storyline and filming (as the camera).

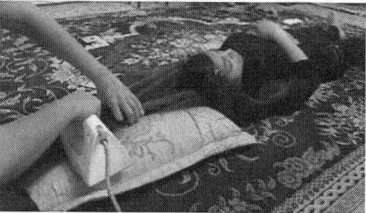
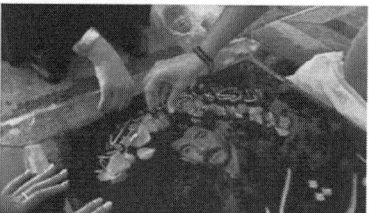

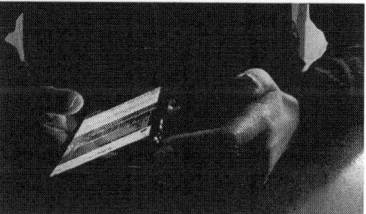

FIGURE 10.5 Images from the *Ghetto NO Ghetto* exhibition opening, Copenhagen, Denmark, 2011. Part of a collaborative photo-diary project showcasing work from young people in Cape Town, Paris, and Copenhagen, together framed as a question around what a ghetto is and who has the power to decide, with what effect.

advantage: these formats allow for communication in registers beyond the scholarly articulated discourse,[4] working as more open invitations into the research and knowledge generated than peer-reviewed scholarly articles (Vium 2018). The smartphone and social media make up part of an infrastructure of conversations wherein informal feedback and analysis can take place in new ways.

A new iteration of analysis is possible through the sensory immediacy of images and the systematic use of feedback, elicitation, and parallax effects, looking at the same thing from different perspectives (cf. Ginsburg 1995, Otto 2013). Image-based and written representation is not the end point of research in this approach, but rather a catalyst for accelerating reflection and dialogue between researchers and their informants or collaborators. Establishing dialogical sites of knowledge-making requires reconfiguring conventional distinctions between knowledge producers and knowledge recipients.

In many cases the digital dimension is increasingly peopled with informants: fieldwork partners, collaborators, colleagues, and everything in between. This points to how the analytic modality "at the desk" is radically changing with smartphones and new technologies: we confer with informants; we are continuously presented with and updated on developments from the intimate micro to the macro. This challenges our initial understanding of a given phenomenon and adds layers to it. As anthropologists we are part of bringing forth representations of people, their environments, and the phenomena that we and they are invested in. I use the phrase *bringing forth* (Heidegger 1977) as I believe this happens in an interplay of entities, technologies, actors, and (digital) materials, with the anthropologist accountable for the representations brought forth and sent into circulation. These representations enter into a flow of images and knowledge and immediately reach the people we work with, as well as other stakeholders in their lives, with impact beyond our control.

People choose what they want to disclose to an anthropologist, and they are in charge of what to reveal (cf. Strathern 1999, 7), but what a person shares with an anthropologist is not necessarily what they wish to disclose to other project participants or their own followers/friends online. If the anthropologist then shares this information in an increasingly technologically mediated and hyperlinked world, it may nevertheless reach the everyday realm of the informants. In previous collaborative photo projects, I increasingly interacted with participants on Facebook and via text messages, sometimes organizing Facebook groups where we could all post information and remarks, yet "private" communication was still possible through the Messenger, and many preferred this. Questions pertaining to who has the rights/access to knowledge demand ethics and sensibilities in terms of visibility, vulnerability, and differing notions of public and private. These ethics and sensibilities have consequences for our informants in terms of how issues of concern to them, as well as they themselves, are made public. This issue goes to the heart of the ethnographic endeavor: how to see and to know—and how to represent or, rather, evoke the ethnography to different audiences in an ethical and accountable way (Waltorp, Vium, and Suhr 2017). No recipe or fail-safe guidelines are in place, but digital communication technologies and our increasingly mediated world make having these considerations and discussions on a continuous basis with the people we work with more crucial than ever. This is a good thing, with the promise of reconfiguring fundamentally how anthropology and representation within and beyond the discipline are practiced.

In this chapter I have sought to exemplify the technique of multimodal sorting. This analytic technique emerges through smartphones and the image-making and -sharing technology of social media and computer software. These technologies are part of our analytic framing both in the field and at the desk. "Inhabiting the infrastructure" is another way of describing being attuned and paying systematic attention to realms and categories that we might not have been familiar with when embarking on the fieldwork. This opens us up to other analytic insights.

Allowing myself to inhabit the infrastructure of digital technologies as part of fieldwork opened up to me different ways of knowledge-making and analysis. One example is the existential crisis of a close informant, Amal, whose eight-year-old daughter had been kidnapped by her father. Paying attention to shifts in Amal's mood and shifts in the ways in which she communicated during telephone conversations, in text messages, and face to face involved "inhabiting the infrastructure" (Waltorp 2017). Instead of a profile picture on her WhatsApp profile, a short text was displayed: "Crying is the only way your eyes speak when your mouth can't explain how things made your heart broken." Through digital technologies Amal sent tentative, hopeful, and despairing images into the world—open-ended requests that might do unforeseen work. Sharing and posting images of herself enacting and being a good Muslim woman and mother was a way for Amal to lobby with her former family-in-law in Jordan to return her daughter to her. In analyzing these events, social media such as Snapchat and Instagram emerged as future-making devices for Amal, and they played together with *du'a* (prayers) and nightly dream images—the technological infrastructure merging here with other flows of images in/across the individual (Waltorp 2017; 2020).

Every fieldwork implies different cosmological beliefs that we must be open to taking into account—whether they become figure or remain ground. In this case it was Islamic notions of predestination, du'a, and dreams that made up part of the infrastructure and the flow of images. In another fieldwork it will be something different. Each field is its own configuration. The cosmology, the physical environment, the politics and layers of stories and histories of the place are other elements that make up the assemblage that you interrogate—the infrastructure of seeing, thinking, and knowing in which the digital is an integral part. The ethnographer is always part of this assemblage as it stabilizes momentarily. Paying attention to that which you did not know or master beforehand demands patience. An iterative approach invites a reconfiguring of the questions we ask—and "problems have the solutions they deserve depending on the terms in which they are stated . . . stating the problem is not simply uncovering, it is inventing" (Deleuze [1980] 1991, 15–16). A fundamental part of ethnographic fieldwork and anthropological analysis and conceptualization is the constant search for better questions to ask. This becomes possible in analysis through movement and "immersement" in the field and in analysis. This ethnographic effect is able to work on us when we pay acute attention to encounters in the field and to our data material, in its various modalities, at the desk. Multimodal sorting is one technique, as I've described here. Possible steps are proposed in the following Protocol.

PROTOCOL

- Select the images your informants have shared and that you have made/collected and want to work with. Be expansive.
- Sort them in several forms or framings: as collage, as montage, or according to themes and categories that you have chosen on the basis of previous knowledge. Be aware of—and play with—the automatic function of a particular software you are using (e.g., iPhoto, Adobe Premier Pro, Adobe InDesign), and pay attention to how it inevitably sorts and frames the material.
- Query your groupings and framings and ask, What are the apparent and unapparent patterns and logics that undergird the groups and/or (temporal) sequences? How is the software part of the analysis and "logic," with what implications?
- Share those tentative "prototype" analytical forms (and their logics) with your informants to enrich, challenge, and transform them through feedback.
- Continue to explore conceptually material in multiple modalities alongside each other. Reiterate the preceding steps, share with different audiences, and benefit from feedback.

1. I am aware that the term *Middle East* did not originate from people living in that area (Marks 2015) and that it situates me geographically in the northern part of the world, therefore I am among those for whom this area becomes, relatively, the middle east. The same goes for other geographical terms used, such as *South Africa*.

2. For a discussion of considerations related to the use of the term *informant*, see Waltorp, forthcoming.

3. In *Anthropology as Cultural Critique* George Marcus and Michael Fischer (1999, 137) suggested contemporary anthropology as defamiliarization wherein critique and cross-cultural juxtapositions were the techniques. I suggest that we can play with this technique in the analytical process, in the multimodal sorting of our material.

4. The film *Manenberg* (2010), which I codirected with Christian Vium from the South African township of the same name, reached an overwhelmingly large audience in the area, courtesy of the Nigerian street vendors selling popular film and music on DVD to locals. The Facebook page of the film has more than five thousand likes, predominantly from people in the region, eliciting feedback though this platform.

Categorize, Recategorize, Repeat

These dossiers sprang up spontaneously, serendipitously, whimsically . . . Occasionally, [one] would suddenly and without warning, overlap with [another] . . . in quite unexpected and surprising ways, parities and conjunctions appearing between contexts that, on the surface of things, seemed to have nothing in common. When this happened, I'd feel a sudden pang, a bristling in the back of my neck: the stirring, the reanimation of a fantasy that . . . all the various files would one day turn out to have been related all along . . . The answer would become clear once all the dossiers hove into alignment.

—Tom McCarthy, *Satin Island*

Ethnographic analysis literally begins and ends with categories. We gather data according to preestablished categories of theoretical and comparative concern, and we also require that the way our subjects categorize salient features of their experience shape what we record. Of course, ethnographic analysis starts before we ever enter the field, and it is constantly folded back into the process of data collection. But it is generally not until fieldwork is more or less complete that we engage in a self-conscious and deliberate process of organizing snippets of data into categories—identifying particular instances of some behavior as tokens of types of phenomena that interest us theoretically. Some of these categories will be obvious either because they are predetermined by the design of our research or because they reflect such salient native concerns. As reading field notes and transcripts is also a process of discovery, the necessity—or irrelevance—of some categories will come as a surprise, reflecting previously unremarked patterns in the data. Finally, as we write up, we inevitably face a big, cumulative problem of categorization: What is our case study an example of?

Depending on whether you approach the analysis of ethnographic data as a process of formal coding or informal indexing, a variety of tools are available. The popular approach of grounded theory (Charmaz 2006), for instance, and the kinds of qualitative data analysis software (QDAS) that incorporate it, are effectively tools for simultaneously categorizing data and, in the process, originating categories. I remain somewhat skeptical that fieldworkers who perform participant observation, and who thus come to embody their categories of analysis through prolonged immersion in the field, require such sophisticated tools, but they do need some kind of granular procedures for registering word-by-word, line-by-line interpretations of textual data. In what follows, however, I want to talk about categories on a macro rather than a micro level. The first section discusses high-level categorization practices in ethnographic analysis; the second, categorization practices as objects of ethnographic analysis. I illustrate both sections with examples from ethnographic and ethnohistorical projects of my own, and I propose some exercises in ethnographic analysis based on my experience. Although I draw examples primarily from the deskwork phase of my research, the techniques of what I might call "cognitively distributed categorization" that I describe here are equally applicable to the fieldwork phase of research—and could potentially bridge fieldwork and deskwork.

FILES

In a way, the best statement I know of on the importance of macro-level categorization concerns among the simplest of all classificatory technologies: the filing cabinet. In his brilliant essay "On Intellectual Craftsmanship," C. Wright Mills ([1959] 2000) makes a number of recommendations about how a filing cabinet and its hanging folders can be used to integrate the categories of one's qualitative research with the categories of one's lived experience. For Mills, a good filing system is the social scientist's lifework, an entelechy unto itself. This probably means something a bit different for a sociologist engaged in research on social problems relatively close to home than it would for an anthropologist engaged in cross-cultural analysis, but I think the basic point holds true. The way we sort data, ephemera, notes to ourselves, clippings, articles, and so on into sets for storage and recall not only reflects our conceptual priorities at any given moment but shapes the course of future projects. As Mills puts it: "The use of the file encourages expansion of the categories which you use in your thinking. And the way in which these categories change, some being dropped and others being added—is an index of your intellectual progress and breadth. Eventually the files will come to be arranged according to several large projects, having many sub-projects that change from year to year. . . . The maintenance of such a file is intellectual production" (199).

We have so many formats of material to work with today, and so many platforms for maintaining them in some kind of orderly archive, that it can be difficult to go about this kind of intellectual production in a manner that coheres transmedially, across the various media we use. My preference, when I am really proceeding in an orderly fashion, is to have a set of physical hanging files, which in turn contain manila folders that can move between them, and an arrangement of digital folders on my computer that more or less mirrors the arrangement of the hard copies. Files that I am not using at any given time are placed in a cabinet for long-term storage, while the files I need for immediate use are in a milk crate on or under my desk. The crate represents a writing project or projects.

I prefer to work with the paper files because it gives me a low-cost opportunity to play around with a variety of ways of organizing and reorganizing materials. Moving organizational units forward and backward or intercalating them in new ways is an exploration of conceptual order. Mills puts it this way: "As you re-arrange a filing system, you often find that you are, as it were, loosening your imagination. Apparently this occurs by means of your attempt to combine various ideas and notes on different topics. It is a sort of logic of combination, and 'chance' sometimes plays a curiously large part in it" (201). Somehow, dragging and dropping digital files just doesn't provide the same satisfaction as spreading out the documents in a file I'm working with, shuffling them into piles, annotating them with sticky notes, and sorting them anew into manila folders.

Here I want to reflect a bit on the role that my personal filing system played in the conception of my recent book, *Magic's Reason* (2017). The files tell the whole story. When I was writing my first ethnography, a study of entertainment magic in contemporary France, as a dissertation and then a book (Jones 2011), I found myself struggling to draw connections with influential anthropological theories of instrumental magic (witchcraft, sorcery, etc.). This struggle was a problem of ethnographic analysis. A wise mentor (Fred Myers) suggested I look at ethnographic representations of shamanic practices involving sleight of hand. Gradually, my reading notes and photocopies on this topic congealed into a hanging file that I labeled "Indigenous Illusionism," with subfolders for particular cultural areas: Inuit, Kwakwaka'wakw, Algonquian, and so on. Using the term *illusionism* rather than *magic* in the folder heading was a way of specifying that my concern was sleight of hand in non-Western traditions, making this file commensurable with a much larger set of files I already had on Western practices of sleight of hand.

A manila folder devoted to a North African Sufi order, the 'Isawa, grew so thick so quick that it soon needed a hanging file of its own, then another, and another. At that point I still didn't have a cogent research question, but I was beginning to amass an ample historical archive of nineteenth- and early twentieth-century depictions of the 'Isawa. Notorious figures in French colonial culture, the 'Isawa's spectacular feats of self-mortification had drawn the widespread attention of ethnographers and stage magicians alike—not to mention journalists, tourists, artists, photographers, and others (see figure 11.1). Many French sources emphasized a cross-cultural contrast between, as they put it, the sophisticated trickery of Western entertainment magic that enlightened Europeans didn't really believe and the crude trickery of North African Sufis that unenlightened Arabs actually *did* believe.

Tracking back to my files on "Indigenous Illusionism," I saw similar patterns of invidious epistemological contrasts between Western entertainment magic and ritual practices depicted in the ethnographic record. A hypothesis was beginning to take shape: perhaps the status of magic "tricks" (to put it rather crassly) was functioning in these texts as a placeholder for a much larger argument about disenchantment and also potentially *reënchantment* as world-historical processes. It was time to begin a new hanging file, which I called "Regimes of Enchantment." There I began to assemble what we might call theoretical resources reflecting contemporary anthropological perspectives on disenchantment, enlightenment, and modernity as cultural constructs alongside classical sources (Tylor, Frazer, Weber, etc.) that theorized these issues with specific reference to different kinds of magic. From the confluence of these folders, an initial article on the 'Isawa took shape. My argument was that "by unfavorably comparing Algerians' supposed credulity toward the alleged trickery of indigenous ritual practices to their own attitude of incredulity toward conjuring as a form of disenchanted entertainment, the French used magic as a powerful marker of cultural difference and divergent social evolution" (Jones 2010, 71). This interpretation had emerged quite naturally from my filing system.

FIGURE 11.1 French representation of 'Isawa snake-handling ritual. *L'Illustration*, 1897. Courtesy Firestone Library, Princeton University.

EXERCISE I

Filing systems typically develop organically through gradual processes of accretion. Some files spontaneously take shape as you collect data: when I was doing fieldwork, I found I needed files (or comparable storage systems) to organize collections of different sorts of ephemera. Sometimes those collections gave rise to taxonomies that served as the basis for future analysis. For instance, I collected hundreds of magicians' business cards, which I played around with sorting into a variety of configurations based on iconographic types. This kind of filing is a way of generating categories that can inform research questions and, consequently, data collection: I ultimately made a much more intentional study of professional self-presentation, even shadowing a photographer who specialized in the kinds of publicity shots magicians use in their promotional materials.

If you're anything like me, you may make lots of files all at once in a paroxysm of housekeeping (during both fieldwork and deskwork), when your analog or digital desktop gets too messy to bear it. As folders fill up with documents and files, you may move things around in subfolders to tidy up or start a new folder to control overflow. Does this reactive approach to file-making do justice to Mills's ([1959] 2000) description of filing as a form of "intellectual production" in which "imagination" and "curiosity" play such crucial roles? What if we approached filing more proactively in the intentional spirit of discovery?

You might go about this in several ways. Take an existing file (or a stack of jumbled material) and reorganize it into a new filing system. If you want to do this without disorganizing an established system, make a copy of a folder on your computer, and then play around with reorganizing the contents—you can delete it when you're done. I like to make folders based on the structure of arguments; for this, make an outline first, and then create files and folders corresponding to the headings and subheadings. I sometimes also represent real or imagined files with sheets of paper of different colors, and their contents with sticky notes of different colors. The proxy files can then be sorted into rows or columns representing larger folders. This strategy makes it especially easy to visualize the contents of one's filing system, its overall architecture, and its redundancies or lacunae. I'm sure there are magnificent ways to do this on a computer. QDAS packages such as Atlas.ti, for instance, have special affordances for this kind of visualization (and have the added advantage of allowing you to create—even as you collect data—nonexclusive folders spanning different kinds of media files). For now, I still prefer this artisanal, "slow-file" approach. Also, it's important to remember that anything can go into your files as long as it jogs some association.

During the deskwork phase of writing up, I find that when I'm suffering from writer's block, focusing on organizational tasks seems more manageable than generating even the mangiest prose. Filing is an ideal outlet. You only need to produce a few words—headings—and then sort documents accordingly. Frankly, you don't even need headings. They can follow rather than precede classification. I hope that thinking of filing as a form of ethnographic analysis doesn't impede the guilty pleasure of organization as a way to avoid writing but rather opens up another, less daunting creative avenue that leads naturally to future occasions of writing.

As a ludic form of ethnographic surrealism—and a game that could be fun to play with students—you might take a stack of unrelated documents and try to find a filing system that reflects some underlying anthropological pattern. Sometimes I like to try to reverse engineer the filing system that other social scientists may have used to produce their works. For instance, what kind of filing system might Erving Goffman (1959) have needed to assemble the range of anecdotal minutiae, newspaper clippings of *fait divers*, and literary examples he brings together in a book like *The Presentation of Self in Everyday Life*? This might also be an instructive activity to undertake with advanced students.

Here is a more ambitious suggestion. Of late, I have become interested in the *Zettlekasten* filing system developed by German sociologist Niklas Luhmann. Sönke Ahrens (2017) provides an excellent survey of this approach, which essentially consists of writing observational or reading-based notes in a detailed, deliberate form and then systematically storing them for use in future writing projects. The ambition is that projects for essays, articles, and books might ultimately emerge from the gradual clustering of discrete notes around otherwise unanticipated nodes. This is obviously a system that requires considerable long-term investment in building a personal archive of ideas—the apotheosis of Mills's vision of the self-as-file. Electronic tools have been designed specifically for the Zettlekasten method, and I imagine that platforms such as Evernote or OneNote could be repurposed to this end. I am not yet in a position to opine the feasibility of a system such as this, but at least as an exercise of the imagination, I have found reflecting on the Zettlekasten filing system as a model of how to approach long-term intellectual work quite invigorating.

ANALOGY

My story could have stopped there had the initial success of my filing system not betrayed me. After the first article emerged from what was still somewhat undefined as a larger project, I was primed to begin working on a book. My filing system, however, seemed oriented to the contours of a book that was never meant to be, with the 'Isawa case study as one chapter, and other chapters devoted to various traditions of indigenous illusionism and histories of colonial contact. Unfortunately, I couldn't manage to expand any of those other folders in a manner proportionate to what I had done in researching the 'Isawa. For a variety of historical reasons, the available archives were simply not as rich with texts and images. Succumbing to the inertia of the filing system, I effectively gave up on the project and relegated all of the files to deep storage.

Five years would elapse before I revisited those files. Looking at them with fresh eyes (after several years of teaching ethnographic methods, I should add), I recognized the possibility for a new way of organizing the material I had already collected around a different theme: analogy. The issue that most intrigued me about French representations of the 'Isawa was the sustained use of a cross-cultural analogy between modern, disenchanted magic and primitive, enchanted magic to construct an account of cultural difference. Inspired by more recent ethnographic work among Algerian 'Isawa (Andézian 2001), I became convinced that this analogy was inaccurate, tendentious, and racist; from an ethnohistorical standpoint, however, I could see how culturally productive it had been in buttressing French accounts of civilizational supremacy.

Perhaps more importantly, it struck me that this material reflected a basic methodological issue for any ethnographic analysis: whenever ethnographers apply analytic concepts such as "magic" cross-culturally, they are inevitably making analogies between things they think they already know and things they're in the process of trying to know more about. A number of influential methodological statements frame such analogy-making as the essence of ethnographic analysis. As Roy Wagner (1981, 9) puts it, "the relation that the anthropologist builds between two cultures," results in "an analogy, or a set of analogies, that 'translates' one group of basic meanings into the other." Positing a cross-cultural analogy is also a mode of categorization—in the case I was considering, one that framed French illusionism and 'Isawa rituals as somehow examples of the same thing ("magic") but with crucial differences. Was this a cautionary tale about the perils of using analogy in cross-cultural comparison?

With this question in mind, I realized that ethnographers weren't the only ones in my data making analogies between primitive and modern magic. In fact, modern Western magicians played an active role in shaping these conceptual associations, and the magicians I worked with in contemporary France were still quite interested in discussing parallelisms between the modern magic they performed and the primitive magic they attributed to nonmodern Others. For a variety of reasons I hadn't systematically analyzed this topic when working on my first monograph. At that time I didn't quite know what to do with it. I hadn't indexed the relevant field notes, transcripts, texts, or ephemera with a relevant code word (such as *primitivism* or *exoticism*), much less sorted them into a self-contained file. I went back to my ethnographic data, began to assemble the relevant documents, and started a new set of hanging files called "Dangerous Doubles." This rubric—pointing to the elaboration of binary oppositions between the primitive and the modern in representations of magic—allowed me to bring together ethnographic, historical, and theoretical materials previously dispersed in separate files.

Marilyn Strathern (1992b, 47) argues that "culture consists in the way people draw analogies between different domains of their worlds." My new filing system was helping me see that, among Euro-American anthropologists and magicians alike, comparisons between Western popular culture and non-Western ritual practices were a way of enacting a shared understanding about what it means to be modern. In the case of these analogies, I found it very helpful to draw diagrams based on a model developed by cognitive psychologist Dedre Gentner (1983). This model focuses on how patterns selected from a familiar "base" domain are mapped onto patterns in an unfamiliar "target" domain, generating an abstracted pattern of similarity and difference in the form of a concept. So, for instance, the literary text is a base domain that Clifford Geertz famously maps onto human culture, generating the conceptual abstraction of culture-as-text (see Hoffman 2009). In my case, the diagram looked something like the sketch in figure 11.2. To be clear, this diagram does not represent my own theoretical viewpoint but rather my analysis of the way that "modern" magic served as a base domain for analogies targeting "primitive" magic in prior ethnographic accounts, giving form to the so-called intellectualist conception of magical thinking as an error in causal reasoning (see Tambiah 1990).

Taking Strathern's observation one step further, I began exploring how connections between the various domains in which people draw analogies could also be culturally organized. I called my comparison between

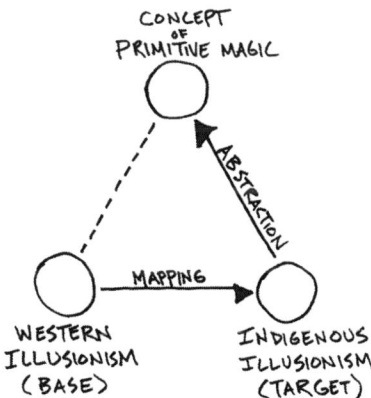

FIGURE 11.2 Diagram illustrating how an analogy between Western entertainment magic and non-Western ritual magic informs the anthropological concept of magic.

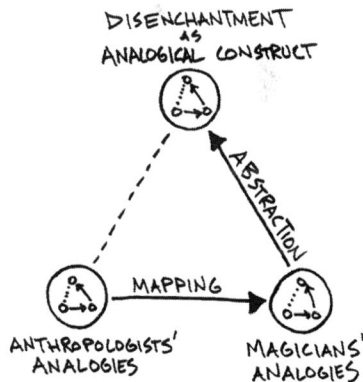

FIGURE 11.3 Diagram illustrating how a meta-analogy between anthropologists' analogies and magicians' analogies informs the concept of disenchantment as a global historical process.

analogy-making practices in anthropology and analogy-making practices in magic a "meta-analogy." Again, adapting Gentner's model of analogical mapping, I diagrammed this meta-analogy along the lines reflected in figure 11.3, producing an image of how comparisons between putatively enchanted and disenchanted illusionistic practices, drawn by experts in different domains, reinforced a more general ethnotheory of disenchantment as a historical condition distinctive of Western modernity. Through these diagrams a book was taking shape, one that would focus on "a style of reasoning about 'primitive' magic shared by both 'modern' anthropologists and 'modern' magicians as Euro-American cultural producers working in the context of colonial and postcolonial ideologies of racial and civilizational hierarchy" (Jones 2017, 162).

Some of my keenest insights when working on *Magic's Reason* came from trying to visualize the analogical relations my subjects were discursively and representationally enacting. I did this through my own diagrams but also literally by placing imagery reflective of native analogies into diagrammatic relationships. For instance, by looking at nineteenth-century French representations of the 'Isawa, like that in figure 11.1, alongside contemporaneous magic posters, I began to better understand how writers and artists were using the trope of "trickery" to draw tendentious comparisons between two ostensibly unrelated domains: mass spectacle and ecstatic ritual. Situating this analogy in practice led me to focus analytically on the types of semiotic labor involved in producing and maintaining such intertextual associations.

EXERCISE II

The meta-analogical approach is a very peculiar type of ethnographic analysis that probably wouldn't fit many projects. It was particularly apt in my case because I was examining dynamic interconnections between the intellectual history of a European social science and the cultural history of a European entertainment industry, both with strong exoticist tendencies. Still, precedents exist for this kind of analysis—Strathern's (1992a) *After Nature* and Herzfeld's (1989) *Anthropology Through the Looking-Glass* come to mind—and I hope that we will continue to see projects in this vein. The specific example of meta-analogy, however, points to a more general component of ethnographic analysis that could have a place in almost any project.

Anthropologists are not the only ones who categorize. Whomever it is that we study, they will also inevitably be engaged in practices of categorization. Categorize the categorizing practices—be they discursive or embodied—emergent in your data. What are the native categories, and are they enacted or "entextualized" through labels, concepts, metaphors, or other devices? What kinds of situations or events occasion acts of categorization, who are the relevant actors (e.g., authors, intellectuals, bureaucrats, administrators), and what are the patterns of consensus or conflict? In making a filing system you have probably already used native categories; now make sure you also include native categorization practices—for instance, recurrent analogies—as file headings.

If analogies are as common in your data as Strathern's definition of culture predicts they will be, try to use base → target → concept diagrams to represent how they function. Look for repeated patterns; find a base domain that people draw analogies from. Depict it on the lower left of your page. What target domain do they use the base to illuminate? Depict that on the lower right of your page, and then connect them with an arrow. What kind of abstraction does the analogy generate? Depict it on the upper middle of your page, as the apex of a triangle, with an arrow leading up to it from the target. Now situate the image in social life: Where and when do the processes of mapping and abstraction occur? What kind of cultural lives do analogical abstractions go on to have? Once you find some analogies, you might even try to diagram more complex relationships between them, such as meta-analogy. Like the organizational practice of filing, drawing, sketching, and diagramming are great ways to originate categories and, in the process, unlock the imagination.

PROTOCOL

- Identify a macro-category that recurs in your thinking. It could come from theory, from powerful field experiences, or from the argument you wish to make. Make a physical or digital folder for it.
- Identify and make copies or some other representation of items (artifacts collected from the field, notes, transcriptions of interviews, ephemera, etc.) that speak to the category.
- Arrange the items within the folder to create subcategories and other types of groupings.
- Focus on the contents of those subfolders/categories: What are the horizontal relations between the items? Are these patterns, contrasts, commonalities, analogies?

- Let the folders and their contents rest: five days, five weeks, five years. It is up to you.
- Open the folders again and reacquaint yourself with the conceptual relations between items.
- If necessary, reorganize your subfolders, or change your categories.

Bonus:

- If in the process of rearranging the items in a folder you begin to think in analogies, you can draw a "base → target → concept" diagram to clarify the analogies at play:
  - Find the base domain from which people are drawing patterns for comparison; draw it on the lower left side of the page.
  - Identify the target domain people are trying to illuminate; draw it on the lower right side of the page.
  - Connect the two with an arrow and identify the particular patterns of both similarity and difference that are being mapped from base to target.
  - If the mapping gives rise to an abstraction that reappears elsewhere in your data, identify that abstraction; draw it in the upper middle of the page to form a triangle.
  - Connect the target and the abstraction with an arrow, and try to identify the moment, process, scene of social life where this abstraction plays out.
- Repeat and enrich as necessary to unlock the empirically grounded imagination

....

CHAPTER 12

BRIT ROSS WINTHEREIK AND JAMES MAGUIRE

Sound Recording as Analytic Technique

Rooms without sound—anechoic chambers—are facilities that are built to test the acoustics of materials. The walls of such chambers are constructed to suck in noise rather than reflect electromagnetic sound waves. Imagine what being in a room without sound feels like. How might it affect you? Some say it is a disturbing, unpleasant experience, a sickening, migraine-inducing, vertigo-provoking moment. They say that when sound waves are eliminated, you are left with a body deprived of one of its basic navigational modes. A body whose sounds are not refracted by its environment loses its sense of orientation. When a body cannot orient itself, it stops being a site of potentiality, perhaps even of life.[1] It becomes unrelatable.

We use the anechoic chamber here to make a contrast with another kind of room where we have experimented with sound-based ways of navigating ethnographic material. This soundproof room is built into the back of our university's largest auditorium. It is small, rectangular, and painted bright green. Unlike the anechoic chamber, this room does not eliminate sound—it merely dampens it—but at the same time the green room is an amplifier and a space for making relations. Whereas an anechoic chamber makes bodies unrelated through a lack of sound, sound recording relates the sound-bodies of ethnographers and imagined listeners. In the process of making and recording sound, we engaged with our ethnographic materials in ways that we take to be analytic. In this piece, we explain why we consider this to be the case. We also describe how you might use our experiences with sound recording in analyses of your own ethnographic materials.

We began making sound recordings because we wanted to experiment with analysis through the public dissemination of research. Our ideas about the analytic purchase of sound recordings were not concrete, and we did not have very specific plans for how we would structure our communication. Moreover, our ideas about the audience were vague. Our resources for embarking upon this experiment were a joint research project on the data center industry, a podcast training course that the first author had taken, and a lot of enthusiasm for trying something new.

In what follows we first describe our sound-recording experiences, focusing on the ambition to create a podcast on data centers and the processes of locating data. We then reflect on the recording work as a "moment of immersement" (immersion) at once "totalising" and "partial"—that is, *pace* Strathern, "a totalising activity which is not the only activity in which the person is engaged" (1999, 1). We find Strathern's notion of immersion very useful because it helps us grasp "intimacy" as a specific form that relations can take. The form of intimacy we are especially curious about is the one between ethnographers and ethnographic materials, which itself is enabled through another kind of intimacy that arises between ethnographers and their imagined audience. The intimacies that were made in, and amplified by, the green room and its recording infrastructure were premised on a collapse between "the field" and "the desk." We end the chapter by presenting a description of a technique that you can try if you are interested in experimenting with immersion through sound recording. As will be clear, recording and listening are both important elements of this analytic technique, as is the presence of an imagined audience. Publishing the recording in the form of a podcast can be a next step and may be a good thing to do. But you could use and adapt the technique we propose without ever actually releasing a podcast, as long as you have produced it with an audience in mind.

WHY PODCAST?

In our current research we are investigating why Denmark has recently become a data haven for Big Tech corporations; Apple, Facebook, and Google have rushed to the cool climes of the north to store the vast bulk of their European data streams. But the data centers of Big Tech are an opaque research object; secrecy is the norm, and concealment is the operative mode of engagement. While this impinges on our ability to gain access to the field, we have found workarounds: interviews with local government officials, state agencies, and data experts, as well as visits to data center construction sites where we peek through security fences and snap photos. Data conferences and data center working groups have also become inroads and entry points.

But we also had broader concerns about the status and role of ethnography in "datafied" worlds: How can ethnography get to grips with complex data relations? "Being there," as a primary ethnographic move, is further complicated in a world characterized by complex data ecologies, as data itself is both located and distributed at one and the same time. Data centers are part of complex digital infrastructures that generate and distribute data across vast geographical expanses. Where data reside at any one particular moment—their location—is difficult to pinpoint through standard modes of assessing an entity's geography. As such, ethnographic colocation is difficult to establish. As our workarounds highlight, data center ethnography is not impossible, and others are doing it (Hogan 2015; Vonderau 2017). But bodily engagement—an important part of our previous research-method assemblages on the volcanic landscapes of Iceland and the windswept coastal plains of northern Denmark—is made extremely difficult by such a distributed research object.

We imagined that making a podcast would help us to create a different kind of access and set up a space where we could be copresent with the phenomenon we were studying, without necessarily being colocated in the usual sense of the word (Beaulieu 2010). Said differently, in our attempt to investigate and analyze digitally mediated infrastructures, we would perform our own digitally mediated analysis. Sound recordings are a way of conjuring a space and a narrative with, and about, the ethnographic material as a means of opening it up for analysis. We imagined that the "empirical base" for our analysis would be recordings from on-site visits at data centers, microphone-based conversations, and extended interviews with interlocutors and colleagues during invited visits to the university. As we began recording, we became more aware of the ethical issues of the recording process, thinking about how to use these sound clips in partially edited formats. And such ethical awareness arose precisely because of the green room's capacity to perform as an analytic space. Nothing happened "automatically"; no information was at risk of being publicized that had not been through careful scrutiny and curated rendition. Making ethnographic data public was simply nowhere near an automated process.

Sounds and sound recording have always played an important role in the production of ethnography. This role can be seen in a more mundane sense as ethnographers work through sound when recording and transcribing interviews. But the ethnographer's body is also always immersed in a multiplicity of sound worlds as the slow process of orientation and navigation unfolds in unfamiliar terrains. Sound, one could say, both signals and elicits, complementing and disrupting action and thought simultaneously.

We both have carried out ethnographic research in landscapes where sound was taken seriously as a crucial mode of orientation and as inspiration for further analysis—by us and by the people we were working with. James, conducting energy research in Iceland, spent much time trekking through volatile volcanic sites alongside geologists as they used the sounds emerging from deep within geothermal wells as an acoustic method for generating knowledge about subterranean forces (Maguire 2017). We both took part in the development of a sound-based energy walk in the landscapes of northern Denmark: hikers were guided through these windy landscapes via recordings that sensitized them to the multiplicity of landscape sounds connected to energy infrastructures (Winthereik, Watts, and Maguire, 2019). In the years after the energy walk had been installed, Brit was often in contact with a person who lived in the area and who had taken it upon himself to engage locals and tourists in questions around wave conversion technologies and sustainable energy raised by the energy walk. That the walk was inviting the public to experience the landscape through sound was important because it excited our interlocutor and enabled him to interest others in the theme of energy. Sound allowed Brit to maintain the link with this field site and its people. These examples are modes of immersement, ways of forming relations in a space through the senses: vision, sound, smell, and so forth.

Venturing into podcasting was another exploration in sound for us; this time however, it was more explicitly connected to our ways of thinking and doing analysis. Currently podcasts are being mobilized as academic technologies in a variety of settings. Most common in anthropology is podcasting in order to disseminate and communicate research; this form adopts somewhat of a telling style. Also popular is using podcasts in order to generate conversations within and across disciplines, primarily by adopting an interview style. More explorative still are setups whereby anthropologists tailor ethnographic methods to the form of a podcast, conducting mini-fieldwork and discussing the findings with the audience. In this instance ethnographic methods are structured around the podcast as a platform for public engagement, a style that, instead of communicating anthropology to the public, performs ethnography through podcasting.

Our intention is to use podcasting for a broader, yet-unknown audience as part of our methods assemblage by adopting it for ethnographic analysis. This version is one that merges the generation of ethnographic materials with their analysis. Analysis is thus a process that happens "in public," performing rather than communicating ethnography while at the same time paying particular attention to the analytic possibilities of sound and sound-based infrastructures.

IMAGINING AN AUDIENCE

Once we made the decision to set aside time for engaging with our ethnographic material through sound recording, one of the first things we did was to make a jingle. The jingle introduces every podcast episode within the frame of a longer series. Making the jingle took a very long time. First, neither of us had any experience of developing a clear message that could be performed in forty seconds. Second, as we listened to our own voices during the recording sessions, we became somewhat alienated by them and by how they seemed to misfire in various way. We stumbled over words. Where to put the emphasis in this sentence? Even the sound of our own names was suddenly weird and unfamiliar.

We experienced sound recording as very different from analysis through writing. This resonates with work from colleagues (Watts et al. forthcoming) who, in their depiction of the making of a graphic novel, argue that drawings and visual arts can enrich the silent spaces of language. Rather than an enrichment, we experienced silence as awkward moments, and even though we were able to remove them during editing, the awkwardness had put a mark on our voices that could be heard in what followed each pause. So, what is uttered during recording is but one small component of the assemblage of affective moments that occupied, and amplified, relations in the recording studio.

In these affective moments, the embodiment of thinking became visible, as did the tendency we have of obscuring this embodiment through observations. After a few recording sessions we noticed how the speed and tone of our individual voices changed, and how we modulated our pitch in relation to one another as stories intensified and deintensified. We had many conversations about our choice of language; we both speak English and Danish, but James is a native English speaker while Brit is a native Danish speaker. At first, we focused very much on the barriers we would encounter by doing the podcast in a second, rather than native, language. As it turned out, language skills were just one of the elements in a much more complicated infrastructural setup that included other issues of power, such as differences in academic seniority. So, although words are essential in podcasting, their dominance as sole mediators of meaning (in comparison to textual modes of analysis) is lessened as the embodied practices required to produce them are heightened. Words are calibrated and rearranged as sound instruments—but only as part of a broader infrastructure through which intimacy between ethnographer and audience circulates. Although much infrastructural analysis attempts to make visible that which is deemed invisible, our turn toward sound and its various modalities (pitch, tone, inflection, etc.) allowed us to observe that sound recording makes heard certain things that are unheard in writing. This idea brings us to listening as an important aspect when using sound recording as an analytic technique.

RECONFIGURING ACADEMIC AUTHORITY

Sound recording is as much an act of listening as it is an act of making sound. You listen while you do the recording, when you review the raw sound files, and when you edit. Because the recording is done with an idea of an audience in mind, you listen in the presence of somebody else. One of the first things an experienced podcaster will tell you is that in podcasting, everything hinges on your capacity to create an intimate relation with the listener. This kind of intimacy is produced in public and through your capacity for relating through the tone of your voice.

Knowing this meant that every act of listening also became an evaluation: How well were we doing with respect to enrolling an audience through the tone, intensity, and melody of our voices? Recording felt risky. We felt that putting ourselves into a format that would remain in the digital ether indefinitely was an analytic practice that differed very much from other modes. It is this sense of risk that is embedded into the analytical infrastructure that forms between ethnographer and ethnographic material, and an imagined, unknown audience. Who is this audience to whom we were reaching out? The answer is that we still don't know, and even if we sometimes think we can pin it down, it tends to change. Our podcast activities ran on the working imaginary of "a public," and what interested this public would change according to what we discussed in the green room.

Interestingly, sound recording as analytic technique is not weakened by the fact that its configuration is constantly in flux; in fact, this flux is a key part of its publicness. Despite greatly improved editing technologies, the sense of liveliness that comes with podcasting does not dissipate. Performative awareness of accent, tone, cadence, pitch, and so forth is married with a sense of another "other" reverberating within the sound room—the academic persona. As we narrated and organized the recorded sounds "on the fly," the classic idioms and registers of academia became increasingly difficult to attain—and they are, quite possibly, also unnecessary. Figuring a relationship with a podcast listener and delivering a conference paper, for example, are entirely different processes. As avid podcast listeners ourselves, we know that what we produce will be present in the audience's lives, for the most part, through digitally mediated headphones. We are "with" them on trains and buses, in parks and on bicycles, in cars and kitchens. Listeners can very easily be among others while among us, totalizing, yet partial. And yet, although we transmit sound signals that they pick up, what binds us together, to our minds, is our willingness to risk a specific version of academic authority. Seeking to craft a more public relation to our ethnographic material complexifies our relation to this very material as the usual academic sureties of reflection and feedback dissipate in a stream of immediate dialogic consciousness. So, as we slip and falter through various analyses, we find that our anxious relations to ourselves, each other, our material, and our audience are also generative of a moment of acknowledgement of what the ethnography might be about.

It is here where the analytic purchase of podcasting, vis-à-vis other modes of doing analysis (writing, drawing, making analogies), lies: in the amplification of insights that are generated in, and as, risky formulations. In collapsing the relation between field and desk in order to do analysis in public, one's authority is put at stake. Part of reconfiguring this authority is inverting sensory hierarchies in order to allow other, nondominant senses back into our modes of analysis. Podcasting enlivens us to the role of our senses when engaging with the messiness of data. It is a process that emphasizes our sensory relation to data and that dares to draw the world into this mesh of sense and sensibility. Sound recording does not replace fieldwork; it is not a way of avoiding the difficulties of negotiating access to hard-to-get-at social and physical spaces. Instead, the activity makes a different form of analytic labor possible, as captured by Michel Serres in *The Five Senses*. Serres argues: "The true labour in research and in the humanities lies in an adequate, sensible and fearless approach to whatever affects us" (2008, 156). He proposes that language and logic remove us from knowing through the senses, and that as researchers we need a second language that "intimately tastes" (2008, 156).[2]

In our context, podcasting is a language that intimately tastes. It answers a particular hunger from within academia to find alternate modes of doing analysis while at the same time engaging the public in discussions that are relevant, timely, and willing to risk being imperfect. These risky formulations, though made in relation to a (for now) unknown public, will, we hope, begin to generate an emerging audience as it figures out its tastes in relation to ours. At the same time, in moving away from the more traditional spaces of research communication, podcasting becomes a performative move as we try to apprehend digitally mediated worlds through digital means. What we are eager to point toward is that, as an ethnographic method, podcasting collapses the field-desk dichotomy, compressing data generation and analysis within riskier sound chambers. So, although our usual modes of analysis consist of multiple iterative steps that take field data and run them through an analytical infrastructure consisting of coding, analyzing, writing, reviewing, rewriting, and publishing, such sound-chamber compression makes heard the tensions, contradictions, and gaps that are the conditions of possibility for the working of those infrastructures. In two particular podcast episodes, the guests asked for a copy of the sound file, not as a means to screen and approve the recording, but because they felt a moment of dazzle (Strathern 1999, 6). In trying to emphasize the infrastructures of sound that are necessary to the production of podcasts, we are trying to bring forth some of our own analytic infrastructures.

What is important to note is that as relations between us as ethnographers and our ethnographic material are formed through these infrastructures, new responsibilities and accountabilities emerge. We have no way of knowing whether James would have become interested in setting up a new project on platform collectivities, for example, had it not been for these experiments with sound and the conversations with guests—part of the aforementioned dazzle. Attempts to relate to "a public" through this form of ethnographic analysis, however, are brought about by the fact that this public is not so much "out there" as "in here" with us.

This realization augmented analysis in the sense that it was in the green room that we began asking ourselves about the material infrastructures of data. The urge to know what data are—what they look like, feel like, how they translate from the moment you strike a key on a keyboard to the moment they "land" in a data center—developed during a recording session as we listened to the excitement at certain moments during our conversation. Recording made what was known—or about to be known—emerge in the relations we have just described as an infrastructured setup that included ethnographic material (in this case, data) and an imaginary, ever-changing public. Attending to relations and their forms as an analytic modality is attending to what is in the world, ontologically speaking. It is not about passing judgement as to which relations are "intimate" or "detached"; it is not about how they can best be characterized. Rather, it is about what takes place once you make space for engaging with your ethnographic material through sound recording. A possibility opens for a narrative that requires you to take various kinds of intimacy in relations seriously. Thus it complexifies how you know you know, because you observe yourself differently as a participant of this opening. At first you are critical about almost anything—from the tone of your voice and how you pronounce your own name to your lack of knowledge about this or that topic. Then you explore that space. You learn how self-critique becomes embodied by inflections in your voice. Observing this, and experiencing how letting go of such criticism is productive of a desire to explore that which you don't know, or don't know you don't know, can reconfigure your relation with your ethnographic material.

GETTING STARTED

A sound recording can be made anywhere, but taking account of an imagined audience necessitates setting up a space that is instrumented and sealed off from the mundane noises of our world. It is the sealing off that makes it possible to establish a sound that is pleasant enough that prospective listeners would continue listening. Recording equipment is also necessary. The podcast course for academics that Brit took introduced her to a fairly easy-to-use sound editing program (Hindenburg.dk), but it was James's continued conversations with the university's communication department that enrolled a media specialist from that department. He found a sealed-off space for us (the green room); he procured a professional microphone and gave us a list of tips and tricks for minimizing noise, common verbal tics that detract from the listening experience, and ways of using the editing program to optimize our time. For beginners, the recording apps that are now available on any smartphone and an additional microphone can help you get started. Getting familiar with platforms for sharing sound and podcast apps are next steps when you have produced something that you would like to share. Then your podcast can be embedded on websites and circulated via social media platforms.

As we mentioned above, podcasting is a language that "intimately tastes," a language not solely concerned with linguistics but of learning to be affected, of thinking through how logic, sense, and technologies such as microphones construct spaces whose artificiality brings us closer to our senses. Or do they remove us from the world we seek to describe and analyze? Or both? We are not going to answer this question in any finite way, but we invite you to try the exercise below in the hope that you will take up the challenge and try out sound recording for ethnographic analysis.

PROTOCOL

- Talk about your research in two minutes, ideally to an academic friend or someone that you trust.
- Make a two-minute sound recording of your story on any recording device. It is important that the recording be no longer than two minutes.
- Listen to the recording, possibly several times.
- Now answer the question: What part of the recorded story attracted you most, and why?
- Write down keywords that will support you in making a new recording (again, a maximum duration of two minutes).
- As you make the second recording, be particularly aware of the part(s) of the story that attracted you most in the first recording. Focus your attention on telling this part in a way that is attractive to a potential audience.
- If you feel like it, make a longer recording about your research and publicize it.

NOTES

1. In physics, potential energy is the capacity of a body to do work as a function of its position in electric, magnetic, or gravitational fields (Helmreich 2013).
2. See also Schulze 2020.

PART IV

INCOMMENSURABILITIES

Substance as Method (Shaking Up Your Practice)

By due attention, more can be found in nature than that which is observed at first sight.
—Alfred North Whitehead, *The Concept of Nature*

This is a workshop. The idea is simple: Pick a substance related to your work that you don't *directly* care about, that you haven't paid due attention to, and find out how others learned to see more in it. Learn from them how their substance challenged them to rethink their theories and methods and, from that, consider how your theories or methods might also be rethought.

OBSESS!

This is an exercise in specificity and kinds. I call it "substance as method" (SAM). It is not a method to replace all other methods; it is not a replacement for ethnography nor a kind of ethnography in itself. This method is a tiny one next to those we do, but it has a chance to help us think and practice research differently, because it shows us different worlds. It begins by picking an adjacent substance.

Think about your research object (your subject, field, actions, the things that matter most to you), and then think about the substances around them. Make a list of ten to twelve secondary objects—materials that are part of other things, things or effects that are close but not central. Don't list things that are precious to you (this is not an "implosion" project; see below). Substances are not usually singular objects but rather something like a material, a substrate, a kind, a species, and so on. It could be a particular kind of wood, an element you've heard mentioned, a work tool. When

I was working on fracking, I made a list: drill bit, worker's compensation contract, deep ground sonar, bromine (that comes up from drilling), plastic tarps lining water pits, handheld computers, man camps, pipeline pipes, bulldozers, tap water.

Then pick the fourth or fifth one. I picked *bromine.*

Your assignment is to then do some research: Locate specialists who care about that substance and read some of their work (scientific papers, newsletters, treatises about working with that substance, textbooks, etc.). Read quickly and widely. Because you chose a secondary substance, you don't know much about it. You are not trying to become an expert—it is okay if you don't understand all the technical language. Rather, you are realizing for yourself that there that there are specialists who spend a good portion of their lives caring about and investigating that substance— specialists such as scientists, technicians, workers, engineers, artisans, artists, fans, managers, and so on. For me, they are the kind of people who, if you asked them about bromine, would have a lot to say. A lot. They are geeks about it. They don't just know about it, they grapple with it in their life, they adapt to it, they have to invent concepts and theories to account for those interactions: vocabularies specific to the substance. Jane Bennett (2010) draws on accounts of metalworkers whose "desire to see what a metal can do" led to "intense intimacy with their material," which led them to discover new structures and a life in metal.

One workshop participant asked about choosing general versus specific substances for this exercise: should she select "candles in general" or "beeswax candles"? The answer is that it is not you who picks the level of generality. Find those other people for whom candles are their obsession and see what their categories of specificity are. The first question you ask yourself of a reading or a person: What is the substance for them? What words do they use, and what do they pick out with them? What are the boundaries (i.e., what is included in "it")? What "kinds" of it do they talk/ care about? The answers may not be what you thought they would be. (That's good! It means you are already learning.)

With regard to candles: Are there people who make all different kinds of candles or do they specialize? For those who think of themselves as inventing new types of candles, do they think of them generically? What are the categories within which they think? Each human will have an emic type of scoping, and you map these as you go along. Not everyone will agree. For my substance, some write books about *bromine,* others *bromides,* others *halogens.* I read in order to notice what their "substances" of concern are: What do they pick out to study? Where do those things begin and end for them? I pick my starting point and then go look and find that it is much smaller or wider or way sideways for them—they put a bunch of other things together that I didn't even think could be "one" topic. That process begins to jostle me out of my categories.

SURPRISE!

The second thing you do as you skim through material or talk to someone is to pay attention to their edges: what don't they know about the substance, what surprised them? What excites them about the substance? What are they challenged by? Where have they run into problems in studying or working with the substance? This is the core of SAM: when someone has been stumped by a substance, but because they are obsessed with it, they refuse to give up and are forced—by the substance—to rethink their own concepts and tools. The key is that the substance resists the specialists' work and curiosity; it requires extensive exploration in order to understand its properties, and different and sometimes new tools are usually needed in order to figure out what it does, how it relates, or connects, or does things, and how it refuses to do other things. Its verbs are recalcitrant to speculation and need empirical work. The specialist often comes to realize that the substance might have types (e.g., types of bromides) and may behave totally differently in different environments or when connected to certain other substances. The substance puts the specialists' categories into variation. This point is where the substance becomes its own metaphor.

I read a book on halogen bonding in which one of the researchers told a story about their realization that bromine had been crucial to a number of pharmaceutical discoveries and yet their computer simulations weren't showing it. They realized that their software had built-in assumptions that noncovalent halogen bonds were *like* noncovalent hydrogen bonds in water—but they hadn't looked closely enough. When they did, they found that halogen bonds were slightly different, and that slight difference actually made them ideal for making "inhibitor" drugs. The researchers needed to rethink their entire notions of bonding and likeness, redo their tools, and create a new type of bond: "X-bonds" (because X is often used as a stand-in for halogens). Their substance, in other words, demanded its own variation; it was its own metaphor.

The second practice is thus to locate those specialists ("philiacs," lovers of the substance) who care so much about a substance that they let it surprise them as such; they are humbled by it. As they persist in their pursuit of it they create knowledge, remake themselves as knowers, and mutate the world toward the substance. They become interested in the duration of the engagement with being stumped, the hesitations. In one case I read through an entire textbook, and only a few paragraphs jumped out as interesting to me: those in which the author had to tell some history in order to explain why something that is now so obvious was overlooked for so long. Much of it was too technical for me in terms of chemistry, but I could follow the grammar of surprise: chemistry worked just fine, until it didn't. Chemistry as they knew it worked just fine for bromine until they were looking at its role in macromolecules, and X-bonding, when they realized that modeling on water had led them astray. They had assumed it generalized. Nope. They had to undo their notion of bonding.

Depending on your substance, you may need to delve into the "gray literature," written for and by people in a particular industry. These publications are where people exchange job news, and they create an extraordinary map of what those people care about. You can use these texts to map their areas of concern and what they think is important—which are often quite unexpected—and what they care less about, which they indirectly identify by not discussing it (e.g., fracking companies couldn't care less about activists—our activities barely show up on their radar when compared with geological speculations and what competitors are doing, as the latter affect their bottom line much more). You can see in that gray literature the things that drive and challenge them. The things that they find necessary to talk about. These are lively edges where disagreement and invention are taking place.

Or, you may need to read white papers or protocols. In one workshop a student was curious about the USB sticks that her informants used to exchange pictures. She looked up the USB protocol white paper and attended to what was necessary to talk about. It was all about the balance between speed and durability and error rates. Here is a device that you stick into and pull out of a computer so many times that it had been given a life span. Errors are not a problem; they are what USB does in continually sending data back and forth and testing them for errors. The issue is the speed of errors, not the happening of them. Error is a flow rate put against a proper transfer rate. These failures are balanced at an acceptable level. SAM is used here to read the protocol as a record of what its developers were struggling with— that is, why they had to specify it: because disagreements and misunderstandings occurred. The text records things that can vary but shouldn't, that can go wrong, the things that need to be standardized. That means that underneath what the writers said is all this variation that needed to be made into one whole. To the extent that you don't see the standard as one among many is the extent to which you've accepted the normality of that standard, that concept, that substance.

RESONATE!

"The encounter between two disciplines doesn't take place when one reflects on the other, but when one discipline realizes that it has to resolve, for itself, a problem similar to one confronted by the other." —Gilles Deleuze, "The Brain Is the Screen"

The third step is to resonate with the surprise of others. As much as substances can spawn new theories, new software, and new methods among researchers caring for their specificity, we can also note how all of our theories are in correspondence with often implicit substances. Literally *in correspondence*, because we think with conceptual prototypes (core examples). In my case, while reading about how bromine created different notions of bonding, I began to notice how deeply my notions of connections (among professionals, among companies) depended on a binary of "direct" versus "indirect" (through communication channels or through structures such as capitalism). The USB sticks led me to wonder about my connections as having life spans and error rates, rather than as being true or good or bad.

When I looked at studies of how bromides function in landfills, I learned that researchers discovered that the concept of "breakdown" needed to be broken up, because landfills have four very different layers, each of which engages in a different transformation. Bromides sometimes broke down into constituent parts, sometimes they bioaccumulated in creatures and became more complex, sometimes they went from toxic to relatively nontoxic, and sometimes they became both more toxic and light enough to fly away into the atmosphere. As these researchers freaked out at this multiplicity of pathways, I started rethinking my comparatively simple assumptions about what it means for a company to break apart or a person to break down. I'd written these words as if I knew what they meant, as if they were relatively simple processes or metaphors.

The third practice of SAM is therefore to use others' surprise about their substance to teach yourself to put your own concepts into variation, especially simple words such as *connection* or *breakdown*, or theory words such as *entanglement* or *neoliberalism*. I like this exercise because it points to our own conceptual shortcuts. What if one of my theoretical terms causes me to overlook the very thing that matters most to me or my informants? Every time I use the word *biopolitics*, I may be overlooking something that matters, because it fits biopolitics "enough" (the way hydrogen bonding fit most of the things these researchers wanted to use halogen binding for, such that when they hit something where it mattered, they overlooked it). So how do even the little words I like—*power, force, cause, entangle, attune*—skip over the challenge?

This is a kind of agitating empiricism. I am interested in all the people who have run up against the failure of their existing vocabulary and theories to deal with a substance. And I am learning from that, because it is rare: in the general way of things I do not have to regularly generate new vocabularies. Especially theoretically speaking, I am mostly pressing against other words (my own words/concepts). Spending too much time in academia, perhaps, I feel as if I don't have enough encounters with things to really question my theories, so I am doing this by proxy. Seeing whether their process might help me think differently.

In SAM, you work on your habits of thinking, but *not* by getting a better description of the substance, *not* by adding multiple perspectives. You listen to find resonance between each of your various struggles with substances. So it is not an empiricism of description; it is not about being more relational with your substance, nor about adding layers or thinking substance as multiple. You are not writing by thinking. You listen to others because you want to challenge your habitual theorizations and bring your own attention to your way of struggling with objects, relations, and worlds. You are provoking yourself, putting your own concepts and methods into variation, not acquiring a new technique.

SPECIFY!

Putting your concepts into variation is a practice of relentless specificity. Always ask: What kind of X is this X? What kind of entanglement is this entanglement? Is it entangled like vines (with or without thorns), or like hair (in need of combing or shampoo), or like a trap (who set it), or like family relations (with what affect), or like a fishing line, or like a story? Your research is the answer to this question. You may decide that *entangle* is not even the right word.

Whenever you find a word coming to your tongue or keyboard, ask yourself whether perhaps you are skipping what matters, avoiding a complex relation that is right in front of you. Instead of staying with its trouble, this word may seem to apply "enough" and may help you avoid naming the thing that you might really want to name there. The word/concept plugs a hole but maybe not in the way you want. Ask yourself what kind of itself it is!

If you want somewhat baroque inspiration, Hans Blumenberg (2016) wrote a fascinating little book called *Paradigms for Metaphorology* in which he discusses words such as *truth* that cannot be empirically grasped and therefore can be accessed only by means of "absolute metaphors" that themselves have a history: Is truth something that you know because it is convincing, or is the fact that something is convincing proof that it is rhetoric and not truth? At different times, each of these has been a dominant absolute metaphor of truth. More than a dozen distinct absolute metaphors of truth exist, each with subtypes. Blumenberg finds that absolute metaphors "owe their 'success' precisely to the fact that they do not permit the question of relation to reality to rise in the first place, since it serves to indicate a basic attitude that first gives what we call 'reality' its gestalt" or feeling (Savage 2016, 143). They give form to our experience (to our phenomenology as Sara Ahmed, 2006, describes). When we think, meditate, poetically write, we do so already within certain relations, within and around the substances we are familiar with (even if we haven't named them as such). But that doesn't mean they can't be replaced with others or corrected with more precise ones.

For more modern inspiration, you can turn to pretty much any of Foucault's lectures that he gave weekly (during semesters) for decades. Read them this time for how he read texts rather than for his takeaways. One of his practices was to approach a text as though it were the only evidence for the meaning of the words in it. If a text used *crime* or *market*, he would come up with a precise definition of those words for that text. It is a technique of turning the document inside out: rather than interpreting it on the basis of what you think the words mean, let it teach you new definitions of all of its words. It often seems like Foucault played a game: make a list of the seven precise characteristics of a word, as it was used. In his book on biopolitics, the result is a specification of markets in the plural: in one text this kind of market appears with these seven aspects, in the next text (or even a few pages later) another kind of market is delimited. I find that this practice of reading confronts me with my own desire to keep words stable, meaning what I already think they mean.

Bennett, in *Vibrant Matter*, calls for something like substance as method: "We need to . . . devise new procedures, technologies, and regimes of perception that enable us to consult nonhumans more closely, or to listen and respond more carefully to their outbreaks, objections, testimonies, and propositions" (2010, 108). Just as she drew upon the history of metal-workers to undo her notion of matter, we, too, can challenge our theoretical terms in resonance with the surprises of others.

A simple mnemonic for this practice is "avoid etymology!" Etymologies stay within your theory, your wordplay horizons, your paradigms. They are incredibly productive of words but rarely jostle your being. Similarly, "resist binaries!" Any binaries you find yourself relying on are clues to where a lapse in thinking occurs: living versus nonliving, life versus matter. These opposites can be turned into new configurations like vibrant matter, but take it further with your substances and ask, What kind of life is this life? What kind of matter is this matter? What kind of vibrant matter is this vibrant matter? The goal is to prevent a satisfying phrase or beautiful wordplay from turning into a reason to stop looking more. Surely these two things are not exactly the same in their vibrancy, so what kind of vibrancy is each?

WORLD!

The world is made from substantive encounters. SAM is about scoping into each person's (or nonhuman's) world: the substances they live for and with. Out of that living have come ways of living and scoping that work, for them. These ways are the effect of hard work. People have struggled with their substance—to shape it to them and them to it—and this is their current relationship with that, so far, until it isn't. The categories they are using are living, lively categories. They didn't get them from someone else, or if they did, they've tested them and shed or modified the ones that didn't work.

Stengers (2014), with Whitehead, dives into the empiricism of each encounter with anything as substance. Every encounter happens at a scale particular to that encounter. They talk about different people walking past a statue differently. Some people walk past the statue and see a navigation tool; they treat it as "always the same" (they ignore almost every alteration of the statue). Then comes the person who takes care of the statue, for whom its decay is what she cares about: every time she walks past she sees a different statue—a chip missing, a stain from rain, and so on. Next is the sculptor who appreciates the type of rock and the tools used to make it, and then the physicist who sees a cloud of electrons and for whom the object's statue-ness is not the issue. These perspectives are all different ways of loving and caring about that statue: different scales, approaches, noticings. These are all different ways of being with the statue—all different kinds of "statue"—that in turn might resonate with different kinds of other objects that I have been overlooking in my world. Worlds are made through these differences. SAM is attending to the world-making in these encounters, and to the encounters that inhabit worlds.

In many ways SAM is the inverse of the exercises in "Writing the Implosion" (Dumit 2014). The world was assumed and mapped in an implosion; with SAM we are figuring out how it was made and continues to be remade. Implosions are based on your chief artifact/object/project of concern, starting from your own point of view and then mapping what you know and don't know. This process provides an understanding of how you came to be the person who cares about and knows the artifact in the way that you do, and how the artifact circulates as that artifact in the world, and how the world as the world you know inhabits that artifact. You don't change yourself when doing an implosion. In SAM we practically change ourselves by finding out the worlds that others live in through their projects. We resonate with their challenges and maybe find out that our artifact isn't what we thought it was, that we aren't what we thought we were, because they and we are more than what their and our (now previous) words/worldings enabled.

Note that seeing more in something is not always better. Stengers (2014), with Whitehead, points out that our habits of seeing and thinking are precisely the effect of our previous encounters up to this point. They are our wager on our own survival (what we are able to attend to in the form that we do). Substance as method is an offering: perhaps you find more here in a way that is helpful to you; perhaps your current terms and ways of engaging and playing are getting in the way. Perhaps a little jostling or shock of surprise will help. We do it because we feel stuck or troubled, not because it is a necessary solution.

In giving workshops on SAM, one concern raised by participants is that it seems we are not following substances at all but how they are rendered in the literature. Why ask others about a substance, and especially, why read what they have said about it? Why not follow the substance ourselves, get our hands dirty, engage with it directly?

As if you could be with the substance itself. No. Only the current you with the encountered substance, your worlded substance. You probably are doing this anyway with your chief objects/artifacts/projects of concern.

You are being challenged by them. For secondary substances it is a much longer road to reach the point where you go beyond being changed by the training and the substance. Recall how the chemists worked productively with bromine for decades and still (in retrospect) missed something. And then at some point, when they asked a different question, bromine said no, and they realized that their basic approach and concepts needed to change. One thing we can learn from others is how their substances taught them to pay attention differently—so that maybe we can pay attention differently to our substances. Texts are never just representations of something that is known but active attempts to use words in order to change others' forms of life (to teach). From texts we can learn from people who are in the position of trying to pass on something they have learned when their world was rocked, their theories were put into variation, and they were jostled by a substance that demanded to be its own method.

PROTOCOL

- Make a list of seven substances that you are directly writing about, then pick the fifth one. Don't engage in etymology or play with it symbolically; doing so stays within your theory, within your paradigms. It is incredibly productive of words, but it rarely jostles your being.
- Follow the substance out to the specialists (or their writings) who live, love, obsess over it, who don't just know about the substance—they can't stop talking about it, how it exceeds them, challenges them.
- Find the moments when the substance surprised them, when they had to invent new concepts and theories to account for their interactions, vocabularies, and methods specific to the substance. These instances are when they realized that their previous ways of seeing assumed a different substance. Instead their substance now demands to become its own metaphor and method.
- Let those moments of their surprise, improvisation, and invention resonate with you, as a practitioner and theorist, and see in your own thoughts, concepts, and methods their substantial limitations, how they might be dependent on other substances. Take these as offerings that may (or may not) be helpful.
- This is not ethnography. It is a way of nudging yourself out of your ethnographic comfort zone (maybe a zone that you don't know

you have). It is about shaking up your own ethnographic concepts and methods so that the ethnography you do practice and write will be more open to the surprises that it finds.

If you want a more fleshed out example of substance as method or to hear more about how weird and troubling bromine continues to be, see Dumit (forthcoming).

....

CHAPTER 14

JUSTINE LAURENT, OLIVER HUMAN,

CAROLINA DOMÍNGUEZ GUZMÁN, ELS RODING,

ULRIKE SCHOLTES, MARIANNE DE LAET,

AND ANNEMARIE MOL

Excreting Variously

On Contrasting as an Analytic Technique

CONTRASTING AS AN ANALYTIC TECHNIQUE

Empirical realities do not speak for themselves. In order to bring them out, analysis is required. How to go about this? How to turn promising fieldwork into salient ethnography? In this text, we propose the analytic technique of contrasting as one possible way. This technique helps ask questions, direct fieldwork, organize materials, and transform these into texts. Contrasting involves searching for tensions, resistance to affirming established theory, eschewing apparent coherence. As an analytic technique contrasting can highlight tensions within the field, among analysts, within literatures, or between field and literature. Its strength is that it does not mush particularities into generalities but cherishes specificities. It does not reiterate what others have written already but elicits distinctions that are worth noting: divergences that may be further explored, discrepancies that may be telling, differences that may be easy to erase but deserve to be made. Rather than resulting in the final word on anything much, contrasting leads to conversations.

Contrasting points to disparities. To show how this works, our collective considered empirical materials collected by the first author, who for her PhD research seeks to learn about practices to do with excretion.[1] The work of contrasting that we typically do when we analyze our own data gains relief when we work as a team. Take this excerpt from Justine's field notes, summarizing an interaction with Sandra, one of her informants. While looking at her toddler, Sandra says: "She usually wants to come with me. 'What are you doing?' she asks when I am wiping. And she wants to give me the toilet paper. So she gives it to me and then we say bye-bye to the poop or to the pee. She is a bit afraid of the flushing, it's loud of course . . . So I warn her. Now we flush, I say. *Spoelen* in Dutch." "Eh, nice. So, she's already interested in the matter?" Sandra: "It's how we learn how to use our body, I guess, no? Just by seeing and imitating!"[2]

Invoking her child's curiosity, Sandra proposes a theory about how we learn to use our body. We do this, she says, by seeing and imitating others. Irina, another informant, presents a contrasting theory about how we learn to use our body. "She always had Pampers, like the really good ones, and then . . . you don't feel it if you pee, I think. So . . . [I gave her cotton underpants] just to let her feel her pants getting wet." So (we conclude from this that) maybe learning how to use one's body does not (just) depend on imitating but (also) on feeling oneself getting wet when peeing. But there are further possibilities. Irina continues: "And then time and again it was like, 'Oh! Too late!' But after she peed in her pants, I put her on the potty. I noticed that every half hour she peed a little bit. So I put her every half hour. And when I went out I put her [in] a nappy. I also picked certain moments, like when she woke up, first go to the potty. Before dinner, after dinner, before going to sleep, before we went out, when we came back. What do we do when we go out? First go to the potty. So she learned, in a few days, to get a bit of control over her peeing." So, while imitating and feeling one's wetness may help "to get a bit of control"—to learn how to use one's body—habits, too (or so we learn from Irina) may assist.

Perhaps these add up: mothers, excerpts, and theories; the imitation, the wetness, and the routines. It might be possible to say that all these things matter together and to fuse them into a coherent narrative, maybe under an umbrella term. For instance the umbrella term of *individual control over one's body* or that of *separation from one's parent*. But—or so we have tasked ourselves to demonstrate—it is also possible to foreground the contrasts. To insist that different repertoires for living with and teaching children coexist. That these incorporate contrasting theories about what it is to learn to gain control over one's body. That they work toward different aims and each harbor their own values. And that, along with that, they have dissimilar effects on what becomes of the child, of the peeing, of the mother, and of the assemblage they jointly form. This, then, is the analytic technique of contrasting: eschewing a coherent narrative so as to focus on differences instead. The result is not an overview, not a grand total, not a Theory with a capital *T* but rather insight into potentially relevant distinctions. What constitutes a relevant distinction depends on the analyst and her analysis. Below follow a few further contrasts that as a team we discern in Justine's field notes. The contrasts we identify—among ourselves, concerns, things, and words, or with the literature—exemplify what we find useful to pursue. There may be many more.

TEAMWORK

The point of collectively analyzing a selection from Justine's materials is not only to jointly explore and clearly elicit the contrasts that these materials hold. From the start we also envision the writing of this text. We orchestrate the occasion in the hope that this may help us to demonstrate how contrasting may work, not just in this case but, mutatis mutandis, in countless others. Perusing the material together, turning it upside down and inside out, we explore tensions within it and among ourselves. When first encountering the material we each bring along our own preoccupations, the literatures we happen to have read. This is how we wondered about plot, audiences, and concerns. Although an individual author can engage in contrasting, our team effort helps us to bring this analytic technique into relief. Putting all of our names above this text, then, seemed not only fair but also true to this method.[3] It prompts us to not reconcile our varying takes but to keep the variation within the ad hoc team alive.

In the other work we do, many of us attend to the material infrastructures in and through which human relations take shape. Taking this preoccupation along with us, it immediately strikes us that Sandra does not just say that children may learn from imitating others but also allows her child to be present as she herself uses the toilet. In the day care center where Justine conducted observations, children likewise witness each other using the toilet. The infrastructure invites this: a row of small toilets and a collection of potties share a joint space. Hence, or so someone in our group suggests, in both cases the situation is orchestrated in such a way that imitating another person's body techniques becomes possible. Someone else wonders about the differences between imitating parents and imitating other children. A third person points to a possible thread that unites the excerpts: all are about the art/work of acquiring a separated body. But Justine warns that the achievement of "becoming independent" is "all over the literature"; it is a classic trope in developmental psychology. Another team member then wonders about the "independence" involved: Independent of whom? Of what? Not of the toilet, for sure, nor of the people, technologies, and bacteria downstream from the place of flushing that are variously involved in cleaning the wastewater. So we look for another phrasing. Instead of saying that each child acquires their own separate body, we agree that it might be better to say that when it comes to excretion children realize different kinds of dis- and re-entanglements.

Which kinds of entanglement might be relevant here? Jointly we come up with a preliminary list (listing is an important tool for contrasting): (1) Spatial entanglement (being together in the place where one excretes) allows for the imitation of body techniques. (2) People's bodily sensitivities may be entangled, at least some of the time: parents say that sometimes they feel the discomfort of their child in their own bodies, but not always—sometimes, they admit, they have no clue. (3) As they are metabolically entangled, a mother breastfeeding a child may need to abstain from foods that would give the child diarrhea. (4) Caring entanglements occur, for instance when a child hands her mother toilet paper or when a father skillfully refreshes his child's nappy so that the floor underneath remains clean. (5) And then there are the entanglements of excreting humans with a myriad of stuff: nappies, potties, toilets, seats to sit on, steps to climb up, water to flush. And so on. Recognizing this diversity of entanglements points our attention in different directions: toward spatial arrangements, sensitivities, diets, cleaning practices, material tools. This list is open: questions, sites, situations, concerns, tensions might be added as the analyst sees fit.

After a few further detours, someone reiterates a contrast between two techniques that may help a child shift from excreting in a nappy to doing so on a potty or toilet: learning to feel (e.g., thanks to wearing cotton underpants or walking around with a bare bottom) versus acquiring a habit (e.g., going on the potty "before we go out," "before bed," "before a meal"). But in the material further techniques are yet to be found: earlier we mentioned imitating; we also come across such things as rubbing a child's back to relax her, distracting a child with a toy, reading stories about children— or bears—using potties, and so on. Justine's informants do not restrict themselves to using just a single technique but combine them. Although it may be compelling to classify parents (for instance distinguishing those who "have a clue" from those who don't), we opt to classify techniques instead. This contributes to (but also builds on) a social science tradition that does not study people but practices. But if within the team most of us share that propensity to foreground practice, that still leaves many other issues pending. Analyzing together, we are careful not to collapse our responses to the materials into a single team view. We keep moving, picking up new concerns, discarding them, picking them up again in a different way. And so the potentialities in Justine's materials proliferate.

CONCERNS

The parents who figure in our materials express a variety of concerns in relation to the excretion practices of their children. At some point the child should cease to need nappies, learning to go to the toilet to pee or poop. Parents are under pressure from others as they work to achieve this feat. One mother tells Justine about her aunts, for whom it is a sign of good parenting if a child is potty-trained by the time she is two years old. Another mentions primary schools, where toilet skills are an entrance requirement for four-year-olds. But the parents don't just hope that their child will acquire the necessary body techniques; they also want to be good parents along the way. This can mean many things: offering structure, giving guidance, setting rules, creating the right circumstances. Parents tell Justine they do not want to force anything, aiming to remain gentle, avoid shaming, keep things light. At the same time they prefer to not bother other people: keep the floor of the rented apartment clean, worry about the effect of diapers on the environment, eat without bothering others with the smell of excrement. And so on. Many norms are mentioned. They may be at work together but they may still be contrasted.

Norms can be identified, but they are not necessarily ours: we do not seek to establish who is and who isn't a good parent. We are neither out to critique, nor to praise. Instead we observe norms of good parenthood at work, finding contrasts between them. We juxtapose them with concerns of our own, such as what kind of entanglements potty practices display and which body techniques are mobilized and taught while engaging in them. In our analysis the parents are informants: they offer information about practices. We may learn from them how, as these practices unfold, children disentangle themselves here, re-entangle themselves there, and variously keep on excreting. The parents and their hopes and fears are relevant to that story, but so, too, are other people and a myriad of things. Hence, a mother who says, "I put her on the potty and she pees," may be primarily interested in norms that adjudicate the *I* who does the putting (am I doing this well?) and the *she* who pees (very good). We, on the other hand, may be at least as interested in values to do with the potty. Is it comfortable to sit on? Does the child like it or prefer a toilet seat? Which body techniques are invited, facilitated, or allowed for by the various things involved in practices of excretion? As we shift our attention from body techniques to the material tools—the things enabling the techniques—we imply a contrast between the parents, who are trying to be good parents, and ourselves, who are researchers also of material infrastructures, of things.

THINGS

But wait a minute. Parents care about things as well. When asked, they tell us about the purple plastic step that helps a child climb up to the toilet seat, the cotton underwear that does not absorb pee. About different brands of nappy, more or less easy to put on, more or less absorbent, more or less expensive. The contrast between informants and analysts lies in the fact that the parents relate those things to their goals and want them to be instrumental. For us, by contrast, tools are not so readily submissive. We wonder what they do to those who use them—even if they do not act alone. The toilet paper doesn't make a mess of itself, but when it hangs from a holder it is attractive for a toddler to play with. The parent who wants to avoid this may collaborate with a cupboard to put the toilet paper someplace high, out of the child's reach. But if, by contrast, the toilet is too high for a child to reach, a plastic step may be brought in to assist. The thin inlay in the cotton nappy can be thrown out when a child has pooped, whereas it can be washed and used again when it has been dirtied by pee only; thus washing machines are involved as well. And so on.

Different things afford and deny their users different possibilities. Both the potty and the step make it possible for a child to keep her underwear clean, but while these things share a similar purpose, their other effects are different. The potty can be transported into the living room, whereas the step only does its work if it is next to the toilet. When carted around, the potty affords the excreting child the comforting presence of others; using the toilet may come with the added pleasure of immediately flushing and thus taking leave of one's excrements: "bye-bye." The potty has to be rinsed every time it is used, whereas flushing allows for a similar degree of cleaning of the toilet. Contrasting the objects helps the analyst to move beyond the question of whether material things act, to specific descriptions of how they act and to what effect.

Traveling between languages is hard work. In Justine's conversations with parents and educators in Amsterdam, the language spoken was mostly English, a second or third language for many of those involved. A few conversations were in French; the odd Dutch word seeped in, as did fragments of Arabic. Of the authors, only one has been an English speaker from the start, but as he grew up in South Africa, other speakers of English tend to quibble with his choice of words. So, writing this text in English requires translation, convergence, adaptation, obedience. At the same time, linguistic differences also form a resource for illuminating contrasts.

For instance: In the everyday English in which our materials are written, children who manage their excretion without the use of nappies are called *potty-trained*, suggesting that some form of training was involved in order for them to achieve this state. In Dutch, by contrast, such children are called *zindelijk*. The word has "thoughtful" in its etymological history, with senses (*zinnen*) resonating in the background. A child who is zindelijk, or so the word suggests, is old enough to be reasoned with. Achieving this state does not depend on dedicated training; the child, rather, is afforded room to grow into it. The French word *propre* is different again; in this context it translates into English as "clean." As does the Arabic word *naḍeef*. Justine's informant Sara analyzed its particularities for us: "The word usually used [for potty-trained, zindelijk, etc.] is *clean*, but I never liked that term, so when I talk, I say she is *without diaper*. You would say for example: 'Yasmine became clean/Yasmine *neḍfat*.' In Jordan for the daycare I had to fill in a questionnaire for registration and one of the questions was if my child was clean. I had no idea what they meant. I was, like, of course she is clean! [*both laughing*]."

But if it is possible to draw contrasts between words from different linguistic traditions, this may also be done between words that are all English. Take the term *excretion*. We decided to use this word, although it only rarely appears in Justine's materials. Parents talk about *peeing* and *pooping*, or even *pissing* and *shitting*—words that sound offensive in an academic English text. *Excreting* has the advantage that it is technical and thus accentuates the difference between day-to-day use of language and academic convention. We hope that it helps, too, in keeping at bay the frowns, giggles, and other signs of unease we encounter when others learn what we study. If the term *excretion* is a formalization, it may help to make our topic respectable, acceptable in academia and writing. *Excretion* has the added advantage that it draws together "peeing" and "pooping," and this serves our analysis. For although the metabolic transformations involved are quite different, they enroll similar things (from nappies to sewage systems) and involve comparable bodily techniques (imitating, sensing, habituating). In this instance, then, we take care to background, hide, a possible contrast and within our word *excreting* draw the different activities of "peeing" and "pooping" together.

For using contrasting terms does not always create space in which to roam, does not always offer the listener or reader freedom, alterity, a choice that is to be celebrated. For contrasting one term with another, one reality with another, one set of values with the next, may seem to set up the future as bending to your choice, but it may also form a binary trap. For instance, adults may ask a toddler in their care: "Do you want to go on the potty or use the toilet?" Here, the child is offered discretion as to the tool, the thing, to excrete on. But at the same time, by stealth, the child is told what to do. Sit, excrete, or at least try to. A binary may sneakily work to turn a question into an instruction.

LITERATURE

Academic analyses talk about materials to audiences. They do not just frame empirical realities; they do so in dialogue with literatures to which their audiences, too, may relate. Hence our reluctance to write about children becoming "independent," which, as Justine remarked earlier, "is all over the literature." We don't want to readily affirm what has been remarked already. Does it seem obvious? Then why not try to doubt it instead? Hence, in contrast with "the literature," we here might want to argue that children who learn to excrete on a potty or a toilet do not become independent at all. Instead, they shift their dependence from nappies to potties and toilets. Hence, rather than celebrating that children liberate themselves from adults, we trace the webs of agencies and attachments in which people and things act and are enacted. In relating to the literature, other contrasts can also be made. Consider for instance the term *inter-embodiment*, which "encapsulates the notion that apparently individuated and autonomous bodies are actually experienced at the phenomenological level as intertwined" (Lupton 2012, 39). Yes, parents "say that sometimes they are able to feel the discomfort of their child in their own bodies." However, using the term *inter-embodiment* to describe this may be precipitous. For this ability to feel what others feel may be fleeting—or, as we have put it: "sometimes, they admit, they have no clue." What is more, in our analysis, feeling the discomfort of another person's body is connected to other entanglements; in our preliminary list we included spatial, metabolic, and caring entanglements. Such specificities are all too easily generalized in theoretical abstractions, mobile terms, of which *inter-embodiment* is one.

There are also contrasts to make with authors to whom we are closely related, such as Abrahamsson (2014), who argues that "shit" does not just happen but requires a lot of work. From professionals who care for people with constipation, Abrahamsson learned that excreting depends on particular ways of eating and drinking, on the ability to relax one's bowels, on not being too scared of the smell of excrement, on feeling safe—and so on. A lot of things are involved: "sewage systems, metaphors, textbooks, doctors and therapists" (125). In our case, too, many f/actors are involved in excreting, but constipation is rarely mentioned. Hence it is not the fact that people and things collaborate that makes the difference between the cases but rather the hows of the collaboration and also the stakes. The parents in our materials do not so much worry about whether defecation will happen but about where, when, and how. They are not concerned about bowel motility per se but about such things as changing a child's nappy in time so as to avoid rashes, or taking enough extra clothing along to be able to change after an accident, or holding a small body over the toilet seat so that it does not fall into the toilet bowl. It is in such specificities that the contrasts lie.

And then there are contrasts to be made with earlier literatures on contrasting. Those literatures may not be about excretion, but for all that they may still add depth to a treatise on "contrasting as an analytic technique." In our literature list you will find a few titles in which this technique has been deployed for analyzing materials closely related to excreting: washing (Pols 2006), tasting (Mann 2018), eating (Yates-Doerr and Mol 2012), cooking (Ibáñez Martín and de Laet 2018), metabolizing (Vogel 2018), composting (Abrahamsson and Bertoni 2014). Others talk about sites and situations, about topics, that may seem to be further away: human disabilities (Moser 2005), animal diseases (Mather 2014), spirits (Jensen and Blok 2013), words (Mann and Mol 2018), the world (Law 2015; Omura et al. 2019). The list could easily be expanded—but as all texts, this one has a word limit too. And we care to still mention that there are, from way earlier, ancestral texts to consider as well. Where to start? With Michel Foucault, Chantal Mouffe, Marilyn Strathern? The more relevant question may be what all these authors used contrasting for: to insist on the possibility to escape from what seems self-evident (Foucault 1969); to argue that politics is not necessarily about reaching consensus but may be shaped as an ongoing negotiation with one's enemies (Mouffe 2005); to keep alterity in focus instead of submitting everyone and everything to Euro-American schemes (Strathern 1991); to avoid the choice between going along with one's field or going against it, as contrasts foreground the criticism, the otherness, within (Mol 1992). In this text we have engaged in contrasting to demonstrate this analytic technique, to show that even practices that seem to go without saying, such as excretion, may turn out to be full of complexity and tensions when they are put into words. What, do you think, might the analytic technique of contrasting allow you to do in your own work?

CONCLUSION

In this chapter we have proposed contrasting as a technique. Rather than helping to reduce rich ethnographic material to a single explanation or argument, this technique foregrounds tensions that resist easy assimilation into a coherent narrative. Rather than adding up fieldwork details into an exhaustive story, this technique works with open-ended lists. Rather than serving this or that theory—let alone Theory with a capital T—it invites playing with words.

Although no recipe exists for how to do work with the analytic technique of contrasting, in the protocol that follows we offer some helpful suggestions. And for now, in conclusion, let us provide a summary. Contrasting assists in making strange what we take for granted: its aim is to rob easily used concepts of their self-evidence. It multiplies versions of reality and ways of understanding what mundane practices are about, rather than reducing them to a one-size-fits-all type of explanation. On a good day, contrasting brings out specificities of the field you are exploring as well as specificities of the disciplinary tradition that forms the background of your analysis. Good contrasts set up productive tensions and will make you think—but, in turn, they depend on good thinking as well.

A crucial move in deploying the technique of contrasting, then, is to resist the urge to assimilate specificities under a single frame. Do not aim to provide a holistic overview that erases tensions and differences, nor try to make your findings fit a grand theoretical term such as *independence*, *inter-embodiment*, or anything else. The point is to resist unmediated rehearsal of established theories. Instead sniff out the tensions that such theories tend to erase. Adapt them, attune them to your case. Along the way it is crucial to carefully disentangle the concerns of your informants (for instance, with being a good parent) from your own (say, with body techniques, dis/entanglements, or analysis). And then, attending to words is essential: instead of translating empirical realities in overarching analytical terms, you might want to remain concrete and stay close to your informants' ways of wording in order to explore where they lead and what they may or may not achieve. Finally, an analysis of mundane practices benefits from being put into relief against the background of a wide and varied body of literatures. Instead of seeking to offer a final understanding of anything much, an exercise in contrasting should result from and invite interesting conversations. Please, be adventurous, not scared.

PROTOCOL

- Look at your material. Stay with it. Suppress the urge to assimilate specificities under a single frame, don't dream of providing a holistic overview, nor try to make your findings fit a grand theoretical term.
- Make an open-ended list of contrasts you encounter in your materials. Do not just try to fit the contrasts we highlighted in this particular case to your site, but consider the contrasts that emerge there.
- Consider the different things, people, f/actors, values that those contrasts bring up or involve, and maybe start another open-ended list. Then, go back to step 2 and expand the list.
- Consider how the different concerns of your informants relate to that list. Be mindful to not just take these concerns on board; instead, think of how to study them (e.g., wonder whether and if so how they transform across practices). Maybe start another open-ended list. Then, go back to steps 2 and 3 and expand those lists again.
- Consider your own concerns. To do this, keep in mind your own position in relation to the site. When drafting your lists, be mindful of how language plays a role, which words you choose (*choose* being a case in point: Do you really want to use that word?), where they come from and how they traveled, and how different literatures and their concerns might be relevant to them. Summarise this, too, in a list. Then go back to steps 2, 3, and 4 and expand those lists again.

- With all those lists at hand, outline an argument/article/text you might want to write. In doing so, however, do not draft a single outline but a few contrasting ones; three tends to work best. Playing with the differences between them will help you figure out what might be the most urgent or most interesting text to write. That is to say: not in general but in your specific site and situation: here, now.
- Also expand this bullet-point protocol list, and don't read it as a linear walkthrough but rather as an open-ended exercise. You may do that alone, but why not with others? Give it a try.

NOTES

1. In this text we use the term *excretion* for practices of both urination and defecation. See the section "Words" for further discussion of this terminology.

2. Excerpt from an interview conducted in Amsterdam in 2017; taped, transcribed, and edited here for readability. All names were changed.

3. Coauthoring, of course, surfaces the collective character of research, which is all too often masked by the fiction of the single author. We met several times and collectively chose the stories for the chapter; all discussed, many of us wrote, others edited, all commented. Gathering everyone a year later for the revision process proved trickier; some sort of togetherness in time and place seems instrumental to collective work.

Facilitating Breakdowns through the Exchange of Perspectives

Two women cannot give birth to the same child. Two men can father the same child. But two women, no.

—Kalou Solok, Baluan elder in the film *Ngat Is Dead*

Normally it may make little sense to formalize into technique or protocol a process that is meant to bring us to a form of knowing that we do not yet know. If "Not to know what one is going to discover is self-evidently true of discovery" (Strathern 1999, 9), how can we describe or give a priori advice about the making of analytical findings?

The challenge, however, can be construed in a different way—a way that seems easier to mitigate. That is, we need not predict how we make findings but rather how to bring ourselves into positions of potential surprise. Thinking of a general way to describe how surprises are brought to emerge, I favor the late Michael Agar's (1986) use of the notion of "breakdown." Agar argued that ethnographic findings come from a focus on the differences that appear in our work when our (cultural) expectations are not met, when what we see or hear does not make sense. *Breakdown* here denotes such disjunctions between the expected and the unexpected. Breakdowns may occur during fieldwork but also after—when making ethnographic discoveries in one's material—during the extension of fieldwork to the "deskwork" of analysis, where the field is "re-created" at the desk (Strathern 1999).

But why settle for "re-creation," when you can bring the field itself back to your desk? The "field" here is of course not just a geographical place, but a network of sociocultural relationships between people, who themselves have analytical skills that can be activated. Turning informants into coanalysts emphasizes and practices the dialogical ideals of anthropological research; in this way, inviting informants into the analytic phase of research is step 1 of my analytic protocol.

Analytic skills can be elicited in many different ways, and those ways depend on the focus, the topic, and the site of one's research. It is necessary to remember that the researcher-informant relationship itself has—implicitly or explicitly—an impact on one's analysis. One way to illuminate this impact is to facilitate reciprocal visits, where informants learn about the researcher's home in ways analogous to how the researcher has learned about theirs. This sharing—step 2 of my protocol—opens up a reflexive space by reversing some of the roles characterizing the ethnographer-informant relationship. Allowing informants to be "reverse ethnographers" (cf. Wagner 1981, 31) supplements traditional ethnographic fieldwork, but it also in itself becomes part of the study (see Walford, this volume).

It is worth remembering here that fieldwork, where an ethnographer visits and gradually becomes familiar with a foreign place and its foreign people (even if they are not always geographically or socially distant), is frequently a process tense with anxiety and social awkwardness, mistakes, and breaks in social etiquette. Many ethnographers, novices as well as those with many years of experience, feel recurrent unease about these "embarrassing" situations. Yet the situations of embarrassment are simultaneously some of the occurrences that teach us the most.

Now imagine if this situation was reversed—the ethnographer becomes the host and the informants are the ones trying to figure out the social norms of an unfamiliar culture. Imagine if this reversal not only created new unfamiliar situations but, as a form of ethnographic mirror, opened new perspectives on those originally unfamiliar situations. If the original encounter, with its dense richness of ethnographic observations of cultural difference, provided generous food for thought on exactly how collaboration is established across the difference between ethnographer and informants, with the frequent challenge of inequality or asymmetry (in terms of status, resources, etc.), then the reversal may do it double. It demonstrates among other things how the awkwardness of guest and host can be mutual. Awkward as it may be for informants to visit you, and for you to visit them, this exchange of roles should remind us and even help us to scrutinize what kind of visitor the ethnographer is and how our social roles develop in the field beyond the general observations of being different in terms of race, age, class, gender, wealth, or authority. The difference in privilege is potentially highlighted in this exchange. This question is very much about the positioning or positionality of the fieldworker in the field and the roles that we gain or are assigned (cf. Halstead 2008). My protocol allows us to remake and to rattle this positioning. It does not negate or reverse cultural difference, but it articulates this difference in a new and I hope generative light. It may also be generative for researchers working close to "home," by enabling a destabilization of their taken-for-granted ideas of what is going on.

Before I move on to describe the remaining steps and how the protocol worked for me in practice, let me dwell briefly on some of the thoughts behind it.

EXCHANGE OF PERSPECTIVES

With inspiration from the work of Marilyn Strathern, we can call this protocol an "exchange of perspectives." It should be understood as the combination of Strathern's thoughts on the temporality of ethnographic bedazzlement with the analogy she makes between Euro-American ethnographic reflexivity and Melanesian gift-giving ceremonies. The latter are characterized in Strathern's terms by exchanges of goods but also of perspective, that is, how each one sees the other person. In those Melanesian societies where gift exchange is prevalent as a form of social interaction, she argues that "in exchanging gifts with one another, persons exchange perspectives, not just as knowledge of their relative positions but as parts of the other that each incorporates" (Strathern 1999, 239). Exchanges between people are seen here as objectifying and revealing the capacities each person embodies—for attracting wealth and for enabling knowledge, gifts, and so on to appear.

Strathern's analogy invites us to think that curiosity about the hidden, and the desire for its revelation, is an important motivation for how ethnographers and Melanesians alike try to understand social relationships, personal capacities, and selfhood (1999, 255). Likewise, engagement with informants in ethnographic research is also a matter of exchange and reciprocity, and what is exchanged may be more than goods or favors (see Otto 2013). Such views, however, are not always out in the open. It takes both patience and ethnographic work to elicit how informants analyze their ethnographer(s) based on what the latter decides or is forced to reveal about themselves (see Bashkow 2006).

In what follows I present how as a member of a team of ethnographers I engaged in a collaboration with informants from Papua New Guinea (PNG), whom we had invited to visit us in Denmark as part of an ethnographic exhibition at Moesgård Museum, a museum of cultural history.[1] Our informants, who had hosted us in PNG, now became our guests. We had lived among them while observing and asking questions about their ways of life, and now they would analogously figure out how we lived in Denmark.[2] This example will explain how steps 1 and 2 worked for me and how the situation of working together on something fairly concrete (the exhibition) can be regarded as step 3 of the protocol: establish as part of the reverse visit a shared project to which your informants contribute their expertise. If nothing else, this can be the actual analysis of some of your data, but it could also be some other activity that enhances your collaborative relationship. The visit and shared project are followed by step 4: discussing with your informants how the reciprocal visits and the shared project changed your respective perspectives and ultimately how their analytical skills are then made active.

FROM DENMARK TO PNG AND FROM PNG TO DENMARK

To elaborate on the aforementioned steps, let me briefly recount how my own research in PNG could be seen in relation to this protocol and how a fascinating breakdown in my understanding emerged as part of the process of exchanging perspectives and working together on a shared project (step 3).

My first major fieldwork—collecting material for my master's degree in anthropology—took place on Baluan Island, Manus Province, PNG, from August 2002 until March 2003. I wanted to study how the knowledge of crafting traditional sailing canoes was subject to ownership. In addition to studying such craftsmanship as a form of intellectual property, my job was also to purchase and ship material for the exhibition and to arrange for craftsmen to travel to Denmark to build a canoe in situ. This fieldwork was followed by a shorter two-month (October through November 2003) visit as part of a small research team who aimed to finish the collections and shipping, and to take part in the making of an ethnographic film about a mortuary ceremony and discourses of tradition (Suhr, Otto, and Dalsgaard 2009; Otto 2013). The revisit finalized many of our preparations for the exhibition; the rest was done from afar after our return to Denmark.

Six men came to Denmark in May and June 2004. Five were craftsmen and one, Joe Nalo, was an artist and museum curator who came from another village in Manus. Nalo had depicted, among other things, canoes and other traditional elements of social life (see Raabe 1997). His art would enhance the exhibition with its interpretations of Manus culture. It had not been easy to organize their visit, and it was not without unease either, because of my unfamiliarity with hosting informants. How would they manage the time in Denmark, where they would be on their own and would not know the local language? How would they be treated by Danes at a time when public rhetoric about foreigners was turning toward the xenophobic? Of a personal—and perhaps silly—nature was my anxiety around introducing them to my parents. Our visitors, having cared for and looked after me while I had been in PNG, were, after all, also family to me. Would my two families, normally so far apart geographically and having little knowledge of each other's ways of life, find a common ground or even something to talk about? (Of course, they did . . .).

Two of the six spoke English very well and had been abroad before (albeit one of them no farther than Indonesia). Only one of the men—the senior craftsman who was in his sixties—did not communicate in English. We invited one of his sons, a friendly middle-aged man who also knew the basic craft. Apart from that, we chose three men who we knew to be trustworthy and knowledgeable about canoe-building and about carpentry more generally. While on Baluan, many men had presented themselves as candidates for the trip and described their skills in various ways. That experience was great for me as a student of the sociotechnical details of traditional canoes and the process of making them, but it was also great for learning about the concomitant political "claims to culture" (see Dalsgaard 2009).

RESULTS OF THE PROTOCOL

I will not linger on the preparations, the selection of craftsmen, or the exhibition itself. This is partly described elsewhere (Dalsgaard 2009; Rasmussen 2013). Instead I want to make two points related to the exchange of perspectives and breakdowns that highlight some of the things I learned from the craftsmen's visit. These two points underscore how the different steps in this protocol are interrelated.

First, the visit (step 4) changed our visitors' understanding of who we were and what an ethnographic project could be like when focused on a museum exhibition. The conversations I refer to in what follows address what the exchange of perspectives and the shared project generated and ultimately how their analysis molded my own knowledge. Some of the men told me toward the end that they had been uncertain and had doubts about the purpose and the reality of what we were doing. The collection and documentation of their material culture undertaken during our visits to PNG had seemed weird to them when still on Baluan, but it became meaningful when they came to Denmark and saw the exhibition setup. We had, for example, purchased the full interior of a kitchen in order to reconstruct a kitchen atmosphere in one part of the exhibition. This had been considered odd by the Baluan villagers, because most of their kitchen utensils could easily be purchased in Denmark—newer and of better quality! Alas, when the canoe craftsmen came to work in the exhibition space, their workspace was next to a room with many familiar items from their home island, and they saw our efforts in a new and different light.

As our guests, the six men explored and experimented with Danish sociality to various degrees. They made new friends and connections among museum staff and other locals, and they collected experiences, stories, names, technologies, and other souvenirs to take back and tell or show their kin at home. We on the other hand became hosts and tried to find ways of accommodating what we thought to be their wishes for a great stay. It was also clear how our informants sought evidence of the efficacy of the exchange by enquiring about our opinions of their work. They appeared eager to make us happy and to show Baluan and PNG in a positive way to a Danish audience, and they also had conversations among themselves about proper ways to behave. Our satisfaction with them as both craftsmen and guests was the evidence of their own agency and effect.

Second, I want to stress how the possibility for the exchange of perspectives (my step 2) was enhanced by actually working on multiple projects (step 3). Collaborating with people over a long period of time and for several different purposes with a joint interest allowed for unexpected discoveries. One joint interest was to make the exhibition, where our informants acted as a form of cocurators through their active contribution, but they also took part in other projects during their visit. One interesting discovery—at least for me—happened outside the exhibition room, when we consulted our visitors about the footage we had shot during our 2003 visit. This was in the process of being edited, and having our Baluan informants around was an opportunity to gain their help with the translations from their local language.

It was during one of these translation sessions that the informant I had asked to help came out with a surprising comment. We were watching a speech given during the distribution of gifts at a mortuary ceremony. On Baluan, where this event took place, descendants are allowed to organize several rituals for their deceased parents. The film we were making was supposed to document one such a ceremony, where a set of siblings would pay their respects to their deceased father.[3] Descent in Baluan is normally counted patrilineally, but establishing the rights of the patrilineage over their inheritance involves giving gifts to maternal relatives. The ceremony referred to was a combination of what otherwise would be two ceremonies. One was called *cement* because it involved cementing the grave and giving it the status of a more permanent memorial. The other was named *pukankokon*, which approximately means "opening the money." Both ceremonies required the descendants of the deceased to give gifts (of money, calico, and food) primarily to the descendant's maternal relatives but also to others (see Otto 2018). This particular case involved competition over who was to be the main recipient—not because there was any doubt who the biological mother was but because the deceased had been fostered by his mother's mother, and the siblings had decided that they wanted to recognize this relationship too. One of the senior men of the mother's group nonetheless contested the choice of dividing the gifts between two recipients. Such complaints are not unusual. Customary ceremonies often involve disagreements over genealogies or interpretations of custom (e.g., Otto 1992, 2011, 2018). In his speech the man with the name Kalou Solok stated the words quoted at the beginning of chapter: that a person could not have two mothers. The interesting part was the contrast he made in passing to having two fathers.

When I first heard this, in person during fieldwork, I did not make much of it. Nor did I grasp the full meaning while I watched the recordings. Yes, of course a person could not have two mothers. I had not seen the part about two fathers as important, because I had simply considered Kalou Solok to be referring to adoption within a family, which is common in Baluan. In the context of understanding Kalou Solok's claim to a larger part of the distribution, it was the denial of two mothers that was important, not what he had said about fathers. Nonetheless, upon hearing the statement, the informant who helped with the translation said something akin to "some old men still believe this silly thing."[4] I asked him what he meant, and he explained that Kalou Solok had expressed an ancient belief that a person really could have two (biological) fathers.

Theodore Schwartz, who worked with Manus people for several decades, wrote that a belief among one of the other language groups of Manus Province (the Titan) had been that several inseminations are required in order to fill the womb of a mother-to-be (1976, 197). That is, repeated sexual intercourse was expected in order for a pregnancy to be fulfilled. Only a small step from this belief allows one to conclude that if a woman has intercourse with more than one man during her pregnancy, more than one father would be contributing biologically to growing the fetus.

I would not have appreciated this if our informant had not helped with the translation and made his offhand remark. This miss was a serious breakdown in my understanding of personhood in Manus. At the time, Strathern's ([1988] 1990) influence on theories of personhood in Melanesia was at its peak. Her framework discussing "the partible person," wherein persons are regarded as "dividuals" made up of the relations that contributed to their creation, made much more sense in a Manus context in light of this discovery. The finding was not central to my research at the time, but it would later gain importance, when it became clear through the work of one of my colleagues how traditional ideas of personhood were closely connected to the possession of skills including that of canoe craftsmanship (Rasmussen 2013). This again became an important background for my understanding of political leadership in Manus, which was the topic of my PhD dissertation (Dalsgaard 2010). I thus learned about Baluan personhood in multiple contexts and through multiple interlocutors including fellow researchers covering different topics.

A POTENTIAL EXPANSION OF THE PROTOCOL

Ethnographic knowing entails, among other things, attaining perspectives that are not entirely visible—even to one's informants—either because the latter take them for granted, because they are morally fraught, or because they are for other reasons difficult to convey in oral discourse. How can such perspectives, then, be revealed? The most important element here is the traditional toolbox of qualitative ethnographic methods. Reversing the guest-host/researcher-informant relationship adds another component to this toolbox and permits an exchange of perspectives whereby hidden forms and experiences are revealed (cf. Strathern 1999, 12). For our case I do not mean to imply that being host/guest entails the same in Denmark as in PNG, nor that interpretation works in the same way. Also, we did not exchange aims let alone positions within a global system of difference, but we did get to elicit the potentials of our relationship from different vantage points. We facilitated the creation of perspectives that included "the other's perspective *as a perspective*" (249, emphasis in original). The perspectives that emerged displayed both self and other through the capacities we embodied—capacities for making canoes and capacities for hosting visitors. This facilitated new lessons for everyone involved, and for me it showed not least how cultural beliefs about procreation and personhood exist and may structure exchanges and relations of influence in Baluan.

Facilitating a reciprocal visit and hosting one's informants seems to be—and is—challenging and filled with anxiety. I think here not only about the revelation to one's informants of who you are as a private person but quite practically how a reciprocal visit may require time and resources that are not available to the ordinary graduate student. Yet, considering the spatial distance that separates PNG and Denmark, it can only be easier to facilitate for other ethnographic researchers working closer to home.

The basic idea of opening up for reciprocal views may be replicated in other ways, which is the potential step 5 of my protocol. Video conversations or the exchange of recordings, though they do not provide a fully embodied immersion, may give a glimpse of life in other parts of the world by showing rather than telling. Manus is today fairly well connected when it comes to social media access, and I have largely used social media to remain up-to-date with some of the more general concerns that my informants are facing (e.g., Dalsgaard 2016). Although they hardly provide a fully reciprocal exchange, social media do give access to some symmetries—seeing each other on the terms and affordances provided by the medium in question.

Most of all I want to stress how productive this technique is in its full form, because it puts informants into an unfamiliar environment, allowing them to be dazzled and to experience puzzlement through the researcher and vice versa. It elicits questions about the unfamiliar, highlighting what is taken-for-granted by both researcher and informant. It immerses us in a reversal of roles with new dialogic realizations.

CONCLUSION

Ethnographic insight relies on discoveries. Such insight entails finding or realizing mandated or occasioned breakdowns, sometimes answers we are looking for, but often that one thing we do not know we are looking for or do not yet know the importance of in relation to our analyses (Strathern 1999, 5). I have discussed the exchange of perspectives as a specific way to facilitate such breakdowns but without implying that this precise technique did or could stand alone. My experience has been only one particular unfolding of it. For other ethnographers it will work differently. This technique and its research process may still work without a foundation of traditional long-term ethnographic fieldwork but probably not without an approach that emphasizes ethnography as a collaborative endeavor. Working with informants across multiple projects and questions, at different locations, and over different periods of time (cf. Dalsgaard and Nielsen 2015) has been a comprehensive exercise, but there could be—as mentioned with regard to digital media—other ways to facilitate the exchange of perspectives.

While the research protocol or technique that any given student of social phenomena needs must depend on the puzzle they are confronted with, I do think that much can be gained from inviting your informants or research partners home and reversing, or at least "shuffling," the differences between the roles of ethnographer and informant. My brief suggestion, then, for a technique that others should try is to work with your informants on multiple projects, invite them home to exchange perspectives, and learn something unexpected from them!

PROTOCOL

- If your analysis is about people and their sociocultural relationships, then invite them to be part of what you do.
- Perhaps the most provocative, the most awkward, but also the most stimulating act is to invite your informants or research partners to your home. If you succeed, discuss how they attempt to be good guests, what puzzles them, and what analyses they make of you and your home.
- To find a common ground from which you can mutually assess how the relationship develops, engage in a shared project or make something together. The project can be big or small, but it should ideally be something in which your visitor has a certain expertise.
- Consider and discuss with your informants how the reciprocal visits and the shared project have generated changes in your respective perspectives.

- Experiment with using digital tools for inviting informants or research partners home, and try to facilitate the collaboration either instead of or as an extension of a reverse visit. For example, consider what is mutually revealed about you through social media such as Facebook.

NOTES

1. The research and the exhibition were organized by Ton Otto, who also supervised my work. Apart from him, several other researchers and research partners provided thoughts and input to this process, especially Christian Suhr.

2. I shall be the first to admit that my inspiration from Strathern is a reductionist rendering of the comparison she makes. Some aspects of the respective perspectives (ethnographer/informant) could never be exchanged for us. The reversal was thus hardly perfect, but that does not make it irrelevant or ineffective in our mutual revelation.

3. What facilitated the filming was that one of the siblings was Ton Otto, whom the deceased had adopted during an earlier fieldwork. The help Ton gave to his adopted siblings was our entry to inside perspectives on the organization of such ceremonies (Otto 2013).

4. I was too perplexed to write it down verbatim.

Analogy

In 2010 and 2011 I undertook ethnographic fieldwork with scientific researchers and technicians involved in a scientific project based in the Brazilian Amazon, called the Large-Scale Biosphere-Atmosphere Experiment in Amazonia (LBA). The main task of the LBA team has been to collect and make available scientific data from the Amazon, which it has done for the past fifteen years by means of an astonishing array of projects in various scientific areas. In this short piece I concentrate on one important aspect of the LBA's work, measurement, and use my attempts to analyze it as an illustration of how analogy can work as a descriptive-analytic tool.

It would be to state the obvious, perhaps, to say that measurement is one of the most common activities in scientific practice, and in the case of the LBA this measurement is done by using all sorts of instruments. The researchers and technicians of the LBA spend a great deal of time out in the forest—setting up instruments, keeping them clean, fixing them when they break, and downloading data from them to be taken back to the LBA head office for analysis—and therefore, as a keen PhD student embarking on their first long-term fieldwork, so did I.

The more I thought about it, however, the more measurement seemed to present me with a problem—namely, that I couldn't work out how to describe it in a way that felt ethnographically appropriate. On the one hand, I could turn to the literature existing at the time in science and technology studies (STS) and anthropology on quantification and measurement, which was mostly based on the premise that instead of neutrally representing a world "out there," practices of measuring, counting, and numbering actually have a hand in sculpting and shaping the worlds that they measure, count, and number. This argument is often made in order to challenge the monopoly that science claims to have on truth or "knowing how the world really is"—and in one sense I am likewise committed to challenging such ontological singularity. But on the other hand, in order to argue that measurement creates, enacts, or in any way generates that which it measures, I felt as though I would have to conveniently ignore what the researchers and technicians I worked with understood they were doing. These researchers clearly held the phenomena they were studying to be independent of their practices of representation. In the cases in which their instruments did affect the thing they were measuring, as when a thermometer got too hot and therefore measured its own heat as well as the ambient heat, then this was considered to be an epistemological problem that could be fixed, not an ontological one.

So, I am talking about an ethnographic puzzle that is possibly specific to studying science, and probably then only certain kinds of science.[1] I didn't want to describe measurement in the way that scientists might describe it themselves, but nor did I want to argue that science is in fact nonrepresentational if you just look closely enough. In STS and anthropology this problem generally has been resolved through a sort of deliberately naive empiricism: science is "both" realist "and" nonrepresentational; that is, as Bruno Latour (1993) would have it, scientific "facts" are both "given" and "made," or as can be seen in Donna Haraway's (1988) powerful notion of "feminist objectivity" in which scientific knowledge is necessarily both objective and situated. As inspired as I am, however, by both of these scholars and others, this move somehow just did not seem ethnographically adequate to me.[2]

It was reading Marilyn Strathern's work that alerted me to the possibility of experimenting with analogy as a means to negotiate this puzzle. Strathern uses the notion of analogy both as technique or method and as an object of study; here, I am thinking of the use she makes of it in order to understand both Melanesian and anthropological, Euro-American knowledge practices at the same time, through each other (Strathern [1988] 1990, 2001). One of the problems she is trying to overcome is how to "think" Melanesian worlds through Euro-American anthropological concepts without reducing Melanesian worlds in the process. Her answer, at least in my reading, was to understand both anthropology and Melanesia as necessarily emergent from the relation between them[3]—and a particular kind of relation at that: an analogical one. In a certain sense, then, Strathern made them into analogies of each other. But importantly, this does not make them the same: "Analogies both conserve and extend. What makes this type of relation nonreductive is the fact that the origins of the two elements to an analogy or comparison are not merged. The power of thinking one thing through another lies in conservation, in keeping their ancestry apart. At the same time, the understanding of each is extended by introducing the other into its description" (Strathern 2006, 91).

Conservation—but also extension and, I would add, transformation. I realized that the question I was struggling with—What constitutes an ethnographically appropriate description?—was not necessarily one of deciding between (cosmo)political loyalty or descriptive faithfulness; rather, it was about what sort of extension or transformation I wanted my description to be. This is how I understand and use analogy in my work: deliberate descriptive transformations that both extend and conserve what I want to understand. To cultivate this as a technique means we need to develop careful and thoughtful forms of descriptive displacement, conservation, extension, and transformation. As we shall see, my attempts are nowhere near as elegant as Strathern's analogical practice, but they nevertheless allowed me to sidestep the problem I was facing and start to ask different and possibly more interesting questions.

ETHNOGRAPHIC OPENINGS

Turning this into a protocol or set of instructions is hard—not least because it is not really mine so much as Strathern's that I have repurposed—but if there is going to be a step 1, then it would be around how you see your ethnographic material.

Two ideas about measurement that emerged from my own material struck me, and they paved the way for the analogy I ended up drawing. In both cases it was something particular that snagged me and held me, and then opened out into something else as I tacked between the "field" and the "desk."

The first emerged from trying to understand how the instruments measure the world. The researchers in the LBA use all sorts of meteorological instruments that measure all sorts of phenomena, from rainfall to carbon flux, but I take just one example here: a hygrometer, which measures the humidity of the air. A hygrometer "works" because air humidity outside the instrument has a relation to a property of a material inside the instrument. In modern electrical hygrometers, for example, a semiconductor, lithium chloride, is inside the instrument; in older hygrometers this semiconductor was a human or goat hair. The changing humidity affects the conductivity of lithium chloride, or the length of the hair; thus lithium chloride lets more or less current through it according to how humid the air is, or in the older instruments, the hair expands or contracts depending on the humidity. The conductivity of lithium chloride, or the length of the hair, therefore varies with the variation of humidity in the air. So, the first thing that happens in a hygrometer, and in most meteorological instruments, is that a continuous property out in the world is transformed into a continuous property inside the instrument—in the case of modern hygrometers, into a current. In old hygrometers that used hair, the hair was attached to a stylus that rested on a revolving drum of paper; as the hair expanded or contracted, the stylus drew a line on the paper as the drum turned.

For that continuous property in the instrument to become a measurement, however, it has to be read against a scale and thereby turned into data. In older hygrometers the line that was traced on the paper was read against a scale. In modern hygrometers the electrical current transforms into data within another element of every electrical sensor: the analog-to-digital converter. As one of the technicians in the LBA explained to me, an analog signal is converted into digital code by assigning one value in the continuous signal to 0 and another to 1 in the binary code. Then, whenever those values are registered, they are converted into ones and zeros. What we call "measurement" therefore can be seen as a transformation from a continuously varying current, to a digital signal, to a set of discrete data points.

During my fieldwork I started to notice that this transformation of the continuous into the discrete, for most aspects of measuring natural processes, was important for the researchers I worked with, and not just within the instruments themselves. Alongside the mechanical minutiae of analog-to-digital conversion in the instruments, I had many conversations at different times with different researchers as to how one decided on the limits of one's research area, or how to fraction air samples into different molecular quantum frequencies by using laser technology. During one particularly arduous conversation I was confused about how one makes air, an invisible ether as far as I was concerned, into "parcels" (which is how the researchers refer to them). The researcher I was talking to tried patiently to explain, and then stopped and said, "Look . . . the air is continuous. But the measurement is not continuous. The measurement is broken [*quebrada*]. Measurement does this. Ten times per second, the instrument measures the parcel. It doesn't measure continuously." Measurement "breaks" a continuous world into discrete data.

The second ethnographically derived idea that snagged me was metrological uncertainty, which I encountered when I accompanied a broken instrument from the LBA to the calibration laboratory in Brazil's Space Research Institute (INPE) in São Paulo State. Calibration is the process by which the error and uncertainty of an instrument are calculated precisely by comparing them to the universal standards for the units the instrument measures. For example, if a thermometer needs to be calibrated, you might use a standardized thermal chamber. You place the thermometer inside the chamber, and vary the temperature inside; you can then compare the thermometer's readings with the set temperature within the chamber. This process, however, is not a simple matter of correspondence between something known (the thermal chamber) and something unknown (the thermometer in question). The standard instrument—here, the thermal chamber—has itself been calibrated in a larger, national metrological laboratory according to standard, accredited instruments that in turn have been accredited by other national or international metrological laboratories that have the capacity to generate absolute metrological standards. So many of the standard instruments at INPE are in fact part of a chain of calibration (Walford 2015) that stretches to metrological laboratories and instruments in Switzerland and other parts of Europe, which instruments themselves have to be calibrated regularly. In other cases, and particularly with meteorological instruments, the calibration lab at INPE often cannot afford standard instruments, and so the INPE meteorologists have to do the best they can with the instruments they have—using brand new ones, for example, which have been calibrated in the factory and hardly ever used.

One interesting thing about this chain of calibration, and in fact the whole calibration process, is that the absolute standards, the instruments, the computer that stores the measurements, even physical processes that are themselves being measured, such as heating and cooling—all generate uncertainty in the act of measurement. As one of the metrologists tells me, "Nothing is pure . . . the minute you start measuring, that's it, there's no way round it" (Walford 2015, 70). So, at every stage of the calibration chain, the act itself of measuring or calibrating produces uncertainty, which then needs to be logged and passed on with the instrument. Therefore all instruments carry with them an uncertainty "factor," indicating the deviation of whatever measurement they give from what metrologists call the "conventional true value,"[4] which is itself necessarily uncertain. Thus at the core of measurement in observational science lies an inescapable and iterative gap between the world and the measurement of it. This gap is "measurement uncertainty." So, these were the two aspects of measurement that really intrigued me: that measurement "breaks" the world and that "no measurement is pure."

Before I go on I'd like to draw attention to three things: first, my field is distributed in that I drew not only on people in the field who explained things to me and things I observed at my field site, but also on instrument instruction manuals I read on my own, information I found on how hygrometers work, and online research into calibration laboratories. I consulted textbooks and read Wikipedia articles. This work continued when I was back from the field and included talking to people in the LBA. Thus I was constantly negotiating how my field "kept going." Second, because of this, I ended up looking for a sort of patterning across this distribution—things that seemed to hang together, the "geology underlying surface diversity" (cf. Strathern 1996, 18). What might "count" as important ethnographic material did not depend only on what my interlocutors told me or what I observed or experienced in the field, but on this elicitation of a certain pattern or shape from all the material at my disposal, material that kept being added to. And third, what this then means is that I was not trying to accurately represent or describe "what measurement means for scientists"; nor was I trying to describe, once and for all, what measurement "is." I was trying to translate it—that is, transform it—in a particular way. Ethnography—the way I think of it, at least—is a relation (among many other possible ones), and as such it makes other relations possible.

With this in mind, the two snags I was caught on offered what I think of as an opening in order to effect exactly such a translation.

MYTH AND MEASUREMENT

The idea that measurement is about the transformation of the continuous into the discrete did not present itself to me as a fait accompli; I came upon it half by accident and half deliberately, as an opening to develop an analogical relationship with what seemed to be a very different set of conceptual coordinates: Amerindian origin myths, which I had encountered while pursuing a separate research project some time before. The realization that measurement is about the transformation of the continuous into the discrete immediately triggered a memory of this.

According to most mythologists who work with indigenous Amazonian peoples, the transition from the continuous to the discrete is a crucial dynamic that animates Amerindian mythical thought and practice. Claude

Lévi-Strauss discusses the importance of the introduction of discreteness in myth, particularly in terms of the introduction of the ability to create systems of signification—that is, systems that are constituted by extensive differences between things such that those things can be combined to make meaning. This indicates the passage, in mythic tales, from the continuous world of difference into the "discontinuous world of distinction and opposition" (Wilden 1972, 245) and is at the heart of Lévi-Strauss's structural analysis of myth and his analysis of the passage from nature to culture that he suggests myth charts. As Lévi-Strauss points out, discontinuity has to be introduced in order that things might be conceptualized (Schrempp 1992, 21). The more recent ethnographic literature on Amerindian myth describes, for example, how in much Amerindian mythic discourse the precosmological world is characterized as one of undifferentiation, or as Eduardo Viveiros de Castro puts it, a domain of "qualitative multiplicity" such that "everything seeps into everything else" and in which difference is internal, rather than external, to each mythic entity (2007, 157–58). Thus everything has the potential to be what it is not, which is why in those times everything could transform into everything else. In very general terms, it is from this primordial substrate—where transformation rather than essence constitutes existence—that the cosmos is created. This transformation is often done by the hero of the origin myth, who in one way or another introduces differentiation, which essentializes the various human and animal groups that today populate the world. Thus, as Bruce Albert tells us, in one Yanomami myth the mythic hero Omame made the Yanomami what they are by "putting an end to transformation" so that they no longer turned into animals such as "tapirs, armadillos, and red brockets" (Albert quoted in Kelly 2012, 3). Anthropologist José Kelly, who like Bruce Albert works with the Yanomami, adds another important facet to this. He shows us how the end of the precosmological time of undifferentiation is marked in Yanomami myths by specific types of differentiation, constituted by the introduction of particular dialectics that structure the cosmos—the differences between human and animal, opacity and visibility, the earth and the sky, for example (Kelly 2012).

Returning to measurement then, I realized that I had created an opening for an analogical relation between myth and measurement. If measurement seemed to emerge from my ethnographic material as a sort of transformation of the continuous into the discrete, and if myth seems to emerge from anthropological analysis as the transformation of the continuous into the discrete, what might I learn from trying to think the one through the other?

So, thinking measurement "with" myth, we might see measurement as the introduction of difference; and not only as the introduction of difference, but a certain kind of extensive difference; and not only extensive difference, but a very particular sort of extensive difference, a dialectic—the dialectic between nature and culture. Measurement, understood through origin myth, introduces the dialectic between nature and culture into the (continuous) world (thus transforming it). Measurement emerges from this analogy as the introduction of the relation between nature and culture into the world.

But this is not to say that measurement and myth are "the same thing." If we turn to the second idea that snagged me, then we might say that this relation, or dialectic, that measurement introduces between nature and culture takes the shape of measurement uncertainty. If uncertainty is the endless, iterative gap between your measurement and the world you seek to measure, is this gap that both makes measurement possible and makes it impossible at the same time. One might push the analogy even further and say that, in a "world before measurement" there was no such thing as uncertainty; to borrow from Latour's discussion of a very different context, "Nature" had never been asked, before Western science came along and measured it, whether or not it was the "true" one (Latour 2009, 471–72).

Now, this may seem a little farfetched to some ears, and so be it. I think this technique will either intrigue you, or it won't. But if nothing else, it does point to an interesting way for me to reconsider the problem with which I started: whether measurement represents worlds or constructs them—that is, whether measurement is representational or nonrepresentational. Thinking measurement through myth suggests that it is measurement that introduces the possibility of representationalism in the first place—the possibility of being "real" or "a representation." Measurement becomes an everyday, but profound, technology of the instantiation of the relation between what is real and what is not.

There have of course been several different and much more illustrious examinations of the relation between scientific thought and mythic thought, but these differ, I think, from what I am doing here in part because my concern is specifically to maintain the differences between the two to a certain effect. Myth is not "scientific," nor is science "mythical." I am not arguing that measurement and myth are the same "thing in the world," of course. Rather, myth provides a logic—an analogic, let's say—that we can think measurement with in such a way that allows us to extend its premises, to see things we might not see otherwise, and at the same time refuse its claims to ontological primacy. Measurement emerges as neither representationalism nor nonrepresentationalism, but as one means of introducing the relation of representation itself.

The glaring question, which I do not have space to address here, is to what extent this analogy works both ways—that is, if I here tried to think "measurement" through "myth," how might I "think" myth through measurement? Is it impossible to do one without doing the other? Or are all analogies not necessarily equal?

As a technique, analogy (as I have practiced it, at least) depends very much on your own material. You can never be sure what opening might let you in, and you can never be sure where it might take you. In the spirit of this volume I provide a protocol below (even though this rather open-ended technique might not sit that well with the demands of a protocol) and a list of the characteristics of analogy that might be useful to think through. "One cannot predict . . . what might be illuminating as an axis of comparison. (Nor does it follow that all comparisons or analogies are illuminating.) And here is something to say to the question about relevance: there can, in this sense, be no predetermination of 'relevance,' no predetermination of 'usefulness,' before the comparison has been tried" (Strathern 2006, 91).

PROTOCOL

- Look for "snags" in your ethnographic material. These are "openings."
- Look for patternings guided by those openings. Can you detect resonances or interferences across your material?
- Work out what it is that is snagging you in these patterns. Does the snag that it seems to belong speak to a very different setting? Does the snag actually cross between contexts? Are you reminded of anything?
  - If so, explore that relationship, even if it seems a bit wacky. (For example, another analogy I am currently working on is Facebook data and organ donation.) This might allow you to think around any particular crisis of representation or description you might be going through.
  - An analogy is a relation that works in multiple directions all the time, whether you like it or not. This means that when you are

talking about one thing you are also talking about more than one thing (and one of those things is usually yourself).

- Analogies are everywhere—anthropologists are not the only ones who make analogies or describe them—but you can apply some more deliberately than others, and sometimes you have to ensure that you are being as deliberate as possible.[5]
- Analogies are a particular way of using relations between things in order to describe those things: "[i]deally, one would exploit the extent to which each talks past the other" (Strathern [1988] 1990, 9).

NOTES

1. As Karen Barad (2007) has demonstrated, quantum physics, as presented in the work of Niels Bohr for example, does not have the same commitment to a pre-existing underlying reality as the observational environmental sciences tend to.

2. In fact I later realized that my unease was misplaced, as I shall explain shortly.

3. But Strathern ([1988] 1990) makes clear that although the ethnographies we write may be "fictions," the people they are about are not.

4. A "value attributed to a particular quantity and accepted, sometimes by convention, as having an uncertainty appropriate for a given purpose." International Organization for Standardization, "Annex B: General Metrological Terms," accessed June 20, 2018, https://www.iso.org/sites/JCGM/GUM/JCGM100/C045315e -html/C045315e_FILES/MAIN_C045315e/AB_e.html/.

5. This one is a bit like Viveiros de Castro's (2004) notion of "controlled equivocations," and it would be interesting to consider the extent to which we might think of such controlled equivocations, in the sense Viveiros de Castro uses, as analogies.

Decolonizing Knowledge Devices

Do not believe in untainted random choices; believe in attaching value to things and people. Initial inflections always exist that configure a predisposition for embracing an ethnographic research. Whether you are conscious of them or not, conditions will always precede your specific research and especially your fieldwork. How can you get a hold of your primeval conditions? Where and how do they stand? What and whom do they show and hide? You cannot create knowledge without intervening, without changing the world and yourself. Without changing your world. And, most important—maybe especially if you are in a colonial country—what and whose world are you aiming at (intervening in)? Two initial steps allow us to approach this problem.

First step: Think about and feel the part of the world around you. What bothers, excites, and puzzles you? Is your feeling difficult to configure? Try to identify and make a list of the inhabitants of the world around you. These inhabitants can be people or things. Be concrete and specific—books, computers, home appliances, cars, friends, colleagues, practices, jobs, institutions—and include scientific and cultural inhabitants as well. How are they where they are? What do you know about them? What are they made of? What specific skills and institutions are necessary to bring them into the world? Under what conditions might you have access to them? Many inhabitants of your world will appear. Be selective in trying to find those that resonate more with what bothers, excites, and puzzles you as an inhabitant of (or someone concerned with) a colonial country.

To the extent that you succeed in carrying on this task, the more the list of these selected inhabitants will express an initial specificity of your research that otherwise might not be so clear (even to yourself). In other words, the exercise of constructing the list will probably make you more able to make those primeval (colonial-concerned) conditions more problematic and less natural. The inhabitants you select are not determinant, and they are not the only ones, but they are indicative of the nature of your problematic encounter with a mode of existence. They configure a broad and imprecise scenario that you find and build of the origins of your work. Almost as if your research is entering your own kind of cosmology of the world your research is entering. In my case I achieved the following list of "knowledge devices," inhabitants of the world where my work/research/intervention took place.

STEP 1 KNOWLEDGE DEVICES

Brazil, as a colonized country, received from abroad a whole parade of modern entities: not only humans—European colonizers and African slaves—and technological artifacts from metal axes and muskets to microscopes, cars, and cell phones, but also scientific entities such as electrons, the law of gravity, and the double helix, and entities of collective organization and management, such as the nation state, nongovernmental organizations, credit systems, universities, professions, public policies, human rights, and representative democracy. I attribute a common name to these entities: knowledge devices.

In cosmological terms a demand exists for names (nouns, substances, actors) when a collective encounters or imagines a detachable entity in a world of unbaptized variations, that is, an as yet shapeless part of reality. For example, the name *electron* was attributed to an entity whose shape was at the time still unestablished.[1] To be a collectively thinkable and sharable part of reality, to become an inhabitant of a world, an entity demands a name to refer to the provisional juxtapositions of heterogeneous elements that configure it. That is an ontology. Names institute situated, stable, sharable knowledges. Extrapolating the list above, I propose that the names of modern entities that inhabit the part of the Brazilian world of my research designate knowledge devices. In other words I take them as means, tools, or "devices" to achieve ends, and they respond to certain demands (Foucault 1977). In this way I have made it clear for myself that the actuation of knowledge devices that come from abroad to my colonized country bothers, excites, and puzzles me. Indeed I find that I am not alone: "A maladaptive conceptual apparatus undermines the scientific knowledge of numerous problems in underdeveloped countries" (Santos [1978] 2013, 31).[2] This naming leads us to the second step.

Second step: Stop for a moment. Meditate in tune with the specificity you were able to identify. Look and feel around again, now zooming in and focusing more on your own relations, connections, and limits. It is time to situate your research, the knowledges you are about to create, and their associated interventions. It is time to choose where, when, and with and for whom you intend to work. They will be your territory. Locate this territory; it will be your area of interest, the area in which you will turn some matters of fact into matters of concern. To produce knowledge is to intervene. The choice of a territory is embedded in your life. If we live on a thousand plateaus, we have no other possibility but to start in the middle.[3] Have in mind your resources, in the proper sense of the word— that is, what you can do and what you can make others do. Gearing up for the ethnographic research, you should soon make your chosen territory more visible with readings, conversations, generic observations, theories, and experiences that are juxtaposed by authors, including experts. This builds a panoramic view of your territory. Panoramic exhibitions are taken as though they offer a wide-ranging picture and complete control over the territory; they seem to review with authority the "whole situation," even though they cover as much as they show: "Full coherence is their forte— and their main frailty" (Latour 2005, 189). Nevertheless, even though they can be misleading, panoramic exhibitions of the territory will prepare you for the political-sociotechnical task ahead: that of intervening in knowledge in favor of decolonization. The panoramic view is of crucial importance to the scale of the intervention you have in mind because it provides an occasion to see the "whole situation" *as* a whole, even though it appeals to knowledge devices that you, as a research-activist, might seek to make problematic.

I chose the evaluation of graduate research programs in Brazilian universities as my territory.

STEP 2 A PANORAMIC EXHIBITION OF MY TERRITORY

Graduate education and research in Brazil are organized in graduate programs (*programas de pós-graduação*). Most graduate programs are affiliated with a university and associated with a department, school, coordination, or center at the university. Well-established graduate programs, however, acquire substantial autonomy from their host university. Although they continue to confer diplomas and titles on behalf of the university, they independently manage the funds they receive directly from government agencies.

A decisive element in Brazilian graduate academic studies is that every four years a central government agency, CAPES, evaluates the programs.[4] Each program receives a grade on a scale from zero to seven. Programs with a grade of three or less are subject to being closed. Well-established "programs of excellence" have grades of six or seven. CAPES sorts the programs by area, and each area has its own specialized evaluation committee that evaluates all programs in that area. Each program takes place in one—and only one—area and is evaluated by the committee of that area. CAPES chooses the members of the area committees, considering a list of candidates who receive the most votes from the community in the area. A certain inertia acts on the assignment of the grades, so that a program's grade will rarely be altered drastically. The most common change is one point up or down on the scale. But the classification is relative and competitive in the sense that for a program to get grade 7, for example, it is almost mandatory that some other program will be downgraded from grade 7 to grade 6.

A second very important element is that the financial resources of the programs are allocated by this same agency, CAPES. A higher grade substantially increases not only the amount of financial support given to the program but also—and this is crucial—its autonomy in the use of such resources. Administrative operating conditions vary significantly according to the program's grade, and programs with grade 6 or 7 not only receive more generous resources directly from CAPES but also enjoy incomparably greater freedom in administering these resources. In relation to their hosting university, these programs achieve complete autonomy as the managers of these resources.

Therefore increasing or maintaining its CAPES grade becomes the main goal of a Brazilian graduate program. Programs must meet several minimum infrastructure conditions (such as rooms and computers for teachers and students, access to libraries) and a set of indicators such as number of students and time to complete master's and doctoral degrees. Although room exists for a small qualitative text, evaluations are made through an online platform, Sucupira, a set of entries in tables that translates each aspect of the evaluation into a numerical value.[5] In this evaluation system the determining factor for achieving grade 6 or 7 is the number of publications in a set of selected periodicals (called the Qualis of the area) divided by the number of participating professor-researchers in the program. This value is the decisive indicator in the competition.

FACING THE COLONIALITY OF POWER

Ethnographic research is a powerful tool to face the coloniality of power embedded in colonial enclaves widespread around the world.[6] The ethnographic moment is a relation in the same way as a linguistic sign can be thought of as a relation (joining signifier and signified). We could say that the ethnographic moment works as an example of a relation which joins the understood (what is analyzed at the moment of observation) to the need to understand (what is observed at the moment of analysis). The relationship between what is already apprehended and what seems to demand apprehension is of course infinitely regressive, that is, it slips across any manner of scale (minimally, observation and analysis each contains within itself the relation between them both). (Strathern 1999, 6)

WHAT IS ALREADY APPREHENDED

In 2017 the Brazilian graduate programs in a technoscientific (TSC) area were evaluated. An important program in a major university, which had received grade 7 from CAPES, was concerned to keep its grade.[7] One year in advance the college suggested the program form a special committee and asked each researcher-professor to write a paragraph about each of their four foremost papers published over the previous four years. During a second meeting the group chose Professor R as the coordinator of the committee. People were leaving the room as Professor V talked with Professor R.

> V: It's great that you're the committee coordinator. Less than a month ago we had concluded the need for a special committee to prepare for the [CAPES] evaluation and today we have a coordinator. It is not often that we act so quickly. I agree with the impression left in the last evaluation that we are not as well positioned as we used to be.
>
> R: I think that in the end we all agree on that. For many years we have been at the top of the scale, but now other programs are publishing as much as we are. We have a more mature group, but we are

somehow failing to differentiate ourselves to compete in a number of publications against the younger faculty programs.

V: It is so indeed. The evaluation ends up reduced to a paper count, a number without a history, or with a very limited history. In our college, we have never made our own evaluation of the CAPES evaluation as a measure of ourselves. Institutionally, we accept a supporting role in defining what we are. The journals in which papers score higher points are suggested by the programs themselves, but each program suggests the journals in which its own faculty publish. This part of the process contributes to isolating each program as an endogenous island. Moreover, there is the problem of an overwhelming pressure to publish in English. We are witnessing the odd situation of journals of Brazilian academic associations publishing in English here in Brazil, a country where most academics do not speak this language.

R: Hmm . . . But this is true everywhere, not only here; it's international reality. We cannot go against this. We must publish more in English. The problem is that we are not sufficiently differentiating ourselves from the other programs in our area. More and more programs have indexes like ours.

V: Well, this is exactly the point I would like to talk to you about: making a difference. The newest programs follow the CAPES rules like a catechism. We are also imprisoned by a lack of criticism within the limits of the CAPES rules and referrals, although there is general dissatisfaction and a growing impression that there is something unsatisfactory about them.

R: Hmm . . . CAPES's rules bring objectivity to the evaluation.

V: Dissatisfaction is general. Grades 6 and 7 are increasingly criticized. The view that these rules are not producing consistent results is becoming prevalent. Even here we are having difficulties, right? The CAPES evaluation director herself recognized this when she was here last month, remember?

R: Yes, but how to evaluate without objective rules?

V: I'm not saying we should not have rules. I agree that there should be rules, though I think it's time to rethink them. However, it's not about the rules that I want to talk to you, at least not now. My point is about something else. It is about the issue of lack of difference mentioned in the last meetings. My point is that our program does have a differential, something that I think is valuable to be presented as an important asset for CAPES evaluation in our introductory text next year.

R: Cool! And what do you think is the difference?

V: I did a brief survey. It seems that graduate programs of TSC in Brazil do not appreciate interdisciplinary lines of research. Well, we do . . .

R: Hmm . . .

V: I mean, at least we have several students working in the emerging field of science and technology studies.

R: I did not know about other programs failing to have this kind of interdisciplinarity. It may be so. But for evaluation . . . the papers . . . CAPES rules are designed to objectively evaluate who produces the most results in TSC. We're talking about mathematics, algorithms, new materials, resonances, artificial intelligence, etc., you know, not concepts from the social sciences or social phenomena.

V: We have already accumulated several research results, master's and doctorate, where it is revealed that concepts and techniques of TSC, everywhere are interwoven with so-called social phenomena.

R: It is difficult to agree that the functioning and efficiency of an algorithm, for example, depends on the social conditions in which it was generated.

V: My point is that our program should announce the fact that we also invest in other understandings of technical-scientific knowledge as a positive difference. At the meeting, Professor A reminded us that university U's program does not adhere so uniformly to the CAPES rules, and, despite this, there was no sign that they would fail to keep grade 7.

R: Frankly, I did not find that very relevant. I do not see how it can help us.

V: The different understanding I want to bring in is that the efficiency of an algorithm, and indeed of any system, certainly depends not only on the social conditions in which it was generated but also on the social conditions in which it is applied.

R: We are a TSC program; we deal with facts and not with other understandings. This may be sociology, philosophy, or even psychology, but it is not the kind of understanding that the TSC world proposes.

V: Of course, TSC deals with results, operation, efficiency, effectiveness, etc. But note that most of the concepts and techniques we use are generated under social conditions different from the social conditions in which they are applied here in Brazil. What if it is true

that the social conditions of the place where they are applied affect
their functioning, efficiency, effectiveness, etc.? Wouldn't we have
cast a shadow on our own work if we ignored this truth?

R: Where are you heading? We have so far succeeded in staying out of
ideological questions.

V: My proposal is that our program show the line of research in science and technology studies as an important differential over other
graduate programs in the TSC area.

R: You look so confident! I cannot make this kind of decision by myself. How do you think the program could do this?

V: The comments I have made, although very brief, suggested ways
to do this, but they went unnoticed. If it is in the interest of the
committee, I can write two or three pages that could be part of the
introductory text to the CAPES evaluation.

R: Fine, I'll talk to the "colleagues" and I'll give you an answer soon.[8]

[After a few days R and V met casually in the hall (they had adjacent
offices).]

R: I talked to the "colleagues" about your proposal, but they think that
research mixing TSC with human and social sciences is irrelevant to
the CAPES assessment. You do not have to bother writing those two
or three pages.

The program was favorably evaluated in 2017, ignoring Professor V's alleged value of strengthening its connections to its local environment. The
program kept its CAPES grade 7 for another four years.

WHAT SEEMS TO DEMAND APPREHENSION

How and why did this happen? Here I enunciate, inspired by Paulo Freire,
the concept of a "generative" knowledge device—a knowledge device that
(1) is easily grasped as necessarily taken into account in everyday life in
the territory, and (2) whose operation is based on and can be decomposed
in operations of derivative knowledge devices that more directly demand
space and time in the sensible world and are therefore more readily apprehended in the territory. These derivative knowledge devices, in their turn,
may become "generative" knowledge devices themselves, in a regression
whose end will be determined by the conditions of your research.[9]

Professor R and the "colleagues" have a powerful knowledge device acting as their ally. It is a knowledge device that oversees the organization of

graduate research programs; that is, a knowledge device that operates the division of labor in the production of academic knowledge in Brazil. That device is the Table of Areas of Knowledge, published by CAPES, and I take it as an initial "generative" knowledge device in the process of decolonizing (some) knowledge devices in Brazil. This table is issued at two levels: Table 17.1 shows the high-level table and comprises the forty-nine research areas at Brazilian universities, corresponding to the forty-nine CAPES committees. Each committee autonomously oversees a community isolated in its "area of knowledge," with its own practices, politics, and hierarchies. Programs strongly adhere to the categories specified in the table. We know that in any classification system, when a new element does not fit into the already established categories, the entire classification is at risk. Criticism is timid, and challenge to the established hierarchy is minimal. ("I talked to the 'colleagues' about your proposal, ... You do not have to bother ...," said Professor R.) This is understandable, because the same committees that evaluate the programs also issue judgments on the distribution of re- sources to the programs in the area. In fact, the Table of Areas of Knowl- edge is a dominant knowledge device shaping public policies for creating scientific knowledges at Brazilian universities. It organizes and evaluates the graduate and research programs, and CAPES actively supports and widely disseminates it. Each area listed in table 17.1 has various subareas of expertise; table 17.2 lists the twenty-five subareas of expertise that, for CAPES—and hence for purposes of evaluation and funding—compose the TSC area of knowledge in Brazil. According to the prevailing ideal, a TSC program is evaluated and gets funds strictly in response to publishing in these specific areas of expertise.

What am I doing? Inspired by Paulo Freire, I take the CAPES table as a generative knowledge device and I start to "decode" it: "Its 'decoding' requires moving from the abstract to the concrete; this requires moving from the part to the whole and then returning to the parts" (Freire 2000, 96). The evaluation that had been previously apprehended will begin to demand apprehension again as thought flows back to it from its infinitely regressive decoding. This regression may take the researcher and the col- lective involved in the research to "limit-situations" that are not "the im- passable boundaries where possibilities end, but the real boundaries where all possibilities begin" (Pinto 1960, 284, with Freire 2000, 89fn).

The CAPES table is the current Brazilian local partial replication of the result of a historical Euro-American process that sidetracked Brazilian lo- calities. Beginning in the nineteenth century the professionalization of the

TABLE 17.1 CAPES Table of Areas of Knowledge/Evaluation

1. Anthropology/archeology
2. Architecture, urbanism, and design
3. Art
4. Astronomy/physics
5. Biodiversity
6. Biotechnology
7. Computer science
8. Food science
9. Political science and international relations
10. Agricultural sciences I
11. Environmental sciences
12. Biological sciences I
13. Biological sciences II
14. Biological sciences III
15. Sciences of religion and theology
16. Communication and information
17. Law
18. Economy
19. Education
20. Physical Education
21. Nursing
22. Engineering group I
23. Engineering group II
24. Engineering group III
25. Engineering group IV
26. Teaching
27. Pharmacology
28. Philosophy
29. Geosciences
30. Geography
31. History
32. Interdisciplinary studies
33. Public and business administration, accounting sciences, and tourism
34. Languages and literatures
35. Mathematics/probability and statistics
36. Materials
37. Medicine I

TABLE 17.1 (*Continued*)

38. Medicine II
39. Medicine III
40. Veterinary medicine
41. Nutrition
42. Dentistry
43. Urban and regional planning/demography
44. Psychology
45. Chemistry
46. Public health
47. Social service
48. Sociology
49. Zootechny/fishery resources

Source: CAPES, "Evaluation," accessed January 31, 2017, http://www.capes.gov.br /avaliacao/instrumentos-de-apoio/tabela-de-areas-do-conhecimento-avaliacao/.

role of scientists fragmented the *république des savants* of the eighteenth century into an increasing number of areas of specialized research communities, which were formed by professional experts from a given area of knowledge. These experts are now postulated as the only audience for relevant scientific objectifications. "CAPES's rules bring objectivity to the evaluation," said Professor R.

"This same historical process that disjointed the république des savants in a 'multiplicity of separate research communities' also produced the cultural untying of the natural sciences, the cultural entrenchment of the human sciences, and the growing constraint of the relations between the two" (Geertz 2000, 135; see also Lenoir 1998). The dominant Euro-American epistemology teaches us that this division of areas guarantees that the ideas of one community can be increasingly refined to reach levels of purity that are impossible if the domain of each community is not precisely demarcated. Hence, those in the area of TSC should seek their own island of knowledge, keeping a distance from "other understandings" and acknowledging that "research mixing TSC with human and social sciences is irrelevant," as Professor R and the "colleagues" stated.

But it seems that what we see as fertile ground for knowledge creation is much more an archipelago between whose islands relations are complex and branched, and whose possible mutual interactions are endless. The

TABLE 17.2 Arbitrary Example (To Keep Anonymity) of Specializations in an Area of CAPES' Evaluation

31200001	aerospace engineering
31201008	aerodynamics
31201016	space aircraft aerodynamics
31201024	aerodynamics of geophysical and interplanetary processes
31202004	flight dynamics
31202012	trajectories and orbits
31202020	tability and control
31203000	aerospace structures
31203019	aeroelasticity
31203027	fatigue
31203035	projects of aerospace structures
31204007	materials and processes for aeronautic and aerospace engineering
31205003	aerospace propulsion
31205011	combustion and flush with chemical reactions
31205020	rocket propulsion
31205038	flow machines
31205046	alternative engines
31206000	aerospace systems
31206018	airplanes
31206026	rockets
31206034	helicopters
31206042	hovercraft
31206050	satellites and other aerospace devices
31206069	certifications of aircraft and components
31206077	maintenance of aerospace systems

Source: CAPES. Tabelas de Áreas de Conhecimento/Avaliação, http://www.capes .gov.br/avaliacao/instrumentos-de-apoio/tabela-de-areas-do-conhecimento -avaliacao. Accessed January 31, 2017.

awkward effects of reductionist CAPES rules seem to be recognized when Professor V claims that "the view that these rules are not producing consistent results is becoming prevalent" in Brazil. The Brazilian archipelago of scientific communities is relatively very small, and it is likely that most of its islands result from initial individual Brazilian students who went abroad (in overwhelming proportions to the US, England, France, and Germany) and returned to engage in institutional research. These novices brought from abroad not only their knowledge but also their research problems, which imply a collection of maladaptively situated, colonized knowledge devices for setting up laboratories, research practices, careers, and operational schemes of recognition and evaluation.

Well-established knowledge devices are stabilized as the "real" and scientific facts, and they tend to function at levels that are reached after innumerous mediations that select, combine, and articulate inscriptions to express variations in terms of differences and resemblances. A labor of division preceded the present division of labor in scientific constructions of knowledges. Knowledge devices cast a veil over the mosaic of asymmetries, hierarchies, and heterogeneities that are kept in place by the coloniality of power in order to make up a colonial scientific world. Professor V denounces the coloniality of power by claiming that, in Brazil, "institutionally, we accept a supporting role in defining what we are." Taken as sanctified knowledge, in fact, the CAPES table guarantees the emptying of the issues. "You do not have to bother writing those two or three pages," announced Professor R, following CAPES' reductionist catechism of knowledge construction.

On the one hand, the coloniality of Brazilian academic powers maintains a subaltern dialogue with the West to create local scientific communities. As is well known, science is capable of dialogues only in its own terms. To establish themselves and to be linked to the modern sciences, Brazilian academic communities must access and try to replicate the disciplinary knowledges that make up the modern sciences, be they the natural sciences or the human and social sciences. The world has expanded—civilization is no longer Western but planetary—but the disciplinary organization and norms in the production of scientific knowledge remain within the parameters of Euro-American epistemology. Over the five hundred years of colonization, denying epistemological possibilities to the "savage," "backward," "underdeveloped," and presently "noncompetitive" Brazilians became so strong as to make people doubt their own wisdom, when their wisdom is not articulated in Euro-American educational institutions and languages.

On the other hand, for Brazilian academic communities to integrate into and serve the local population, they must attend to local particularities, not only "tropicalizing" the disciplinary structures of Euro-American models but sometimes straying from them and creating new ones of their own. They must handle "cases in which the 'frontiers' of knowledge are no longer located on the known but in the production of knowledge itself" (Mignolo 2000, 4). This may require not only interdisciplinary but also a-disciplinary expressions. Westerners themselves acknowledged that "the peoples from 'other' civilizations and with 'other' forms of knowledge are claiming a gnoseology that they have been taught to despise" (Mignolo 2000, 300; see also Viveiros de Castro 2014).

TOWARD "LIMIT-SITUATIONS"

Of course, knowledge devices are not isolatable entities. More tasks lie ahead in order to decolonize a knowledge device such as the CAPES table. This requires proceeding toward a limit-situation, which is, as noted above, not an impassable border but rather a moving configuration of unpredictable heterogenous elements. The issue predictably enters explicitly political arenas. In general, Brazilian academics are "colonized-colonizers," subaltern-dominants. They are subalterns inside the cage of the CAPES table, which their Euro-American "peers" inhabit in a differentiated condition. They are dominant amid lay Brazilians as the spokespersons of the CAPES table (scientific knowledges). Their mixed feelings about decolonization movements are noteworthy.[10]

What demands apprehension in the CAPES table leads the researcher, together with the participants in dialogues, to find and apprehend the CAPES table's derivative knowledge devices such as "peer reviews," "citation indexes," and "patents"—a task beyond the limits of this chapter. In order to proceed, it is necessary to select, historicize, accomplish the ethnography, and reconfigure the derivative knowledge devices that will support a situated analysis/intervention.

Dominant Western knowledge devices acquired their disseminated forms in parts of the hegemonic West through a process that is not blind to colonialism as an object of study but is indeed blind to epistemic colonial differences and possible different epistemological dimensions (Mignolo 2000, 38). The relations between geopolitical location and the production of knowledge emerge in the intersection of modes of existence. They can be discussed in the encounter of panoramic, clean characterizations and local, impure ethnographic stories.

Differences and resemblances must be formed not as opposites but as the results of contrasting combinations and articulations of diverse inscriptions. Differences and resemblances can embrace, complement, situate, and give form to each other. No opposition exists between ethnographic stories, which reveal differences, and panoramic exhibitions, which enact resemblances. It is important to make them act together—with and against each other—and thereby configure what a common reality is. And what it is not.

PROTOCOL

- Focus on entities around you (things, people, facts, theories) in light of the coloniality of power. Try to select the entities that most strongly provoke your feelings, those that bother you the most, excite you, surprise and astonish you. Many entities will appear.
- Do not make random choices. Try to assign value to entities and debug your list. This will help you choose your territory, that is, a space-time-culture that you will detach as the part of the world where your research will happen.
- Next, learn more and study your territory. Read and listen informally.
- Then compose a panoramic exhibition of your territory. Make it as complete as possible given the availability of resources. Resources should be a concern from the outset; evaluate both your resources and with whom and for whom you will work. None of this is rigid or definitive, but keep a clear idea of these elements at every point in the research process. The territory is not a prison. It is possible for you to expand or reduce it throughout your search.
- You are now ready for the ethnography. The effort here is to observe a situation lived in your territory and to record as much as you can on the different positions facing coloniality. This is the moment of observation in which you will see how coloniality is apprehended in your territory.
- Now (and intertwined) comes the work of writing, the analysis in which you will identify, from the specifics observed during the fieldwork, what demands apprehension in your territory. These are the starting points of interventions of your research. And it is here that the concept of a generative knowledge device is a powerful tool. The choice of the first generative knowledge device is important. It is through it that you will more easily arrive at other generative devices linked to the material daily life of your territory.

- The contours of how the colonialities of power act in the territory will gradually gain sharpness. If successful, your work will translate imperial matters of fact into matters of concern in the territory.

NOTES

1. See Latour (1987), based on Hoddeson (1981).
2. The original was published in French; see Santos (1971).
3. Deleuze and Guattari (1987).
4. Coordenação de Aperfeiçoamento de Pessoal de Nível Superior, created in 1951.
5. Plataforma Sucupira, version 3.32.1, https://sucupira.capes.gov.br/sucupira/.
6. Mignolo (2000) provides a commanding argument about the inadequacy of postcolonial approaches when it comes to Latin America.
7. I have made minor changes to ensure the anonymity of the program and professors.
8. Professor V used the Portuguese word *pessoal*, which in the context here means a restricted circle of colleagues. It is implicit that who is going to be consulted about the matter will remain at the discretion of Professor R.
9. Paulo Freire (1967) defines "generative words" as "those that, broken down into their syllabic elements, provide, through the combination of these elements, the creation of new words." Methodologically, in teaching illiterate people to read, Freire (1967) chooses a first generative word in "informal meetings with the residents of the area to be reached." "Only when the group, with the collaboration of the coordinator, has exhausted the analysis (decoding) of the situation" given by the first generating word does the creation of other generating words—words placed, for example, in a specific work situation of the participants—begin with greater ease. Freire's (2013) *Education for Critical Consciousness* is a recent edition of an English translation of his 1967 *Educação como prática da liberdade*.
10. See, for example, Schwarz (1988). In resonance with the ambiguity concerning Brazil's scientific and technological dependence, see da Costa Marques (2005).

Writing an Ethnographic Story in Working toward Responsibly Unearthing Ontological Troubles

An ethnographic story entitled "Bus Passenger" opens my essay. This story is the data in a science and technology studies (STS) ethnographic project that reveals some of the ontological troubles that Aboriginal Australians need to negotiate on a day-to-day basis while living in a contemporary Australian city. Bus companies decree a normative category that standardizes the entity "Darwin bus passenger," which Aboriginal Australians going about their everyday life experience as an ill-fitting category.

As a story, "Bus Passenger" is a decomposition of experience. It takes the tangled whole of experience and pulls on just one thread. The story is an abductive, whole-parts type of generalizing. Three comments follow the story in a form of qualification. Each comment speaks to a need for ethnographers undertaking such an ethnography of concepts to develop particular practices in learning to write such stories knowingly, in decomposing experience to generate ethnographic data. My first comment proposes that ethnographers need to learn to attend to ontological constitutions in reading and writing. In beginning to write a story, start by wondering how the figures of the author-in-the-text and the reader-in-the-text are being rendered as ethnographic knowers. In writing, be attentive to the places where author and reader participate and are co-configured.

Writing an ethnographic story involves negotiating two tricky passes. The second and third comments relate to these. In writing your story, how will you show that you recognize "physical stuff" as a lively participant in the situation you are describing? In learning to negotiate this "stuff" as a participant in collective action, you respect your inchoate experience but resist the fallacy of experiential immediacy: the idea that objects and their knowers are given ontologically before experience. Writing an ethnographic story should express this.

Then in actually writing we need to be careful in deploying words as we (re)experience our inchoate experience of experience. Our stories are always *re*-presenting rather than representing. This re-presentation is making passage with words in composing an "experience-as-story" that keeps open myriad possibilities for mutual ontological co-constitutions of knowns and knowers in the resituating experience in interpretive writing and reading.

When your story hangs together well enough, you have inferentially assembled your data. In making something of your data, however, in presenting your story as a generalization that can intervene, you are only halfway there. Three further interpretive steps are necessary in order to complete your argument. The six steps of the protocol articulate epistemic practices of using ethnographic stories to intervene. I attend to the first three in this text.

BUS PASSENGER

Darwin's buses are an inexpensive way to travel. In my experience they are rarely less than half full, but on the other hand they are almost never crowded. They are comfortable without being luxurious, air-conditioned so that it is usually quite pleasant to step into a bus, the journey a brief respite from the tropical heat. The city is small and its suburbs are few. The buses move in and out of the tiny city center and circumnavigate both clockwise and counterclockwise. Many passengers who use the buses travel in groups, and they often hop on and off buses several times a day, circulating through Darwin's public places. The buses generally buzz with cheerful conversations and have a comfortable, homey feel. Few express buses run, and most buses halt at every stop along a route.

One week I traveled twice a day on the buses, moving along two routes during each journey to and from my office at the university. I find the life on buses interesting, and during this week several incidents occurred that I found disconcerting in the sense that they puzzled me. I felt a need to keep them with me so that I might turn them over, look for places to "get inside" them, so to speak. It seemed they were moments when some sort of undertow broke briefly through the surface banality—the very ordinary experience of traveling on a bus in a small Australian city.

It was a weekday, the start of the work and school day, and I was traveling away from the city center. At a stop some ten minutes into the journey, outside a Catholic secondary school, several children got off and quite a large group of neatly dressed Aboriginal women and children got on. A middle-aged woman paid the bus fares for the several younger women, all the while addressing the brood loudly in an Indigenous language I could not recognize. The children (who travel free on buses) bundled aboard, rushing to get their favorite places, their boisterous tumbling about calling forth shouted admonitions from the matriarch. As it happened, this was the only day that my bus ride featured the presence of transit officers, and one of the officers took exception to this behavior.

According to a government-maintained website, a transit officer can do any of the following:

- Direct a person engaged in unacceptable and antisocial behavior to leave a bus, interchange or bus stops
- Remove a person from a bus, bus stop or interchange
- Ask for a person's name, address, or date of birth if the officer reasonably believes the person may have committed an offense or they can assist in the investigation of an offense
- Direct a person to comply with the rules of behavior on a bus
- Require a person to get off a bus, keep away from a bus station, and use reasonable force if necessary
- Issue on-the-spot fines
- Arrest and detain a person (without warrant) where the officer believes on reasonable grounds the person has committed an offence warranting arrest
- Search and seize dangerous articles from an arrested person[1]

Upon boarding the bus several stops earlier, the transit officers had positioned themselves deliberately. One officer stood near the back door, and a second, a younger and fitter man, stationed himself in the narrow passage that all passengers (bar those who occupy the very front row) must move through to take a seat. The narrowness of this passage meant that those boarding must squeeze themselves past the officer. His position made it easy for him to block passage. The discomfort of passengers joining the bus in these circumstances was obvious, the exception being some children who bent low, put their heads down, and charged. It was this behavior that had provoked loud shouts from the woman paying the fares for her adult family members.

She was still fumbling with her coins, the line of tickets she had purchased fluttering from her hand, as she turned from the driver to pass into the bus. The transit officer shifted his position to confront her, uncomfortably close, preventing her passage. She concentrated on getting the coins into her purse. Very loudly, exceeding the volume of the woman's shout at her brood but with a quite different tone and speaking English, the transit officer barked, "When you board a bus you *must* behave like a bus passenger!"

The bus fell silent; the driver seemed to still the engine. The woman looked at the officer squarely, unmoving and calm. "Yes, *sir*," she said loudly into the silence. Several passengers sitting nearby burst out laughing at her deadpan performance with its perfect comic timing. "Passengers *do not* shout!" he shouted, somewhat lamely, as he stepped aside, with as much ceremony and dignity as he could muster, to let her pass. He was still glowering minutes later.

I was one of the passengers who had chuckled out loud, yet in addition to the amusement expressed in this involuntary act, I felt both offended and puzzled by the episode. It was a tense moment, punctured by comedy and unexpected collective laughter. Was the transit officer behaving in a racist manner? Yes, that and more. He had silently harassed all boarding passengers, succeeding in making his intimidating presence felt all through the bus. That some smaller children clearly had a well-established routine for evading his methods suggested this was not a new experience. And it was clear that the matriarch was no less experienced in dealing with racist transit officers than with boisterous grandchildren. Along with everyone else on the bus I knew that public transport governance had happened; that we all noticed it actually attests to it being a failure of mundane governance. Of course the pain of the experience of racism embedded in this happening of governance was felt by each of the bus passengers, although it differed markedly in degree. And of course others would likely tell the story of the event quite differently. My motivation in telling this story is to (re)enact a happening of governance in order to articulate a situated truth of governance.

Walking across the university campus, from the bus stop to my office, I re-experienced delight in my copassenger's performance; the collective laugh became my start in feeling my way toward a story. *Story*, like its cousin *history*, originates in the ancient Greek idea that narrative as a form of knowing, when wisely deployed, "outs" something, brings something hidden to the surface. My ethnographic story "outs" a happening of the present.

I am almost certain that in the course of reading my story most of you did not concern yourselves with how you as a reader were being ontologically constituted in the text, and that you took my ethnographic story as being about certain designated things: buses and shouts, Indigenous Australian languages and small children, women and tickets, laughter and discomfort, racism. Along with those things, no doubt you assumed the "I" in the text to be ontologically constituted as a sensible individual who experienced those named things through seeing and hearing—a sort of natural knowing subject who is familiar with those real things as given parts of a knowable world. This is not the reading of a trained ethnographer.

In the default reading the ethnographer becomes a duality: the "I in the flesh" ineluctably distinct from, and set against, the "'I' in the text."[2] That sort of reading takes the story as a representation, a picture that claims to mimetically represent a situation "out-there." That reading might indeed be appropriate were you a reader of a social science text that aimed to represent in order to generalize inductively. But this is not my purpose. A generalization is enacted here, but it is not inductive. A different sort of generalization is made here, and I say more about that in my next paragraph. But beware, for making this different sort of generalization is just the start of a quite different set of epistemic practices than those associated with induction.

We might imagine the general human experience of racism as a vague whole, distributed in time and space, or better, as coming to life again and again, repetitively yet subtly distinct in myriad time-places. Each and every experience of racism is a part of the vague, ramifying whole. The story I tell adduces, or brings to the fore, just one tiny part of that vague whole. We could say the story adductively generalizes, but it is more usual to use a slightly different prefix and say that it *abducts*.

Part of learning to generalize abductively is learning how to read differently. Reading my story, I ask you to experience the story differently as you read. I invite you to identify as my specified reader-in-the-text and, like the writer, to ontologically reconstitute yourself. As writer I am committed to becoming a complex, distributed, extended figure—the ethnographic knower. I announce my narrator in the text as coming to life as an extension, as an externalized wordy protrusion inseparable from the narrator in the flesh, albeit taking a radically different form. I am not making the absurd claim that no difference exists between a figure embodied as a walking, talking author and a wordy author-in-the-text. The claim is that as a continuum the figures constitute a singular participant in the collective action of ethnographic knowing. It is a claim made within epistemology—the study of how we can know we know—a claim about epistemic practice in ethnographic empiricism. I urge you to consider this bothersome work of learning to be a different sort of reader as necessary method work in order that we might recognize first-person experience empirics as epistemic practices.

Our ethnographic knowers here are equally the author-in-the-text and the reader-in-the-text.

Part of what I hope to achieve with this section is to urge you, dear reader-in-the-flesh, to consider how you constitute yourself as reader-in-the-text. I am asking you to attend to the ontological happening of yourself as reader-in-the-text. I am proposing the "I" of ethnographic empiricism as a singular particular knower constituted in the circuit of collective action—passing from an inchoate experience you have had to the composition of "an experience" in wording a story or in inferentially cognizing a story you have read. This "I the ethnographic knower" is like all other knowers (human and nonhuman) in that knowing necessarily expresses the tensions between realness experienced as "a happening to" in a particular here and now, and realness experienced in some "expressive outcome" of being in a here and now. That could be a definition of participation.

Focusing on this work brings to light a further concern in the practice of ontological constitution: the conventional formulation has that "I in the flesh" immediately experiencing buses and shouts, women and children as such: as things. Writing an ethnographic story as I articulate it here refuses the easy assumption that named things are immediately knowable as what they are. Significant ineluctable and unavoidable ontological work connects with words: buses as experienced and buses designated as buses. In their methods practices ethnographers need to explicitly and knowingly do this work. But more, they must recognize that the ontological constitution of entities—the knowers and knowns that will emerge in their story—that emerges is just one possibility among many. Good abductive ethnographic stories invite readers to do it differently.

"PHYSICAL STUFF" AS A LIVELY PARTICIPANT IN ETHNOGRAPHY

We find puzzling certain things about the process of experiencing. This is because we are not puzzled enough by the actuality that it is possible to have and to story experiences.[3] That is my maxim for this set of practices in negotiating the first tricky section in the passage from inchoate experience to a written ethnographic story.

I start by asking you to imagine a little old lady, the embodied me, ethnographic storyteller in the flesh, there in a bus, the journey happening to me and around me. Gazing out of the window most of the time, a chuckle my sole utterance during the journey. Imagining yourself into that body, you will understand that it was experience itself that was actually experienced by that embodied narrator.[4] She will later expand her experience of the experience of being a bus passenger by experiencing the wording of experience as she writes the story you have just read. That wordy reexperience of the experience of being a bus passenger is the focus of my next section. Here we imagine experience as a particular little old lady on a particular bus.

The inchoate, sensed beingness of sitting on a comfortable enough seat among others and being surprised when amusement erupts as noise from my throat was experience that happened to the embodied me. Recognizing physical stuff as a participant in the collective action starts by lingering in the journey as an inchoate experience of experience. I did not exit my experience of the journey when I exited the bus. The journey stayed in me and I in it; I played with my experience in my imagination, mostly trying to picture what had happened and when and how things were arrayed with respect to each other in the sequence of happenings, in order to identify some of the significant relations enacted in the event. I kept coming back to the collective laugh, my out-loud chuckle, instantaneous, not something that arose from thought or words. Knowing that the collective laugh happened was at the time simultaneously a knowing that racially inflected governance had happened and that it had been resisted and subverted. Recognizing that I had been moved by the collective action of this bus journey as a performance with a cast consisting of both nonhumans and humans, I delayed as I walked through the lush vegetation of a tropical university campus; literally I tarried in the twain of staying/leaving inchoate, sensed, noninferential knowing in (re-)experiencing experience.

This, my second set of practices, is more specific than the first set I sensitized you to. The beginning lies in recognizing that the ontological constitution of things that happen in a here-and-now is unknowably complex. The possibility for storying a happening begins by a delay in the experience as such. This delay has the ethnographic knower partially refusing the convention of empiricism. Orthodox "immediate empiricism" has truth about things as knowable "straight away" and without any conceptual mediation. Refusing this proposition, the ethnographic knower of my story accepts knowing that we know can be immediate: in experiencing experience as such, merely that I know is immediately knowable.[5] Conceptually, the ethnographic knower cannot know immediately precisely what she knows, or how she knows she knows. These are epistemic matters and lie on the other side of words and require conceptual mediation in inference.

DEPLOYED WORDS EFFECT THE RE-EXPERIENCE OF INCHOATE EXPERIENCE

So, how to carefully stop delaying in an inchoate experience of experience and start writing a story? In this process inchoate experience will become "an experience" and be forever changed as words strung together work like a palimpsest in the experience of experience—setting it in form. My habit in starting is to find someone who will be interested enough to listen to me tell a story. Not that I announce it as a first version of what will become an ethnographic story, although those who are my familiars by now often realize that they are being "used" as co–ethnographic knowers when they find themselves enduring yet another of Helen's tales. In the case of the story I tell here it was a young colleague in the Northern Institute who endured the first version of this story. She showed interest, was suitably outraged at the officer's behavior, and managed to politely change the subject by sympathizing about my undertaking long bus journeys in order to travel the short distance between the university and the city center. Of course, the story did not have the form it has now, but the disconcerting laugh as climax was there.

To dramatize what is at stake in this cluster of practices, I again ask my readers to imagine. Two women feature in my story, the narrator and the accomplished comic as the subject of the story, the latter an Indigenous woman speaking mostly in her first language except when she spoke two English words to great effect. She, along with her group, got off the bus a few stops down the road, and I imagined her and her companions heartily enjoying the moment again in their conversation. I have told my story in English, which designates distinct spatiotemporal entities that act in space and time. The entities designated in Australian Indigenous languages are quite other than those in English and are articulated as enacting quite different forms of being.[6] My reason for imagining this conversation is to remind you that the story could be told in infinitely many ways, including (of course, quite differently) in English. Imagine for example how the transit officers would word their English story; a very different story than I have told would ensue. The point is that there is no way to decide on "the truth" of one version or another. Each story is its own passage through the treacherous fog that separates wordlessness from wordiness.

Let me focus on that passage. To tell a story is itself an experience, and I propose it is the experience of negotiating an aporia. In this section I attempt to articulate what I know from feeling my way with this experience as I subject myself to its happening. I use words to express the rigors and difficulties of attempting to inhabit an a-wordy experience of experience while dwelling among words that at any and every moment threaten to drown that minimal and hard-won experiential capacity to be outside words. In composing I feel myself carefully selecting a way to proceed that will avoid inadvertently opening floodgates and finding myself carried off on currents that take me to places—topics of analysis—that I wish to evade.

It may be that you are unfamiliar with the term *aporia*, and perhaps, too, with the experience of negotiating aporia of the sort I describe in the previous paragraph. Coming to terms with the term while feeling your way into the experience I am gesturing at in writing *aporia*, is the imagining I am asking of you here. The etymology of *aporia* takes us back to stories of ancient Greek gods.[7] The figure who is the subject of those stories is Poros, said nowadays to be "the God of expediency," so a-poria is the state of not being able to work out what is expedient in this here-and-now. As I use the term here, *aporia* is being in a quandary about which word to use in order to effect a story that somehow plumbs the depths of what that experience means when it come to this analytic purpose.

Why is *aporia* a good term here, in telling this story about wording a story? What makes *aporia* useful for me is that in those old stories about Greek gods, Poros's mother, Metis, was a Titan known for cunning and wisdom. For me Poros and Metis provide an indissoluble link between journey, transition, crossing, resourcefulness, expediency. Here we are concerned with passage tracked across a chaotic expanse. A porotic way is never traced in advance; it can always be obliterated before one's eyes, and each time it must be traced anew in unprecedented fashion. In infernal chaotic confusion—in my case the infernal excess of words—the poros is the way out, the stratagem that allows escape from the always threatening impasse, associated always with an attendant anxiety. Effecting passage here—getting a story just so, after much redrafting—is not purification; the mess of the experience as experience is not left behind. It is there in the story, embedded in the strategies, the techne of the wordsmithing.

The story is an abductive generalization; it articulates a part of a vague whole, the world of public transport. But what comes next is contingent. In interpretation it could be used in generating an explanatory account, for example in mobilizing an actor-network theory account, revealing what it would take for an advocacy organization to challenge the bus company's ontological standard bus passenger. This would tell of actor-nets and their network strengths, showing how a particular society is assembled in a sociology of translation.[8] Another way to use the story would be to juxtapose it with another that I could tell involving a well-dressed German tourist, a woman about the same age as my Aboriginal copassenger. This would be to enact a social constructivist framing such as Strathern uses in reifying the object of ethnographic knowledge, juxtaposing a story of Hagen men displaying shells and pigs with a glimpse of the "retreating back" of her companion "humped with a netbag full of tubers, digging stick clasped over her head, a steep path in front of her, hurrying home."[9] The way I hope to use this story is neither of those. Rather, I hope to use the data that is the story in an interpretation that can intervene. The plan is to assemble many such situated truth claims in order to unearth a glimpse of the ontological work that "others" must do to enact difference in modernity.

PROTOCOL

- During fieldwork, cultivate a sensitivity to disconcerting happenings.
- When such a happening stays with you, compose a story of the experience orally and tell that story to a friendly listener.
- Write the story up as an ethnographic vignette, with the disconcertment (in my example the involuntary uttering of a chuckle) as the story's climax. In writing your ethnographic story attend to the three practices I elaborate below. When your story is complete you will have completed the first decomposing element of ethnographic analysis and assembled your data.
- To go beyond what I attend to in my text and put the data to work in making something of your story, first settle on the concept your story turns on. Perhaps you will need to rework your story when you have this.
- Identify the institutional or cultural milieu your story speaks to.
- Be explicit about your metaphysical assumptions; these will determine whether you make a universalizing, relativizing, or situating

knowledge claim about the salience of the happening that your story presents to the institutional or cultural milieu. (I usually write towards making a situated knowledge claim, although it is possible to write a story that can do both relativizing and situating epistemic work (see Winthereik and Verran 2012.)

NOTES

1. Northern Territory Government of Australia, "Transit Officers," last updated June 16, 2020, originally accessed October 8, 2018, https://nt.gov.au/driving/public-transport-cycling/bus-information,-safety-and-alerts/transit-officers/.

2. This is the dualistic self of the autobiographical philosopher in the Western tradition (see Wright 2006). Here "an Outer, rhetorical self, the literary, social, and/or psychological ego represented in texts as the source of one's identity [and authority]" (Wright 2006, 9), is set against an inner "self as referent of particular statements and actions, an internal (Inner) perspective of the self as active creator of one's statements and actions" (5). These two given or found entities, which are metaphysical commitments of such a philosopher, are separated by a "chasm [that] never collapses completely" (9).

3. Wittgenstein (1953). This is a misquote of "We find certain things about seeing puzzling, because we do not find the whole business of seeing puzzling enough" (212e).

4. See Dewey (1905). Dewey acknowledged that this claim that we experience seems "insignificant and chillingly disappointing . . . [in that it] just comes down to the truism that experience is experience, or is what it is" (399).

5. This claim is the one that Wittgenstein is making in the section of *Philosophical Investigations* (1953) from which I derive my maxim.

6. See Verran, the Yirrkala Yolngu Community, and Chambers (1989).

7. Sarah Kofman's "Beyond Aporia?" (1988) is my inspiration here. She takes Plato to task for leaving Metis out of the story of Poros, thus rendering philosophy as pure.

8. See Latour (2015).

9. See Strathern (1999), esp. 13 and 19.

CHAPTER 19

MARISOL DE LA CADENA
with the inspiration of
Mariano and Nazario Turpo
(and some feminist witches)

Not Knowing: In the Presence of . . .

If we keep on speaking the same language together, we're going to reproduce the same history. Begin the same old stories all over again. Don't you think so? [. . .] The same difficulties, the same impossibility of making connections. The same . . . Always the same.
—Luce Irigaray, *This Sex Which Is Not One*

We know, knowledge there is, but the idiot demands that we slow down, that we don't consider ourselves authorized to believe we possess the meaning of what we know.
—Isabelle Stengers, "The Cosmopolitical Proposal"

I was obliged to "not knowing" as practice with Mariano and Nazario Turpo—*with* indicates the togetherness that made "not knowing" a requirement in order to think ethnographically in their presence, physical or not. Presence is the relation within which "not knowing" happens, and in my particular case it includes the three of us: when it is "them," it also includes me. No separable "other" exists in this presence of which I am (and was) the writer. This paragraph condenses almost all that this short piece is going to be about, which includes what preceded it. I will start by briefly describing the latter.

I wrote *Earth Beings: Ecologies of Practice across Andean Worlds* (2015) motivated by (what I considered to be) "a peasant's archive"; Mariano was "the peasant" and "his archive" was a box of assorted documents: letters, receipts, telegram texts, minutes, fliers, newspaper clippings, and more recorded what I (using my main conceptual grammar at the time) thought about as "long years of peasant struggle against the landowner." (I had accessed the box through my sister and her husband; they worked at a nongovernmental organization in the area where the Turpos lived.) My idea was to write an ethnography of this archive—the practices that made it—and in so doing analyze the history the documents told and also discuss "archive" as a concept. When I first got to Mariano's village and talked to him about my idea, he went along with it. A few weeks into our practice he insisted on talking about what was not in the documents, which frequently would also escape history (for example, *tirakuna* [see Box 19.1] safekeeping the papers). At times he would even get annoyed when I insisted on learning from the documents. This "tug of wills"—Mariano's and mine—put at risk my initial ethnographic object of inquiry (the peasant archive and its historical promise) and offered an important ethnographic disconcertment (Verran 2001). Mariano's stories were beyond the limits of the possible; as such, they presented the classical situation that I could have translated through "culture" to explore "his beliefs." This translation would not have been ethnographically wrong; after all, interpreting belief is how we ethnographers know (more about this below). It would, however, have been inadequate to co-laboring. This ethnographic mode required a different *we*: not me with ethnographers, but me and the Turpos. Co-laboring required my categories and Mariano's stories even if they clashed—or as I learned, better if they clashed—for this would not stop the conversation. It would continue and yield unexpected possibilities and the unexpected as possibility!

BOX 19.1 TIRAKUNA

Tirakuna is the Quechua word for earth-beings; they can also be translated as mountains. *Runakuna* is the Quechua word for the people who, emerging together with tirakuna, form *ayllu*, another Quechua word. The Andean ethnographic record has translated it as the institution formed by a group of people who collectively own land. This translation separates subject (people) from object (land) and then connects them through the relation of "possession." Ignoring this definition, which is not wrong, was fruitful: it allowed me to think ayllu as the condition whereby runakuna *with* tirakuna take-place (as in, occur in time and space). To get here I had to start by ignoring mountains and people as nature and humans, and practice "not knowing" tirakuna: using culture, I could not access what they were that was not "belief"—and as Mariano insisted, what was to me (in this case) belief, was *not only* such. (More on *not knowing* and *not only* later.)

Co-laboring was my name for the practices among us (conversations, sensations, feelings, observations, intuitions) that composed a complex togetherness: a contact zone (Pratt 2007; Haraway 2016) in which we understood each other and did not understand each other. This second ethnographic mode, which I call "excess," was as important as understanding and could be simultaneous with it (see Box 19.2).

To get to excess, to sense it, I started with what I had—culture and belief—and sought to displace them. In the anthropological analytical habitus *belief* stands for what can be interpreted (it has meaning), but it cannot be known through empirical evidence because it lacks such. Thus, interpreting the meanings of belief is how what escapes modern epistemic knowledge emerges as known. A mirroring move is possible: "not knowing" can occupy the place that "meanings of belief" stands for, thus displacing it analytically and keeping it in view, relationally and as an analytic step, in order to reveal the process. I explain further: an analysis of the meanings of the Turpos' "beliefs," though adequate to anthropology, would have also left the Turpos' practices behind. Such analysis is insufficient to those practices when taken as not only belief, for they exceed "culture": those practices do and thus are in a way that is not only as the meaning(s) of beliefs. For example: What do you do with a narrative that makes what it tells, a form of storytelling that makes the event (and place) it narrates? What do you do when you ask what "something" is, and the response is that an answer cannot be provided because the answer would not be that "something"? What I did was to let what I was being told affect my analytic grammar, to make it vulnerable to the Turpos' presence, to their stories. I let them breathe relentlessly into my breathing space, making it also theirs, one and distinct at the same time. In that complex breathing space my categories were useful and also insufficient, hence exceeded. My practice was displacement, not replacement (Box 19.3).

BOX 19.3 DISPLACEMENT

I borrow *displacement* from Marilyn Strathern (1988). I also tweak it a bit to use it for what I call the "ontological openings" that may result from a disposition to co-labor with the situation at hand (what I mean by this will be clear momentarily). Displacement results from controlling, without canceling, (the practice of) categories, concepts, or analytics that may overpower, perhaps even kidnap the situation that is up for description. Strathern calls what results from this ethnographic practice "a better description"—one that also indicates the limits and therefore excesses of the displaced categories/practices that, while present yet controlled, cannot further explain away the situation in question, which remains opened to a "better description"—without closure.

Concepts do their work with other concepts: "culture" and "belief" had analytic companions. Their displacement also required displacing other categories: archive, peasant struggle, history, even indigenous. I used them without the power of modern epistemology—and with it, history—to impose requirements in order to decide what is (possible or impossible). Complicating my disconcertment was my early realization that nothing (words, deeds, movements, entities) observed the simplicity of "worlds apart." For one, we shared the history that had generated "Mariano's archive"; it was the history that "Mariano had struggled against," the struggle that I admired and had lured me to him. But history's terms (e.g., its requirement of representational evidence) did not exhaust Mariano and Nazario's terms; doing so—exhausting what they were insufficient for—was what those terms claimed. As required by co-laboring, I aimed at suspending those claims by practicing "not knowing."

"Not knowing" also proposed my conceptualization of excess as that which is beyond the limit of modern epistemological knowledge and its requirement of representation. It all started with Mariano's archive as a complex matter. At first sight it was a box with more than six hundred assorted documents put together by people from many paths of life. The texts, also the texture of the papers, told events that history could subscribe—they were the matter of history. But this object had also become through relations among runakuna with tirakuna, humans with earth beings. The box thus also was—and thus mattered—through conditions that did not leave a historical track. How to make sense of this was not obvious. Habituated to grant history the power to discern what is from what is not, and with culture within reach to explain the latter, my initial scholarly reflex was to separate Mariano from his archive. Mariano's stories would be cultural; the archives, historical. The separation would have even matched the grammatical form whereby a subject (Mariano) owns an object (his archive). Mariano insisted: we could read the papers in the box, but not only! (I still feel his impatience, see his hands moving in the air, as he told me, "You have not traveled all the way here to read what is inside that box, not if what you want is my story.") His insistence made present a matter that was not historical but may not have been without history. Hence neither one—history nor its excess—were to be discarded: they had both made "Mariano's archive" a complex entity for which I experienced my scholarly knowledge—taken seriously—as insufficient. Co-laboring the archive meant accepting it was not only such: an archive in the historical sense. What it was I did not know, perhaps could not know. Responding to this complex object (a historical archive that was not only such) and the circumstances that had made it proposed "not knowing" as a different form of knowing: one that accepts the challenges posed by that which it interrogates. Co-laboring created a fractal space where the Turpos' practices and mine overlapped and diverged: our conversations—also our being together—were, very tangibly, unevenly occupied by our respective understandings. It implied the composition of a "we" that maintained radically present the divergences that made our encounter: "we" would not have been able to converse without those divergences, or our conversation would have been another.

My guess is that this divergence is not infrequent as ethnographic experience; however, it is frequently ignored because acknowledging it would require slowing down habitual knowledge, thereby creating an ethnographic contact zone for "not knowing" that can be perplexing. The reflex is to resort to "knowing": it protects us, often trapping us in what Luce Irigaray calls "the same"—I will resume this last discussion as I close this section.

Co-laboring was certainly perplexing. It required me to acknowledge entities, events, circumstances that *were* but that I could not access with the tools that "culture" and "history" offered. I have already explained why this was the case; now let me add what might be obvious to the reader:

translating my friends' world-making practices into "beliefs" would have canceled co-laboring as an opportunity for a symmetry of practices precisely of the kind that history denied. Moreover, the reason I would have had for a translation into beliefs—lack of evidence—seemed out of place, for evidence there was—the problem was mine if I could not accept it as such! Emphasizing that I was the bearer of "lack," that it was *my* problem if I could not see-feel-sense what was (for example, "evidence," to follow the idea above), was a "classic Nazario move," and he did it humorously. Sometimes he would invent words in Spanish (in his bad Spanish) to mimic what I was saying (with my bad Quechua); this became an internal joke that made obvious our incommensurability and friendship—a unique relation. His humor—laughing at a situation that included all of us, our fractality, our "failures" at mutual understanding, our (im)possibilities—leveled the terrain intimately, if not structurally. Humor also eased my work into knowing in a different way: controlling the reflex to translate into belief what I found no evidence for, being careful with words because they could make what I uttered, and learning to ask questions as a relation proposed within the shared spaces we occupied.

"Not knowing" does not subtract; on the contrary, it has creative returns. The perplexity it produces may be used to control the habit to exercise what Stengers calls "epistemological right" (2000, 80). She uses this phrase to refer to statements that know before the experiment has spoken. If translated to ethnography, "epistemological right" would describe the habit to know better than our interlocutors, depending on who they are, even against what they say-do-know. It is intriguing to think that the exercise of "epistemological right" might be more frequent in ethnographic practice than in the experimental sciences: the experiment speaks epistemological languages; it is on a par with the researcher.

Instead anthropologists speak culture as analytic language and, as the anthropological adage goes, some of our interlocutors have it but do not speak its analytic language; when in such relation, what we know is that they believe.[1] This specific epistemological right includes an us-them distinction that also asserts its right to a position of hierarchical command. (I think of this as epistemism, the hierarchy-making twin of racism that, unlike the latter, remains uncontested and legitimate.) "Not knowing" undercuts this right. It assumes that all statements in such interlocutions may belong to the order of the possible (Savransky 2016) as events "yet to emerge" within modern knowledge (scientific and nonscientific) or as events that exceed the limits of modern knowledge. Hence "not knowing" can help perform onto-epistemic openings: it can be used to slow down the "givenness" of a notion (or an entity, or a practice) and interrogate it as a historical event (in Foucault's sense) so as to open possibilities for what this event (now historicized and therefore liberated from onto-epistemic "givenness" and excluding presence) might not contain, while perhaps also being part of it. Take "Mariano's archive" as the given. Then ask: What made a box with written documents an archive? The answer, naming just a few onto-epistemic conditions: history, the state and its practices (politics, law), the situations these recognize (property, peasants), our scholarly training (yours and mine). Occupied by these conditions, I thought the box as "Mariano's archive"; he in turn occupied it in a way that both coincided with and exceeded my conditions, and from this excess he insisted: tirakuna guarded the box and its papers, which then were with them, like runakuna were. Because he insisted—and Nazario helped me to attend to his father's insistence/excess—I yielded to the possibility that the box (that I had not hesitated to pronounce an "archive") could be not only a historical object. I then let the presence of excess (that which was unoccupied by "archive" and related material semiotics) affect my practice. It was not easy.

As ethnographic practice, "not knowing" meets the feminist assumption that knowledges come with the world they make. Donna Haraway (1988) is my obvious source of inspiration here. Elaborating on Marilyn Strathern's proposition that "anthropology uses relations to explore relations," Haraway also offered that "it matters what . . . thoughts think thoughts, what descriptions describe descriptions, what ties tie ties. It matters what stories make worlds, what worlds make stories" (2016, 12). It matters because scholarly knowledges make the worlds they know; they trap what they perform (Corsín Jiménez 2018).[2] They make their similar. This echoes Luce Irigaray's urge in the first epigraph above: if we repeat the categories that have made our history, even change becomes the same, within the same history. Also, within the same worlding practices: those that confirm reality through evidence of the empirical kind and impose the same requirement on others. "Not knowing" has the capacity to practice the requirement and *not only*, thus suspending the exclusion that the imposition enacts, or at least revealing its process. Not knowing as ethnographic practice *knows in divergence with the same* and escapes it as imposition while being through it.

Not only was a phrase Mariano repeated to make me aware of my inability to sense what escaped what and how I knew. It suggested "not knowing" as ethnographic (and friendship) relation: a fractally shared space where we did not know and also knew together.

"Not knowing" and "not only" are fellow travelers of what Marilyn Strathern called "negativities." That is, the mode of analysis she used to take into consideration the absence (in Hagen, her Melanesian fieldwork site) of certain categories and use such categorical absence to "create contrasts within our own language" (Strathern [1988] 1990, 16) and affect her analyses. Absences, she said, "create spaces that our analysis lacks" and can be used to "stop ourselves thinking about the world in certain ways" (16). I also use absences to affect our conceptual language, but I wish to do something else perhaps more prosaic. My use of negativities, particularly *not only*, wants to indicate that epistemic assertions make presences (for example, nature) that may (the conditional here is important) include the ontological denial, sometimes benevolent yet always imperative, of what exceeds them. The practice of these assertions, which I call "onto-epistemic," can make absent and impossible what does not fit them while also creating tolerable analytic room for those excesses (for example, through culture). Negative qualifiers at the site of denials—a negation of the negation— may work as tool to displace the assertion of what appears unquestionably as "given" and open possibility for the presence of what the assertion (of the given) makes either absent or impossible.

As a tool to perform onto-epistemic openings, "not only" is a device to halt knowing as usual and allow what we know as an archive or a mountain to emerge not only as such, and therefore through requirements that diverge from what makes them archive or mountain. "Not only" suggests that entities, or even the order of things, may also be other than what and how we know they are. It is not a formula to add known possibilities (not only happy, also unhappy) in order to make a list of things, or to denote conditions that combine into being something else (not only black, also white and thus mulatto). Rather, "not only" opens room for presences that could challenge what we know, the ways we know it, and even suggest our impossibility of knowing without such impossibility canceling those presences, for "not only" allows entities to both fold into and exceed each other: like Ausangate, the mountain and earth-being whose overlaps and mutual excesses made me think. Allowing for complex incommensurability, "not only" shares in the vocation of Strathern's (1991) "partial connections." Yet, in addition to stating that anything can be connected with anything else, it also wants to push against the historical onto-epistemic impossibility of some connections. In that sense "not only" proposes what John Law (2004) calls both/and situations, yet not necessarily to replace either/or—rather, to displace them. For example, "not only" works with Mariano's archive as a historical object as it (also) pushes against the impossibility of earth-beings guarding it. Together and in mutual excess, both made what I called Mariano's archive: a historical object and not only. In this specific case "not only" recognizes the empirical (that history needs) and works to open it up toward a divergent mode, which is not "abstract theory" either, yet can become with it. Thus "not only" arrests the analytic urge embedded in the practice of history that wants to cancel the eventfulness of relations, practices, or entities that do not meet the empirical conditions that modern epistemology currently requires in order to "abstract knowledge" from the objects it tests.

Allowing for divergence from modern epistemic knowledge while also being with it, "not only" positively asserts incompleteness. Thus this ethnographic tool for onto-epistemic openings also closes: it closes the prospect of notions, ambitions, and desires for completeness that may drive, for example, ethnographic data collection. Yet it also calls attention to practices (also the practices of notions) that demand completeness, for example, the forces that translate into singularity what Mol (2002) calls "multiple." Considering these forces, one of the tasks of "not only" is to make of singularity an ambiguous condition: "not only" might unsettle the imposition of singularity over multiplicity while maintaining it as possibility. On ending: "not only" and "not knowing" slow down the scholarly habit to use categories without inquiring into their historical worlding capacities. They do not carry dangers of ahistoricity—on the contrary.

PROTOCOL

First a caveat: *not knowing* is not equivalent to *I do not know* if this phrase implies that I will eventually know. In that case *I do not know* would be equivalent to *not knowing yet*. "Not knowing" is an analytic method—a way to practice analysis—not its result. Premised on "not only," it means that what you know (or might eventually know) might be exceeded by that which what you know (or might eventually know) cannot contain (both, as in comprise and control.)

Now the steps, not necessarily sequential. Perhaps it is better to think of them as suggestions to choose from:

- Identify the presences you want to think-feel with. This includes what you are intimate with, your most cherished concepts and ideas. Locate if possible where they are coming from and what other concepts and ideas they come with. This is like opening a black box and encountering a mess inside. Do not organize the mess; just treat it as an entangled piece of yarn impossible to gauge. Touch the knots, get familiar with them, but do not try to untangle them; just touch the connections they make. Same with the presences you are not intimate with: try touching them; feel the borders that keep them out of your reach.
- Make vulnerable your most cherished concepts and ideas. This will risk their becoming with and through those borders that for you seem to make the presences you are not intimate with. This will start the complex contact zone that I talked about above. Once there, begin your "not knowing"; for example, control your impulse to divide what emerges there into binaries (tempting among these might be "empirical" and "abstract," the former perhaps bifurcating into "real" and "unreal.") Let the contact zone be complex and you in it.
- Watch your analytic grammar: as modern scholars our default position (the one we do not think of) tends to be that of subject and object (that is, the specific relational form representation requires). We may want to suspend it (momentarily is fine) in order to think through the presences we co-labor with: Are they expressing another relational form?
- Co-laboring also means you are being co-labored, learning with and perhaps in divergence. This makes fieldwork about us as well: a complex "us" that includes what exceeds it. Co-laboring also places fieldwork always in the here and now of the presences it works with; "the field" is wherever those presences make you work (think and feel). Co-laboring makes co-presence the name of the game fieldwork is.
- Co-presence does not distinguish humans from nonhumans or other-than-humans. With the latter I refer to that which escapes the empirical and the abstract. I invented the hyphenated word.

Be ready to invent words—"not knowing" and "not only" may, at times, require it.

- As co-presence, fieldwork also shapes "ethnographic concepts," which you can think as concrete abstractions. This oxymoronic phrase refers to concepts that do not easily detach from what provoked them, or if they do, they continue to refer back to the here and now of their "conception." Ethnographic concepts evoke what Benjamin says of the story of the storyteller: "it preserves and concentrates its strength and is capable of releasing it after a long time" (1968, 90). An ethnographic concept preserves the strength of what made it; it is that localized strength that makes ethnographic concepts travel.

- "Not knowing" does not want to make "better knowledge" nor to "prove wrong" the knowledges from which it diverges. It can work with them without becoming them; it insists on "not only" as refrain. Both not knowing and not only are tools to hopefully make alliances in and across divergence. Remember the orchid and the wasp? (Deleuze and Guattari, 1987)

NOTES

1. Similarly, the exercise of epistemological right may allow "us" to know that animals do not think, plants do not feel, and rocks lack life.

2. I borrow this notion of trap from Alberto Corsín Jiménez (2018).

MELANIE FORD LEMUS AND
KATIE ULRICH

Questions, Experiments, and Movements of Ethnographies in the Making

We write as students of anthropology about to "go into the field." We have completed all of our coursework and exams, but even so we know that our training is far from over. In engaging with coursework and carrying out preliminary fieldwork thus far, we have grappled, like so many students of anthropology before us, with the various phases of assembling research projects. Part of this grappling extends from the accustomed process of generating ethnography—that is, the supposedly smooth transitions from first educating oneself about a project to developing research questions, initially arriving at one's field site, compiling fieldnotes and materials, and finally writing an analysis. These steps are easier said than done. The assumed certainty of this pedagogical structure fades as different research questions reveal new field sites, new field sites lead to different analyses, and new analyses coil us right back to generate even more research questions. Instead of following order we learn to find excitement and inspiration in inhabiting these constant coils, their interstices and nonlinearities. What we have written here is an attempt, as well as a reminder to ourselves, to explore nonlinearity in ethnographies in the making, that is, to embrace and seek out unconventional movement—where physical movements within a field site and conceptual movements of ethnographic analysis are constitutive of one another, rather than sequential. It is this sense of movement that we feel emerges from this volume. It offers a collection of methods for creating the conditions in which ethnographic analysis can be so transformative—so moving—of one's writing, thinking, and fundamental anthropological being.

Thus these chapters together seem less a list of protocols than a suggestion for a new movement of making ethnographies and ethnographic making. They posit ethnographic analysis as formative for and transformative of our anthropological selves.

The movement we have in mind does not start only with ethnographic analysis. As students we learn what is (and what was and what we hope will be) considered interesting, in part by becoming more familiar with contemporary and historical literatures. We learn what an "intervention" in the literature might look like. We learn what is at stake, theoretically and politically, in different kinds of questions and in the different manners of asking them. We also learn what is "askable" not only in terms of what is considered interesting enough but also in terms of our methodologies and ethical commitments. In other words, we have been learning how to ask questions—questions that have the potential to move us in particular directions.

Movement is crucial in moments of questioning. What has been perhaps most exciting in our training so far are the opportunities we have had to experiment not only with how to ask questions but also with how to engage the answers thrown back at us. In using the term *experiment*, we mean an exercise that consists of setting up certain conditions within which something interesting, unexpected, or perturbing can emerge. We acknowledge that the word *experiment* carries with it many sedimented connotations from colonial science to contemporary innovation. In using it here we take a cue from thinkers such as Michelle Murphy (2017b) who, while interrogating the role of experiments in colonial and postcolonial governance, also emphasized the radical potential of experiments for imagining and enacting worlds otherwise. As she says, when "invested in provoking an otherwise, experiment can be part of decolonial and other radical projects" (Murphy 2017b, 81). Likewise, for us, experimenting with the answers that ethnographic praxis returns to us is not simply a matter of trying out different answers to see how they sound. Experimenting with ethnographic insight is a skill that requires a degree of regimen. It entails the risk of not arriving at a predictable outcome, of not arriving at any one outcome that could have been imagined previously. In science studies literatures, scientific experiments have been described as a form of essentially structured fumbling and bumbling (see, e.g., Rheinberger 1997). This does not, however, mean that experimenting is merely undisciplined exploration or a broad scan. The skill required for good experimentation is the skill and care of introducing the right amount and the right kinds of structure and constraint for the particular context. As Kim Fortun (2009) has argued, constraint can be quite liberating. By pulling and tugging and squeezing some information in just the right way, what unexpected forms of understanding do we encourage to emerge? Thus we might turn to good experimentation as the condition of when something emerges that you did not even know you did not know; this emergence is often generated by purposeful and political attention that counters structures that maintain hegemonic, harmful, and prescribed research narratives. We see the ethnographic protocols in this volume as offering instruction on just this process, urging and stimulating such epistemic emergences or movements through analytic experimentation.

The analytic techniques presented in the chapters show that good experimentation in return generates more and new questions, not just reformulated answers. This prompted us to ask: Like the protocols in this book, what is the difference between a question and an experiment? What happens when we take two things that seem similar and ask how they are different? This very question could be taken as an experiment in itself. Questions like these pause experimentation. They allow one to get a foothold on something, suspending conceptual and analytic movement in order to allow something to congeal. Experimenting, then—for example, through following the protocols in this volume—might be how we introduce movement back into our questions in order to ensure that we do not take this pause for granted or naturalize it as a fixed part of reality. In this way experiments activate and enliven the structure of a question that has become too still in one's thinking: rather than simply asking, "Is this X or Y?" experimenting puts forward, "What happens when I consider X and Y as different?" Thus an experiment is a doing of a question, a way of introducing movement.

Our involvement as co-coordinators of Rice University's Ethnography Studio, established by Andrea Ballestero, has been a productive channel for this kind of experimentation. An intellectual space dedicated to stretching, consolidating, breaking down, and playing not only with our own fieldwork experiences but also the very design of ethnographic studies, the Ethnography Studio has inspired us and other participants to engage with experiment as an analytic and as a method. We see this collected volume as materializing (in written form) kinds of experiments similar to those of the Ethnography Studio. In other words, the ethnographic insights gathered here demonstrate not only how to ask questions in order to generate unexpected information but also, crucially, how to double down and in turn make something unexpected of this unexpected information. This means taking such unexpected information and moving in unexpected theoretical directions with it, rather than settling into theoretical frameworks anticipated beforehand. If immersement is a method that allows the unlooked-for to emerge (Strathern 1999, 3), such exercises and experiments, like those in this volume, can help one then do something with this unlooked-for—beyond slotting it into preexisting theoretical models. This moment is where the potential to provoke an otherwise emerges. Thus, this relation between immersement, fieldnotes, information, analysis, and so on is the movement of ethnographic experiment, the motility that makes ethnography something other than a report or description. We grappled with trying to label this phenomenon: Is it movement between different sites or along more of a continuous trajectory, perhaps one of increasing mediation? Are immersement, experiences, fieldnotes, raw data, information, analysis, analytic, and knowledge all different and processive "stages" or "sites" of what we do as ethnographers? We've come to a conclusion that ethnography lies not in these various forms—immersement, fieldnotes, information, analysis—but in the dynamically experimental relation between them.

Marilyn Strathern writes about this experimental relation, referencing anthropology's two "fields"—fieldwork and writing (or deskwork). With an emphasis on the production of content, Strathern shares that "In a world which thinks of itself as information-driven, there is always too much and too little data . . . The challenge is indeed to the breadth of information one wishes for. It is renewed in challenges posed by new perceptions of complexity" (1999, 4). These new perceptions of complexity arise when we begin to consider the genesis of our ethnographic material. We become involved in the new thoughts, analytics, and questions that arise with each letter, photograph, handout, or picture encountered in the field. A question unearths an answer that provides us with new directions in our studies and new analytics to think with. The protocols shared here continue to teach us about the important relation that dances between ethnographic dazzle and structure, one that "encourages fieldworkers to expect to intervene and to work reflexively and creatively with that intervention as part of the ethnographic process" (Murphy 2016, 442). As we embrace ethnographic moments as an enchanting effect that emerges from particular trajectories and collections of data, we suggest that the essays in this volume also emphasize the mutually dependent relationship, and false dichotomy, between fieldwork and deskwork (Ballestero, Campbell, and Storer 2015).

Although this might seem obvious, we often overlook the movement that brings us from our very first ethnographic question to the final material we produce through our own ethnographic experiments (that which gave us our better questions and our better ethnography).

In part this observation arises from our being PhD students trained in a traditional US program; it remains as creative as possible while still necessarily slicing the program into three main components—courses, fieldwork, and analysis and dissertation—knowing all the while that these separations are easier said than done (and not always useful). On the other hand, we recognize that the field is not solely time for collecting "raw" data (as if raw data could have ever existed) but a time of continuous stimulation and inspiration as well. The materials we have gathered through various thought exercises will be written altogether; we come to information through the time and relationships we find and create with the temporal and spatial dimensions from which these materials lend themselves to us. Fieldwork and deskwork always work in tandem.

Ultimately, for us as students preparing for our long-term fieldwork and what will follow, the techniques collected in this volume provide valuable tools we can take with us into the field and also back to the desk afterward, reminding us that this division is never certain. Experiments like those described in this collection are not in themselves the end result to ethnography; experimenting gives movement to our questions, it does not answer them. Experimenting can help keep questions open to the unsettled and the unsettling, even the beginnings of a radical otherwise. But this collection as a whole also does more. These ethnographic effects are not only illuminative in their individual content; in addition, taken together they provide an instructive space for considering what the ethnographic effect, not only as a protocol but also as a more general mode of doing ethnography, can look like. They not only instruct how to do experiments but also push us to pay attention to experimental design more broadly. That is, it's not only about simply following the protocols in a book like this, but learning how, in turn, to design our own such protocols—continuously challenging what ethnography can, and should, achieve.

Where Would You Put This Volume? On Thinking with Unruly Companions in the Middle of Things

As students in sociology we were always excited about the empirical seminars offered during a term. The research trainings were some of our favorites because of the excitement that would be generated by finding our own research topic, thinking about the kinds of methods we could use, exploring the field, reading the relevant literature, and developing a research question. At the beginning we were always amazed by how many ideas we came up with—ideas that all had different possible outcomes. There were always so many potentially interesting people to talk to and phenomena to observe, practices to dive into. Jotting notes, drawing, conducting interviews, recording sounds, or making videos were some of our data-producing practices. Sometimes we already had a precise idea of what we wanted to do and how we would go about our research; other times we just did not know. Still, within this playful space for learning and guessing, our term papers, and later our master's theses, somehow had to find their ways into disciplinary standards, a task we experienced as doing research about our objects and fields. In this afterword we draw on our experience as students to briefly problematize this approach as building on a particular take on the empirical. We then invite you as readers to engage in and be troubled by a different way of relating to the empirical and analysis that we think this book foregrounds. As student reviewers, we feel that this book generously presents itself as an unruly companion to ethnographic research.

Our first story deals with "aboutness" as a way of relating to and researching reality. It plays out in Germany between a student library, a hospital blood bank, and an ecovillage. As a way to prepare for our master's theses we made several visits to the library, browsing through books we thought might help us get started. Clément would read books on medical sociology and anthropology for his thesis about blood donation; Markus would read books on the sociology of architecture and infrastructures for his thesis about experimental building and living. Both of us eventually found plenty of resources for theoretical insights, and as students we also found it helpful to make use of the many handbooks about doing ethnography. They hold the promise—or so we thought—of giving us timely advice for accessing the field and starting early on with doing fieldwork, for example, how to best plan encounters, to situate ourselves well as ethnographers, or to outline good methods for collecting data. Out of our preparations for fieldwork came a sense of what a good research design might be and of what we could build on for different formats, be it for a seminar, a master's thesis, or a PhD proposal. We took from handbooks their ability to make us feel safe in how we could think of ordering different steps to go about our research—and only in that way would we keep a focused research track. After we spent some time browsing and borrowing books, bringing them home or reading them on the spot in the library, some feeling of being ready eventually took shape. The time felt right to go on with fieldwork.

Luckily, we found ways to move to our fields—a hospital blood bank in a big German city and an "Earthship" project close to a little German town. These movements, however, had unsettled our designs, and during and after fieldwork we were left with a different taste for things and a trouble: doing fieldwork did not quite fit the kind of work that our research designs seem to ask for. Rather, it constantly kept exceeding, deceiving, and reorienting what we had been expecting and preparing for. Although we felt that our "good designs" asked for approval of a reality "out there," we experienced fieldwork as a very different and messy activity. We started hesitating: Had the practice of researching actually been an effective mode of engagement for cultivating "good" ethnographies? What kind of moves, both physical and analytic, did this practice enable us to do? And what did it *not* allow for?

These questions kept haunting us after our respective fieldwork periods. Back at the desk we found it hard to hold still during analysis our time spent in the field. The "empirical" proved to be more slippery than expected: sometimes our memories, notes, drawings, or photos from the field were too talkative; sometimes they seemed too thin to make a point, or would not have anything to say in the moment. We wondered: How was it that our research designs did not help us further in that regard? We felt that somehow they made too little space for hesitation and failed to help us be attentive to the blurring of boundaries between analysis and the empirical during ethnographic fieldwork. For us the central question then became how to craft and inhabit a space for precarious and partial attempts to hold analysis and the empirical together.

This, we think, may require us to leave to the side for a little while "aboutness" as a way of engaging with reality. Aboutness, because it treats analysis and the empirical as separate entities in our designs, presses us to make a point, to draw a conclusion "in advance of the things" themselves. Instead we reminded ourselves of Anna Tsing's suggestion that to situate oneself "in the middle of things" (2015, 160) might be a virtue when it comes to ethnographic practice. Because such a positioning allows us to muddle through with others and does not properly conclude (278), situating ourselves in the middle of things brings the practice of analysis closer to the often unruly and always collective practice that constitutes the "empirical" in ethnography. It allows us to take such questions as the following seriously and as they come: How do we deal with the unmanageable amount and details of our data and with their complexity? How do we manage the heterogeneity of these data, their relevance for analysis? How do we hang on to surprises and serendipity that continuously happen while doing ethnographic fieldwork? It seems that, through situating ourselves in the middle of things, we see more possibilities emerge for learning how to become sensitive to what our research designs often make us overlook.

One way for us to experiment with this was through participating in an interdisciplinary workshop on time and temporalities at the University of Düsseldorf in 2016.[1] For this occasion we brought our two projects together and prepared a single presentation in which we tried to think through the differences of some of the temporal objects of our respective fields and how they come to matter. This process was a lot of fun and quite liberating: we were less bounded to speak separately about our field sites "out there," and at the same time we could engage with and think through some of the details and "excessive" materialities of our ethnographic data that otherwise would not have quite fit our research "objects." It felt liberating in a second sense as well: we did not need to have a last word about this exercise in ethnographic analysis. Rather, the relations we drew between some of our objects originated from the middle of our talks and fields.

Thinking about what it takes to do research in the middle of things durably changed our understanding of what we considered as our literary "companions"—here, the handbooks and guidebooks. Although they invited us to situate ourselves "in advance of things," some of our companions were meant to be good guides in the exercise of crafting ethnographic accounts about what we were likely to find "out there." But we were looking for a different kind of companionship—one that responds to how analysis may look in the middle of the "unruly realities" to which ethnographers are committed. Maybe we would need, likewise, an "unruly companion"?

This is the point where we think the contributions of this book can be very helpful and at the same time also be quite troubling at a moment where ethnographic analysis seems to become more blurred, vulnerable, partial, and contestable. At first we wouldn't be so sure about where to put this book on our shelves or where we would find it in a library. Would it be in the "methods" zone? Would it better fit "basics"? Maybe we put it in the "other" section or even open up a new category called "good to have and fun to read." Second, it was particularly difficult to imagine what our reactions would be in coming across such a book: Would we be interested? The many contributions would certainly have struck us, and we would have an idea about how to use them in different ways. They could serve all at once as a practical guide, as a tool for speculative-theoretical thinking about different fields and objects, or as a set of intimate, carefully written ethnographic stories about some of the epistemic troubles encountered along the way. In short, we could not tell where it should be put or what exactly it should be used for. And this, we thought, speaks to the unruliness of this collection and its pleasures.

One of the main takeaways of the book is its argument against the purity of ethnographic method and analysis. It tackles the idea that one can think in advance about the "right" ethnographic technique for the "right" research object as a kind of theory-informed methodology, or that both the research object and the technique could be somehow artificially kept separate, as the editors make clear in their introduction. It argues, rather, that ethnographic analysis and methods are particularly difficult to disentangle from what is usually called the "field," and that this "field" is hard to keep still at the "desk" during analysis. Turning this volume into an unruly companion means for us that a different kind of ethnographic engagement becomes not only possible but also specifiable, for example, through "thinking through" the multiple devices that are involved in coproducing ethnographic encounters: drawings, jottings, photographs, postcards, drafts, tweets, artifacts, meetings, and so on.

An unruly companion of this kind may not be the best guide toward any "fixed" outcome. But it shows us that intimacy, vulnerability, and partiality are constitutive of what it takes to pay attention in ethnographic practice and analysis. It invites us to follow those situations, events, and artifacts that made us hesitate in the first place about what next step to take—be it during fieldwork or back at the desk. Resonating with Isabelle Stengers's (2018) call to "slow down" your research through cultivating a sense for hesitation, for how analysis and the empirical might hang together in ethnographic practice, the stories presented in this collection are as many invitations to pay more attention to what happens between field and desk. In doing so the collection itself performatively foregrounds possibilities for nonconclusive analytic practices.

For us as students it can sometimes be difficult to make a break during our research projects and engage with analytic practices that might seem a bit "experimental." This reason may be why it can seem at first sight reassuring and more straightforward to go for standardized and clean designs. But we also are concerned by the idea that, for our research, this would have expelled all the fun and excitement of doing fieldwork and bringing analysis in close exchange with ethnographic practice. Instead, we discovered that complexity is not always a bad thing but rather a quite common experience with how we can know the world (Mol and Law 2002). If we didn't want to lose complexity for the sake of simplifying our findings, we needed to make time for elaborating in depth what might also be at stake. The contributions in this collection suggest such possibilities. And they do so in a very accessible way by proposing research protocols that hint at what it can take in practice to give some order to the messiness that surrounds us. In doing so the collection makes itself contestable, partial, and nonconclusive. "Try it out, collectively, and see what comes out" would describe well what is at stake in many of the contributions. It is in that sense that we understand the book you hold as a companion in cultivating an analytic sense of what it means to be in the middle of things.

NOTE

1. Heinrich Heine Unviersität Düsseldorf, "Programm," accessed August 16, 2020, http://www.geschichte.hhu.de/lehrstuehle/geschichte-der-fruehen-neuzeit /unsere-forschung/tagungen/relationen/programm.html/.

Abrahamsson, Sebastian. 2014. "An Actor Network Analysis of Constipation and Agency: Shit Happens." *Subjectivity* 7 (2): 111–30.

Abrahamsson, Sebastian, and Filippo Bertoni. 2014. "Compost Politics: Experimenting with Togetherness in Vermicomposting." *Environmental Humanities* 4 (1): 125–48.

Agar, Michael. 1986. *Speaking of Ethnography.* London: SAGE.

Ahmed, Sara. 2006. *Queer Phenomenology: Orientations, Objects, Others.* Durham, NC: Duke University Press.

Ahrens, Sönke. 2017. *How to Take Smart Notes: One Simple Technique to Boost Writing, Learning and Thinking—For Students, Academics and Nonfiction Book Writers.* North Charleston, SC: CreateSpace Independent Publishing.

Alvarez Astacio, Patricia. 2015. *Entretejido.* Watertown, NY: Documentary Educational Resources. DVD.

Alvarez Astacio, Patricia. 2015. "Moral Fibers: The Making of (Trans)National Fashions in Post-Authoritarian Peru." PhD diss., University of California, Santa Cruz.

Andézian, Sossie. 2001. *Expériences du divin dans l'Algérie contemporaine: Adeptes des saints dans la région de Tlemcen.* Paris: CNRS Éditions.

Archambault, Julie S. 2013. "Cruising through Uncertainty: Cell Phones and the Politics of Display and Disguise in Inhambane, Mozambique." *American Ethnologist* 82 (3): 392–411.

Ballestero, Andrea. 2015. "Theory as Parallax and Provocation." In *Theory Can Be More Than It Used to Be,* edited by Dominic Boyer, James Faubion, and George E. Marcus, 171–79. Ithaca, NY: Cornell University Press.

Ballestero, Andrea. 2019. *A Future History of Water.* Durham, NC: Duke University Press.

Ballestero, Andrea, Baird Campbell, and Eliot Storer. 2015. "What Can Twitter Do to/for the Field?" Platypus: The CASTAC blog. http://blog.castac.org/2015/11/twitter-field/. Accessed February 28, 2020.

Barad, Karen. 2007. *Meeting the Universe Half-Way: Quantum Physics and the Entanglement of Matter and Meaning*. Durham, NC: Duke University Press.

Barad, Karen. 2012. "On Touching—The Inhuman That Therefore I Am." *Differences* 23 (3): 206–223.

Barad, Karen. 2018. "Troubling Time/s and Ecologies of Nothingness: Re-turning, Re-membering, and Facing the Incalculable." *New Formations* 92: 56–86.

Bashkow, Ira. 2006. *The Meaning of Whitemen*. Chicago: University of Chicago Press.

Bataille, Georges. 1985. *Visions of Excess: Selected Writings 1927–1939*. Edited by Allan Stoekl. Translated by Allan Stoekl, Carl R. Lovitt, and Donald M. Leslie Jr. Minneapolis: University of Minnesota Press.

Bateson, Gregory. [1972] 2000. *Steps to an Ecology of Mind: Collected Essays in Anthropology, Psychiatry, Evolution, and Epistemology*. Chicago: University of Chicago Press.

Beaulieu, Anne. 2010. "Research Note: From Co-location to Co-presence: Shifts in the Use of Ethnography for the Study of Knowledge." *Social Studies of Science* 40 (3): 1–18.

Benjamin, Walter. 1968. "The Storyteller: Reflections on the Works of Nikolai Leskov." In *Illuminations: Essays and Reflections*, edited by Hannah Arendt, translated by Harry Zohn, 83–110. New York: Schocken Books.

Bennett, Jane. 2010. *Vibrant Matter: A Political Ecology of Things*. Durham, NC: Duke University Press.

Bernard, H. Russel. 2006. *Research Methods in Anthropology: Qualitative and Quantitative Approaches*. Lanham, MD: AltaMira Press.

Blumenberg, Hans. 2016. *Paradigms for a Metaphorology*. Translated by Robert Savage. Reprint edition. Ithaca, NY: Cornell University Press.

Boellstorff, Tom, Bonnie Nardi, Celia Pearce, and Tina L. Taylor. 2012. *Ethnography and Virtual Worlds: A Handbook of Method*. Princeton, NJ: Princeton University Press.

Borneman, John. 2012. "Incest, the Child and the Despotic Father." *Current Anthropology* 53 (2): 181–203.

Bradley, Richard. 2000. *An Archaeology of Natural Places*. London: Routledge.

Bratton, Benjamin H. 2016. *The Stack: On Software and Sovereignty*. Cambridge, MA: MIT Press.

Brecht, Bertolt, and John Willett. 1964. *Brecht on Theatre: The Development of an Aesthetic*. New York: Hill and Wang.

Brettell, Caroline, ed. 1996. *When They Read What We Write: The Politics of Ethnography*. Westport, CT: Bergin and Garvey.

Buck-Morss, Susan. 2002. *Dreamworld and Catastrophe: The Passing of Mass Utopia in East and West*. Cambridge, MA: MIT Press.

Burke, Tom. 1998. *Dewey's New Logic: A Reply to Russell*. Chicago: University of Chicago Press.

Cantarella, Luke, Christine Hegel, and George E. Marcus. 2019. *Ethnography by Design: Scenographic Experiments in Fieldwork*. London: Bloomsbury.

Charmaz, Kathy. 2006. *Constructing Grounded Theory: A Practical Guide through Qualitative Analysis*. Thousand Oaks, CA: SAGE.

Chen, Nancy N., and Trinh T. Minh-Ha. 1994. "Speaking Nearby." In *Visualizing Theory: Selected Essays from V.A.R. 1990–1994*, edited by Lucien Taylor, 433–51. Durham, NC: Duke University Press.

Cheng, Jesse. 2007. "Life Frontloaded: Advocacy, Anticipation, and Death Penalty Mitigation." PhD diss., University of California, Irvine.

Cheng, Jesse. 2010. "Frontloading Mitigation: The 'Legal' and 'Human' in Death Penalty Defense." *Law and Social Inquiry* 35 (10): 39–65.

Cheng, Jesse. 2017a. "Humanity's Subtensions: Culture Theory in U.S. Death Penalty Mitigation." *Social Analysis* 61 (3): 74–91.

Cheng, Jesse. 2017b. "Mitigate from Day One: Why Effective Defense Advocates Do Not Prioritize Liberty over Life in Death Penalty Cases." *Ohio State Journal of Criminal Law* 14: 231–45.

Choy, Timothy. 2016. "Distribution: Theorizing the Contemporary." *Society of Cultural Anthropology*, January 21. https://culanth.org/fieldsights/distribution.

Choy, Timothy. 2018. "Tending to Suspension: Abstraction and Apparatuses of Atmospheric Attunement in Matsutake Worlds." *Social Analysis* 62 (4): 54–77.

Christen, Kimberly. 2015. "Tribal Archives, Traditional Knowledge, and Local Contexts: Why the 's' Matters." *Journal of Western Archives* 6 (1). https://digitalcommons.usu.edu/westernarchives/vol6/iss1/3.

Classen, Constance. 1993. *Worlds of Sense: Exploring the Senses in History and Across Cultures*. New York: Routledge.

Classen, Constance. 1999. "Other Ways to Wisdom: Learning through the Senses across Cultures." *International Review of Education* 45 (3/4): 269–80.

Classen, Constance. 2005. *The Book of Touch*. New York: Berg.

Clifford, James, and George Marcus, eds. 1986. *Writing Culture: The Poetics and Politics of Ethnography*. Berkeley: University of California Press.

Collins, Samuel G., Matthew Durrington, and Harjant Gill. 2017. "Multimodality: An Invitation." *American Anthropologist* 119 (1): 142–53.

Conklin, Harold. 1980. *Ethnographic Atlas of Ifugao: A Study of Environment, Culture, and Society in Northern Luzon*. New Haven, CT: Yale University Press.

Corsín Jiménez, Alberto. 2010. "The Political Proportions of Public Knowledge." *Journal of Cultural Economy* 3 (1): 69–84.

Corsín Jiménez, Alberto. 2014. "The Right to Infrastructure: A Prototype for Open-Source Urbanism." *Environment and Planning D: Society and Space* 32 (2): 342–62.

Corsín Jiménez, Alberto. 2015. "The Capacity for Re-description." In *Detachment: Essays on the Limits of Relational Thinking*, edited by Matei Candea, Joanna Cook, Catherine Trundle, and Thomas Yarrow, 179–96. Manchester, UK: Manchester University Press.

Corsín Jiménez, Alberto. 2018. "Spider Web Anthropologies: Ecologies, Infrastructures, Entanglements." In *A World of Many Worlds*, edited by Marisol De la Cadena and Mario Blaser. Durham, NC: Duke University Press.

Corsín Jiménez, Alberto, and Chloe Nahum-Claudel. 2019. "The Anthropology of Traps: Concrete Technologies and Theoretical Interfaces." *Journal of Material Culture* 24 (4): 383–400.

da Costa Marques, Ivan. 2005. "Cloning Computers: From Rights of Possession to Rights of Creation." *Science as Culture* 14: 139–60.

Dalsgaard, Steffen. 2009. "Claiming Culture: New Definitions and Ownership of Cultural Practices in Manus Province, Papua New Guinea." *The Asia Pacific Journal of Anthropology* 10 (1): 20–32.

Dalsgaard, Steffen. 2010. "All the Government's Men." PhD diss., Aarhus University.

Dalsgaard, Steffen. 2016. "The Ethnographic Use of Facebook in Everyday Life." *Anthropological Forum* 26 (1): 96–114.

Dalsgaard, Steffen, and Morten Nielsen, eds. 2015. *Time and the Field.* New York: Berghahn.

Dányi, Endre. 2012. "Parliament Politics: A Material-Semiotic Analysis of Liberal Democracy." PhD diss., Lancaster University.

Dányi, Endre. 2013. "Democracy in Ruins: The Case of the Hungarian Parliament." In *The Inhabited Ruins of Central Europe: Re-Imagining Space, History and Memory*, edited by Dariusz Gafijczuk, and Derek Sayer, 55–78. Basingstoke, UK: Palgrave Macmillan.

Dányi, Endre. 2015. "The Parliament as a High-Political Programme." In *Architecture, Materiality and Society: Connecting Sociology of Architecture with Science and Technology Studies*, edited by Anna-Lisa Müller and Werner Reichmann, 99–118. Basingstoke, UK: Palgrave Macmillan.

Dányi, Endre. 2017. "Walking as Knowing and Interfering." *Aggregate* 3, June 12. Accessed February 19, 2020. http://we-aggregate.org/piece/walking-as-knowing-and-interfering.

Dányi, Endre. 2018. "The Things of the Parliament." In *Soziologie Der Parlamente*, edited by Jenni Brichzin, Damien Krichewsky, Leopold Ringel, and Jan Schank, 267–85. Wiesbaden, Germany: Springer vs.

Das, Veena. 2018. "Analysis: Between the Empirical and the Conceptual." *Social Analysis* 62 (1): 9–11.

Daston, Lorraine, and Peter Galison. 1992. "The Image of Objectivity." *Representations* 40: 81–128.

Dattatreyan, Ethiraj G., and Isaac Marrero-Guillamón. 2019. "Introduction: Multimodal Anthropology and the Politics of Invention." *American Anthropologist* 121 (1): 220–28.

Davies, Gail, Beth Greenhough, Pru Hobson-West, and Robert G. W. Kirk. 2018. "Science, Culture, and Care in Laboratory Animal Research: Interdisciplinary Perspectives on the History and Future of the 3Rs." *Science, Technology, and Human Values*, 43 (4): 603–21.

de la Cadena, Marisol. 2015. *Earth Beings: Ecologies of Practice across Andean Worlds.* Durham, NC: Duke University Press.

Deleuze, Gilles. [1980] 1991. *Bergsonism.* New York: Zone Books.

Deleuze, Gilles, and Félix Guattari. 1987. *A Thousand Plateaus: Capitalism and Schizophrenia*. Minneapolis: University of Minnesota Press.

Deleuze, Gilles, and Melissa McMuhan. 1988. "The Brain Is the Screen: Interview with Gilles Deleuze on 'The Time-Image.'" *Discourse* 20 (3): 47–55.

Deville, Joe, Michael Guggenheim, and Zuzana Hrdličkova. 2016. *Practising Comparison*. Manchester, UK: Mattering Press.

Dewey, John. 1905. "The Postulate of Immediate Empiricism." *Journal of Philosophy, Psychology and Scientific Methods* 2 (15): 393–99.

Dewey, John. 1938. *Logic: The Theory of Inquiry*. New York: Henry Holt.

Drew, David. 1992. *Postcards from the Planets*. Oxford: Rigby.

Driessen, Annelieke, and Rebecca Ibáñez Martín. 2020. "Attending to Difference: Enacting Individuals in Food Provision for Residents with Dementia." *Sociology of Health and Illness* 42 (2): 247–61.

Dumit, Joseph. 2014. "Writing the Implosion: Teaching the World One Thing at a Time." *Cultural Anthropology* 29 (2): 344–62.

Dumit, Joseph. 2017. "Notes Toward Critical Ethnographic Scores: Anthropology and Improvisation Training in a Breached World." In *Between Matter and Method: Encounters in Anthropology and Art*, edited by Gretchen Bakke, and Marina Peterson, 51–58. New York: Bloomsbury Academic.

Dumit, Joseph. Forthcoming. "Bromine: A Substance as Method Investigation." In *Reactivating Elements. Substance, Process, and Practice from Chemistry to Cosmology*, edited by Dimitris Papadopoulos, Maria Puig de la Bellacasa, and Natasha Myers. Durham, NC: Duke University Press.

Dumit, Joseph, Kevin O'Connor, Duskin Drum, and Sarah McCollough. 2018. "Improvisation." *Society of Cultural Anthropology*, March 29. https://staging.culanth.org/fieldsights/improvisation.

Durán, Gloria G., and Alan W. Moore. 2015. "La Tabacalera of Lavapiés: A Social Experiment or a Work of Art?" FIELD: *A Journal of Socially-Engaged Art Criticism* 2: 49–75.

Engelmann, Lukas, Caroline Humphrey, and Christos Lynteris. 2016. "Diagrammatic: Beyond Inscription?" Paper presented at conference held at the Centre for Research in the Arts, Social Sciences and Humanitices (CRASSH), December 2–3, Cambridge. http://www.crassh.cam.ac.uk/events/26782.

Estalella, Adolfo, and Tomas Sanchez Criado, eds. 2018. *Experimental Collaborations: Ethnography through Fieldwork Devices*. New York: Berghahn.

Ewen, Stuart. 1990. *All Consuming Images: The Politics of Style in Contemporary Culture*. New York: Basic Books.

Fabian, Johannes. 2002. "Virtual Archives and Ethnographic Writing: 'Commentary' as a New Genre?" *Current Anthropology* 43 (5): 775–86.

Fabian, Johannes. 2008. *Ethnography as Commentary: Writing from the Virtual Archive*. Durham, NC: Duke University Press.

Feld, Steven. 1996. "Waterfalls of Song: An Acoustemology of Place Resounding in Bosavi, Papua New Guinea." In *Senses of Place*, edited by Steven Feld and Keith H. Basso, 91–135. Santa Fe, NM: School of American Research Press.

Flores, Jorge A. 1968. *Alpacas y Cuyes en la Etnografía Andina*. Puno, Perú: Universidad Nacional del Altiplano y Editorial Horizonte.

Fortun, Kim. 2009 "Figuring Out Ethnography." In *Fieldwork Is Not What It Used to Be*, edited by James D. Faubion and George E. Marcus, 167–83. Ithaca, NY: Cornell University Press.

Foucault, Michel. 1969. *The Archaeology of Knowledge*. Abingdon, UK: Routledge.

Foucault, Michel. 1977. "The Confession of the Flesh." In *Power/Knowledge: Selected Interviews and Other Writings 1972–1977*, edited by Colin Gordon, 194–228. New York: Pantheon.

Freire, Paulo. 1967. *Educação como prática da liberdade*. Rio de Janeiro: Paz e Terra.

Freire, Paulo. 2000. *Pedagogy of the Oppressed*. New York: Continuum.

Freire, Paulo. 2013. *Education for Critical Consciousness*. London: Bloomsbury Academic.

Fukuyama, Francis. 1992. *The End of History and the Last Man*. New York: Free Press.

Gan, Elaine. 2017. "An Unintended Race: Miracle Rice and the Green Revolution." *Environmental Philosophy* 14 (1): 61–81.

Gan, Elaine, and Anna Tsing. 2018. "How Things Hold: A Diagram of Coordination in a Satoyama Forest." *Social Analysis* 62 (4): 102–45.

Geertz, Clifford. 2000. *Available Light: Anthropological Reflections on Philosophical Topics*. Princeton, NJ: Princeton University Press.

Gentner, Dedre. 1983. "Structure-Mapping: A Theoretical Framework for Analogy." *Cognitive Science* 7 (2): 155–70.

Geurts, Kathryn L. 2002. *Culture and the Senses: Bodily Ways of Knowing in an African Community*. Berkeley: University of California Press.

Gibson, James J. [1979] 2015. *The Ecological Approach to Visual Perception*. New York: Taylor and Francis.

Ginsburg, Faye. 1995. "The Parallax Effect: The Impact of Aboriginal Media on Ethnographic Film." *Visual Anthropology Review* 11 (2): 64–76.

Goffman, Erving. 1959. *The Presentation of Self in Everyday Life*. New York: Anchor.

Green, William S., and Patrick W. Jordan, eds. 2002. *Pleasure with Products: Beyond Usability*. London: Taylor and Francis.

Gugganig, Mascha. 2017. "Postcards and Ethnography." Colleex, July 28. Accessed July 30, 2020. https://colleex.wordpress.com/colleex-open-formats/postcards-and-ethnography/.

Gugganig, Mascha, and Sophie Schor. 2020. "Teaching (with) Postcards: Approaches in the Classroom, the Field, and the Community." *Teaching Anthropology* 9 (2): 56–65.

Guha, Ranajit. 2003. *History at the Limit of World-History*. New York: Columbia University Press.

Gupta, Akhil, and James Ferguson. 1997. "Culture, Power, Place: Ethnography at the End of an Era." In *Culture, Power, Place: Explorations in Critical Anthropology*, edited by Akhil Gupta and James Ferguson, 1–32. Durham, NC: Duke University Press.

Guyer, Jane I. 2013. "'The Quickening of the Unknown': Epistemologies of Surprise in Anthropology: The Munro Lecture, 2013." *HAU: Journal of Ethnographic Theory* 3 (3): 283–307.

Guyer, Jane I. 2014. "Quickening the Unknown." *HAU: Journal of Ethnographic Theory.*

Hahlo, Richard, and Peter Reynolds. 2000. *How to Run a Successful Workshop.* London: Faber and Faber.

Halstead, Narmala. 2008. "Introduction: Experiencing the Ethnographic Present: Knowing through 'Crisis.'" In *Knowing How to Know: Fieldwork and the Ethnographic Present*, edited by Narmala Halstead, Eric Hirsch, and Judith Okely, 1–20. New York: Berghahn.

Halstead, Narmala, Eric Hirsch, and Judith Okely, eds. 2008. *Knowing How to Know: Fieldwork and the Ethnographic Present.* New York: Berghahn.

Hamilton, Dotty. 2014. "Appetite and Aroma: Visual Imagery and the Perception of Taste and Smell in Contemporary Korean Film." In *Food on Film: Bringing Something New to the Table*, edited by Tom Hertweck, 125–40. London: Rowman & Littlefield.

Hammersley, Martyn, and Paul Atkinson. 1995. *Ethnography: Practices and Principles.* New York: Routledge.

Haraway, Donna. 1985. "A Manifesto for Cyborgs: Science, Technology, and Socialist Feminism in the 1980s." *Socialist Review* 15 (2): 65–107.

Haraway, Donna. 1988. "Situated Knowledges: The Science Question in Feminism and the Privilege of Partial Perspective." *Feminist Studies* 14 (3): 575–99.

Haraway, Donna. 1989. *Primate Visions: Gender, Race and Nature in the World of Modern Science.* London: Routledge.

Haraway, Donna. 2003. *The Companion Species Manifesto: Dogs, People, and Significant Otherness.* Chicago: Prickly Paradigm.

Haraway, Donna. 2008. *When Species Meet.* Minneapolis: University of Minnesota Press.

Haraway, Donna. 2016. *Staying with the Trouble: Making Kin in the Chthulucene.* Durham, NC: Duke University Press.

Harding, Sandra. 2015. "Objectivity for Sciences from Below." In *Objectivity in Science*, edited by Flavia Padovani, Jonathan Y. Tsou, and Alan Richarson, 35–55. New York: Springer.

Hastrup, Kirsten, and Peter Hervik, eds. 1994. *Social Experience and Anthropological Knowledge.* London: Routledge.

Hayward, Eva. 2010. "Fingereyes: Impressions of Cup Corals." *Cultural Anthropology* 25 (4): 577–99.

Hegel, Christine, Luke Cantarella, and George E. Marcus. 2019. *Ethnography by Design: Scenographic Experiments in Fieldwork.* London: Bloomsbury.

Heidegger, Martin. 1977. *The Question Concerning Technology and Other Essays.* New York: Garland.

Helmreich, Stefan. 2007. "An Anthropologist Under Water: Immersive Soundscapes, Submarine Cyborgs, and Transductive Ethnography." *American Ethnologist* 344 (4): 621–64.

Helmreich, Stefan. 2009. *Alien Ocean: Anthropological Voyages in Microbial Seas.* Berkeley: University of California Press.

Helmreich, Stefan. 2013. "Potential Energy and the Body Electric: Cardiac Waves, Brain Waves, and the Making of Quantities into Qualities." *Current Anthropology* 54 (S7): S139–S148.

Herzfeld, Michael. 1989. *Anthropology through the Looking-Glass: Critical Ethnography in the Margins of Europe.* Cambridge: Cambridge University Press.

Hoddeson, Lillian. 1981. "The Emergence of Basic Research in the Bell Telephone System, 1875–1915." *Technology and Culture* 22: 512–45.

Hodson, Elizabeth A. 2016. "Drawing the Anthropological Imagination." Paper presented at Lab 001 at Association of Social Anthropologists of the UK and Commonwealth (ASA) 2016: Footprints and Futures: The Time of Anthropology. Durham University, July 4–7. https://www.nomadit.co.uk/asa /asa2016/panels.php5?PanelID=4668.

Hoffman, Katherine E. 2009. "Culture as Text: Hazards and Possibilities of Geertz's Literary/Literacy Metaphor." *The Journal of North African Studies* 14 (3–4): 417–30.

Hogan, Mél. 2015. "Data Flows and Water Woes: The Utah Data Center." *Big Data and and Society* 2 (2): 1–12.

Holbraad, Martin, Sarah Green, Alberto Corsín Jiménez, Veena Das, Nurit Bird-David, Eduardo Kohn, Ghassan Hage, Laura Bear, Hannah Knox, and Bruce Kapferer. 2018. "What Is Analysis?" *Social Analysis* 62 (1): 1–30.

Holmes, Douglas R., and George E. Marcus. 2005. "Cultures of Expertise and the Management of Globalization: Toward the Re-functioning of Ethnography." In *Global Assemblages: Technology, Politics, and Ethics as Anthropological Problems,* edited by Aihwa Ong and Stephen J. Collier, 235–52. London: Blackwell.

Holmes, Douglas R., and George E. Marcus. 2008. "Collaboration Today and the Re-Imagination of the Classic Scene of Fieldwork Encounter." *Collaborative Anthropologies* 1 (1): 81–101.

Howes, David. 1991. *The Varieties of Sensory Experience: A Sourcebook in the Anthropology of the Senses.* Toronto: University of Toronto Press.

Howes, David. 2005. "HYPERSTHESIA, or, The Sensual Logic of Late Capitalism." In *The Empire of the Senses: The Sensual Culture Reader,* edited by David Howes, 281–303. New York: Berg.

Hu, Tung-Hui. 2015. *A Pre-History of the Cloud.* Cambridge, MA: MIT Press.

Hustak, Carla, and Natasha Myers. 2012. "Involutionary Momentum: Affective Ecologies and the Sciences of Plant/Insect Encounters." *Differences: A Journal of Feminist Cultural Studies* 23 (5): 74–118.

Ibáñez Martín, Rebecca, and Marianne de Laet. 2018. "Geographies of Fat Waste: Or, How Kitchen Fats Make Citizens." *The Sociological Review* 66 (3): 700–717.

Ingold, Tim. 2000. *The Perception of the Environment: Essays on Livelihood, Dwelling and Skill.* London: Routledge.

Irigaray, Luce. 1985. *This Sex Which Is Not One.* Ithaca, NY: Cornell University Press.

Jacknis, Ira. 1985. "Franz Boas and Exhibits." In *Objects and Others: Essays on Museums and Material Culture*, edited by George Stocking, 75–111. Madison: University of Wisconsin Press.

Jensen, Casper B., and Anders Blok. 2013. "Techno-animism in Japan: Shinto Cosmograms, Actor-Network Theory, and the Enabling Powers of Non-human Agencies." *Theory, Culture and Society* 30 (2): 84–115.

Jensen, Casper B., Barbara Herrnstein Smith, G. E. R. Lloyd, Martin Holbraad, Andreas Roepstorff, Isabelle Stengers, Helen Verran, Steven D. Brown, Brit Ross Winthereik, Marilyn Strathern, Bruce Kapferer, Annemarie Mol, Morten Axel Pedersen, Eduardo Viveiros de Castro, Matei Candea, Debbora Battaglia, and Roy Wagner. 2011. "Introduction: Contexts for a Comparative Relativism." *Common Knowledge* 17 (1): 1–12.

Jones, Graham M. 2010. "Modern Magic and the War on Miracles in French Colonial Culture." *Comparative Studies in Society and History* 52 (1): 66–99.

Jones, Graham M. 2011. *Trade of the Tricks: Inside the Magician's Craft*. Berkeley: University of California Press.

Jones, Graham M. 2017. *Magic's Reason: An Anthropology of Analogy*. Chicago: University of Chicago Press.

Kapferer, Bruce. 2017. "What Is Analysis: Between Theory, Ethnography and Method." Paper presented at the American Anthropological Association Conference, Washington, DC, November 29–December 3.

Kelly, José A. 2012. "Figure Ground Dialectics in Yanomami, Yekuana and Piaroa Myth and Shamanism." In *The Culture of Invention in the Americas: Anthropological Experiments with Roy Wagner*, edited by Pedro Pitarch and José A. Kelly, 233–52. Canon Pyon, UK: Sean Kingston Publishing.

Kelty, Christopher M. 2009. "Collaboration, Coordination, and Composition: Fieldwork after the Internet." In *Fieldwork Is Not What It Used to Be: Learning Anthropology's Method in a Time of Transition*, edited by George E. Marcus and James D. Faubion, 184–206. Ithaca, NY: Cornell University Press.

Kennedy, Helen, Rosemary Lucy Hill, Giorgia Aiello, and William Allen. 2016. "The Work That Visualisation Conventions Do." *Information Communication and Society* 19 (6): 715–35.

Kofman, Sarah. 1988. "Beyond Aporia?" In *Post-structuralist Classics*, edited by Andrew Benjamin, 7–44. New York: Routledge.

Korsby, Trine M. 2015. "Hustlers of Desire: Transnational Pimping and Body Economies in Eastern Romania." PhD diss., University of Copenhagen.

Korsby, Trine M. 2017. "The Brothel Phone Number: Infrastructures of Transnational Pimping in Eastern Romania." *Cambridge Journal of Anthropology* 35 (2): 111–24.

Korsby, Trine M., and Anthony Stavrianakis. 2016. "Moments in Collaboration: Experiments in Concept Work." *Ethnos: Journal of Anthropology* 83 (1): 39–57.

Kowal, Emma, Joanna Radin, and Jenny Reardon. 2013. "Indigenous Body Parts, Mutating Temporalities, and the Half-lives of Postcolonial Technoscience." *Social Studies of Science* 43 (4): 465–83.

Kulick, Don, and Margaret Willson, eds. 1995. *Taboo: Sex, Identity and Erotic Subjectivity in Anthropological Fieldwork*. London: Routledge.

Lassiter, Luke E. 2005a. *The Chicago Guide to Collaborative Ethnography*. Chicago: University of Chicago Press.

Lassiter, Luke E. 2005b. "Collaborative Ethnography and Public Anthropology." *Current Anthropology* 46 (1): 83–106.

Latour, Bruno. 1987. *Science in Action: How to Follow Scientists and Engineers through Society*. Cambridge, MA: Harvard University Press.

Latour, Bruno. 1993. *We Have Never Been Modern*, translated by Catherine Porter. Cambridge, MA: Harvard University Press.

Latour, Bruno. 1999. "Circulating Reference: Sampling the Soil in the Amazon Forest Pandora's Hope: Essays on the Reality of Science Studies." In *Pandora's Hope: Essays on the Reality of Science Studies*, edited by Bruno Latour, 24–79. Cambridge, MA: Harvard University Press.

Latour, Bruno. 2005. *Reassembling the Social: An Introduction to Actor-Network-Theory*. Oxford: Oxford University Press.

Latour, Bruno. 2009. "Will Non-Humans Be Saved? An Argument in Ecotheology." *Journal of the Royal Anthropological Institute* 15 (3): 459–75.

Latour, Bruno, and Peter Weibel. 2002. *Iconoclash*. Cambridge, MA: MIT Press.

Lave, Jean. 2011. *Apprenticeship in Critical Ethnographic Practice, Lewis Henry Morgan Lectures: 1993*. Chicago: University of Chicago Press.

Law, John. 2004. *After Method: Mess in Social Science Research*. Abingdon, UK: Routledge.

Law, John. 2015. "What's Wrong with a One-World World?" *Distinktion: Scandinavian Journal of Social Theory* 16 (1): 126–39.

Law, John, and Annemarie Mol. 2002. *Complexities: Social Studies of Knowledge Practices*. Durham, NC: Duke University Press.

LeCompte, Margaret Diane, and Jean J. Schensul. 1999. *Designing and Conducting Ethnographic Research*. Plymouth, UK: Rowman Altamira.

Leder Mackley, Kerstin, and Sarah Pink. 2013. "From Emplaced Knowing to Interdisciplinary Knowledge: Sensory Ethnography in Energy Research." *Senses and Society* 8 (3): 335–53.

Lenoir, Timothy. 1998. *Inscribing Science: Scientific Texts and the Materiality of Communication*. Stanford, CA: Stanford University Press.

Lupton, Deborah. 2013. "Infant Embodiment and Interembodiment: A Review of Sociocultural Perspectives." *Childhood* 20 (1): 37–50.

Madianou, Mirca, and Daniel Miller. 2012. "Polymedia: Towards a New Theory of Digital Media in Interpersonal Communication." *International Journal of Cultural Studies* 16 (2): 169–87.

Maguire, James. 2017. *Icelandic Geopower: Accelerating and Infrastructuring Energy Landscapes*. PhD diss., no. 133, IT-University of Copenhagen.

Mann, Anna. 2018. "Ordering Tasting in a Restaurant: Experiencing, Socializing, and Processing Food." *The Senses and Society* 13 (2): 135–46.

Mann, Anna, and Annemarie Mol. 2018. "Talking Pleasures, Writing Dialects: Outlining Research on *Schmecka*." *Ethnos: Journal of Anthropology* 84 (5):

772–88. doi.org/10.1080/00141844.2018.1486334. Accessed February 19, 2020.

Marcus, George E. 2012. "The Legacies of Writing Culture and the Near Future of Ethnographic Form: A Sketch." *Cultural Anthropology* 27 (3): 427–45.

Marcus, George E., and Michael M. J. Fischer. [1986] 1999. *Anthropology as Cultural Critique: An Experimental Moment in the Human Sciences.* Chicago: University of Chicago Press.

Marks, Laura U 2000. *The Skin of the Film: Intercultural Cinema, Embodiment, and the Senses.* Durham, NC: Duke University Press.

Marks, Laura U. 2015. *Hanan al-Cinema: Affections for the Moving Image.* Cambridge, MA: MIT Press.

Marks, Laura U. 2016. "Real Images Flow: Mullâ Sadrâ Meets Film-Philosophy." *Film-Philosophy* 20 (1): 24–46.

Massey, Doreen. 1994. *Space, Place and Gender.* Cambridge: Polity Press.

Massumi, Brian. 2011. *Semblance and Event: Activist Philosophy and the Occurrent Arts.* Cambridge, MA: MIT Press.

Mather, Charles. 2014. "Avian Influenza Multiple: Enacting Realities and Dealing with Policies in South Africa's Farmed Ostrich Sector." *Journal of Rural Studies* 33: 99–106.

Mazzio, Carla. 2005. "The Senses Divided: Organs, Objects, and Media in Early Modern England." In *The Empire of the Senses: The Sensual Culture Reader,* edited by David Howes, 85–105. New York: Berg.

McCarthy, Tom. 2015. *Satin Island.* New York: Knopf.

McCosker, Anthony, and Rowan Wilkin. 2014. "Rethinking 'Big Data' as Visual Knowledge: The Sublime and the Diagrammatic in Data Visualisation." *Visual Studies* 29 (2): 155–64.

McGranahan, Carole. 2018. "Ethnography Beyond Method: The Importance of an Ethnographic Sensibility." *Sites: A Journal of Social Anthropology and Cultural Studies* 15 (1): 1–10.

McLuhan, Marshall. 2005. "Inside the Five Sense Sensorium." In *Empire of the Senses: The Sensual Culture Reader,* edited by David Howes. New York: Berg.

Melhuus, Marit, Jon P. Mitchell, and Helena Wulff. 2009. *Ethnographic Practice in the Present.* Oxford: Berghahn.

Mialet, Hélène. 2012. *Hawking Incorporated: Stephen Hawking and the Anthropology of the Knowing Subject.* Chicago: University of Chicago Press.

Mignolo, Walter. 2000. *Local Histories/Global Designs: Coloniality, Subaltern Knowledges, and Border Thinking.* Princeton, NJ: Princeton University Press.

Mills, C. Wright. [1959] 2000. "On Intellectual Craftsmanship." In *The Sociological Imagination,* 195–226. Oxford: Oxford University Press.

Mol, Annemarie. 1992. "Migreren en mengen. Over waarnemen, handelen en taal." In *De rol van de intellectueel. Een discussie over distantie en betrokkenheid,* edited by Lolle Nauta and Gerard de Vries, 128–42. Amsterdam: Van Gennep.

Mol, Annemarie. 2002. *The Body Multiple: Ontology in Medical Practice.* Durham, NC: Duke University Press.

Mol, Annemarie. 2014. "Language Trails: 'Lekker' and Its Pleasures." *Theory, Culture and Society* 31 (2–3): 93–119.

Moore, Henrietta L. 2004. "Global Anxieties: Concept-Metaphors and Pre-Theoretical Commitments in Anthropology." *Anthropological Theory* 4 (1): 71–88.

Moser, Ingunn. 2005. "On Becoming Disabled and Articulating Alternatives: The Multiple Modes of Ordering Disability and Their Interferences." *Cultural Studies* 19 (6): 667–700.

Mouffe, Chantal. 2005. *On the Political*. London: Routledge.

Murphy, Keith M. 2016. "Design and Anthropology." *Annual Review of Anthropology* 45 (1): 433–49.

Murphy, Michelle. 2017a. "Afterlife and Decolonial Chemical Relations." *Cultural Anthropology* 32 (4): 494–503.

Murphy, Michelle. 2017b. *The Economization of Life*. Durham, NC: Duke University Press.

Myers, Natasha. 2012. "Dance Your PhD: Embodied Animations, Body Experiments, and the Affective Entanglements of Life Science Research." *Body and Society* 18 (1): 151–89.

Myers, Natasha. 2014. "Sensing Botanical Sensoria: A Kriya for Cultivating Your Inner Plant." *Center for Imaginative Ethnography*. http://imaginativeethnography.org/imaginings/affect/sensing-botanical-sensoria/.

Myers, Natasha. 2015. *Rendering Life Molecular: Models, Modelers, and Excitable Matter*. Durham, NC: Duke University Press.

Myers, Natasha, and Joseph Dumit. 2011. "Haptics: Haptic Creativity and the Mid-embodiments of Experimental Life." In *A Companion to the Anthropology of the Body and Embodiment*, edited by Frances Mascia-Lees, 239–61. Chichester, UK: Wiley-Blackwell.

Nielsen, Morten, and Nigel Rapport. 2017. *The Composition of Anthropology: How Anthropological Texts Are Written*. New York: Routledge.

Niewöhner, Jörg, and Thomas Scheffer. 2010. *Thick Comparison: Reviving the Ethnographic Aspiration*. Leiden: Brill.

Noble, Safiya Umoja. 2016. "A Future for Intersectional Black Feminist Technology Studies." *Scholar and Feminist Online* 13 (3): 1–8.

O'Dell, Thomas, and Robert Willim. 2013. "Transcription and the Senses: Cultural Analysis When It Entails More Than Words." *The Senses and Society* 8: 314–34.

Okely, Judith. 1994. "Vicarious and Sensory Knowledge of Chronology and Change: Ageing in Rural France." In *Social Experience and Anthropological Knowledge*, edited by Kirsten Hastrup and Peter Hervik, 34–48. London: Routledge.

Okri, Ben. 1997. *A Way of Being Free*. London: Phoenix House.

Omura, Keiichi, Grant J. Otsuki, Shiho Satsuka, and Atsuro Morita, eds. 2019. *The World Multiple: The Quotidian Politics of Knowing and Generating Entangled Worlds*. London: Routledge.

Otto, Ton. 1992. "The Ways of Kastam." *Oceania* 62: 264–83.

Otto, Ton. 2011. "Inventing Traditions and Remembering the Past in Manus." In *Changing Contexts, Shifting Meanings: Transformations of Cultural Traditions in Oceania*, edited by Elfriede Hermann, 157–73. Honolulu: University of Hawai'i Press.

Otto, Ton. 2013. "Ethnographic Film as Exchange." *The Asia Pacific Journal of Anthropology* 14 (2): 195–205.

Otto, Ton. 2018. "My Culture, I Perform It, I Can Change It: Film, Audience and Cultural Critique." *Visual Anthropology* 31 (4–5): 318–35.

Pandian, Anand, and Stuart J. McLean. 2017. *Crumpled Paper Boat: Experiments in Ethnographic Writing*. Durham, NC: Duke University Press.

Partidge, Tristan. 2014. "Diagrams in Anthropology: Lines and Interactions." Life Off the Grid Blog. https://anthropologyoffthegrid.wordpress.com /ethnograms/diagrams-in-anthropology/.

Paxson, Heather. 2013. *The Life of Cheese: Crafting Food and Value in America*. Berkeley: University of California Press.

Pink, Sarah. 1997. *Women and Bullfighting*. Oxford: Berg.

Pink, Sarah. 2006. *The Future of Visual Anthropology: Engaging the Senses*. London: Routledge.

Pink, Sarah. [2001] 2013. *Doing Visual Ethnography*. London: SAGE.

Pink, Sarah. [2009] 2015. *Doing Sensory Ethnography*. London: SAGE.

Pink, Sarah, Vaike Fors, and Mareike Glöss. 2018. "The Contingent Futures of the Mobile Present: Beyond Automation as Innovation." *Mobilities* 13 (5): 615–31.

Pink, Sarah, Heather Horst, John Postill, Larissa Hjorth, Tania Lewis, and Jo Tacchi. 2016. *Digital Ethnography: Principles and Practice*. Thousand Oaks, CA: SAGE.

Pink, S., R. Lucena, J. Pinto, A. Porto, C. Caminha, G. Maria de Siqueira, M. Duarte de Oliveira, A. Gomes, and R. Zilse. 2019. "Location and Awareness: Emerging Technologies, Knowing and Mobility in the Global South." In *Location Technologies in International Context*, edited by R. Wilken, G. Goggin, and H. Horst. London: Routledge.

Pink, Sarah, Kerstin L. Mackley, Roxana Morosanu, Val Mitchell, and Tracy Bhamra. 2017. *Making Homes: Ethnographies and Designs*. Oxford: Bloomsbury.

Pink, Sarah, and Jennie Morgan. 2013. "Short-Term Ethnography: Intense Routes to Knowing." *Symbolic Interaction* 36 (3): 351–61.

Pink, Sarah, Minna Ruckenstein, Robert Willim, and Melissa Duque. 2018. "Broken Data." *Big Data and Society* 5 (1). doi.org/10.1177/2053951717753228.

Pinto, Àlvaro B. 1960. *Consciência e realidade nacional*. Rio de Janeiro: Ministerio da Educação e Cultura, Instituto Superior de Estudos Brasileiros.

Pols, Jeannette. 2003. "Enforcing Patient Rights or Improving Care? The Interference of Two Modes of Doing Good in Mental Health Care." *Sociology of Health and Illness* 25 (4): 320–47.

Pols, Jeannette. 2006. "Washing the Citizen: Washing, Cleanliness and Citizenship in Mental Health Care." *Culture, Medicine and Psychiatry* 30 (1): 77–104.

Posavec, Stefanie, and Giorgia Lupi. 2016. *Dear Data*. London: Particular Books.

Postigo, Hector. 2012. *The Digital Rights Movement: The Role of Technology in Subverting Digital Copyright*. Cambridge, MA: MIT Press.

Postrel, Virginia. 2004. *The Substance of Style: How the Rise of Aesthetic Value Is Remaking Commerce, Culture, and Consciousness.* New York: HarperCollins.

Pratt, Mary Louise. 2007. *Imperial Eyes: Travel Writing and Transculturation.* 2nd ed. London: Routledge.

Price, David H. 2019. "Scharlette Holdman." Anthropology News website, 31, December 17. doi.org/10.1111/AN.1083. Accessed September 30, 2020.

Raabe, Eva. 1997. "A Modern Pacific Painter and His Tradition." *Pacific Arts* 15/16: 61–67.

Rabinow, Paul. 2003. *Anthropos Today: Reflections on Modern Equipment.* Princeton, NJ: Princeton University Press.

Rabinow, Paul. 2011. *The Accompaniment: Assembling the Contemporary.* Chicago: University of Chicago Press.

Rabinow, Paul, and Gaymon Bennett. 2012. *Designing Human Practices: An Experiment with Synthetic Biology.* Chicago: University of Chicago Press.

Rabinow, Paul, George E. Marcus, James D. Faubion, and Tobias Rees. 2008. *Designs for an Anthropology of the Contemporary.* Durham, NC: Duke University Press.

Rabinow, Paul, and Anthony Stavrianakis. 2013. *Demands of the Day: On the Logic of Anthropological Inquiry.* Chicago: University of Chicago Press.

Rabinow, Paul, and Anthony Stavrianakis. 2014. *Designs on the Contemporary: Anthropological Tests.* Chicago: University of Chicago Press.

Rabinow, Paul, and Anthony Stavrianakis. 2016. "Movement Space: Putting Anthropological Theory, Concepts, and Cases to the Test." HAU: *Journal of Ethnographic Theory* 6 (1): 403–31.

Rabinow, Paul, and Anthony Stavrianakis. 2019. *Inquiry after Modernism.* Oakland, CA: ARC / Wilsted and Taylor.

Rasmussen, Anders E. 2013. *Manus Canoes: Skill, Making, and Personhood in Mbuke Islands (Papua New Guinea).* Oslo: Kon-Tiki Museet.

Rheinberger, Hans-Jörg. 1997. *Toward a History of Epistemic Things: Synthesizing Proteins in the Test Tube.* Stanford, CA: Stanford University Press.

Rouch, Jean. 1978. "On the Vicissitudes of the Self: The Possessed Dancer, the Magician, the Sorcerer, the Filmmaker, and the Ethnographer." *Studies in Visual Communication* 5 (1): 1–8.

Rutherford, Danilyn. 2012. "Kinky Empiricism." *Cultural Anthropology* 27 (3): 465–79.

Sanjek, Roger. 2016. "From Fieldnotes to eFieldnotes." In *eFieldnotes: The Makings of Anthropology in the Digital World,* edited by Roger Sanjek and Susan W. Tratner, 3–27. Philadelphia: University of Pennsylvania Press.

Santos, Milton. 1971. *Le métier de géographe en pays sous-développé; un essai méthodologiqu.* Paris: Distribué par les Éditions Ophrys.

Santos, Milton. [1978] 2013. *O Trabalho do Geógrafo no Terceiro Mundo.* São Paulo, SP: Edusp—Editora da Universidade de São Paulo.

Savage, Robert. 2016. "Translator's Afterword. Metaphorology: A Beginner's Guide." In *Paradigms for a Metaphorology,* edited by Hans Blumenberg, 133–46. Reprint ed. Ithaca, NY: Cornell University Press.

Savransky, Martin. 2016. *The Adventure of Relevance: An Ethics of Social Inquiry.* London: Palgrave Macmillan.

Schrempp, Gregory A. 1992. *Mythical Arrows: The Maori, the Greeks and the Folklore of the Universe*. Madison: University of Wisconsin Press.

Schulze, H. 2020. *The Bloomsbury Handbook of the Anthropology of Sound*. New York: Bloomsbury Academic.

Schwartz, Theodore. 1976. "The Cargo Cult: A Melanesian Type-Response to Change." In *Responses to Change: Society, Culture and Personality*, edited by G. De Vos, 157–206. New York: Van Nostrand.

Schwarz, Roberto. 1988. "Brazilian Culture: Nationalism by Elimination." *New Left Review* 167: 77–90.

Sedgwick, Eve Kosofsky. 2003. *Touching Feeling: Affect, Pedagogy, Performativity*. Durham, NC: Duke University Press.

Serres, Michael. [1985] 2008. *The Five Senses: A Philosophy of Mingled Bodies*. London: Continuum.

Shanks, Michael. 2004. "Three Rooms: Archaeology and Performance." *Journal of Social Archaeology* 4 (2): 147–80.

Simpson, Bob. 2006. "'You Don't Do Fieldwork, Fieldwork Does You': Between Subjectivation and Objectivation in Anthropological Fieldwork." In *The SAGE Handbook of Fieldwork*, edited by Dick Hobbs, and Robert Wright, 125–38. London: SAGE.

Skeide, Annekatrin. 2019. "Enacting Homebirth Bodies: Midwifery Techniques in Germany." *Culture, Medicine, and Psychiatry* 43 (2): 236–55.

Sneath, David, Martin Holbraad, and Morten A. Pedersen. 2009. "Technologies of the Imagination: An Introduction." *Ethnos* 74 (1): 5–30.

Stavrianakis, Anthony. 2015. "From Anthropologist to Actant (and back to Anthropology): Position, Impasse, and Observation in Sociotechnical Collaboration." *Cultural Anthropology* 30 (1): 169–89.

Stavrianakis, Anthony, Paul Rabinow, and Trine M. Korsby. 2018. "In the Workshop: Anthropology in a Collaborative Zone of Inquiry." In *The Composition of Anthropology: How Anthropological Texts Are Written*, edited by Morten Nielsen and Nigel Rapport, 169–92. Oxford: Routledge.

Stengers, Isabelle. 2000. *The Invention of Modern Science*. Translated by David W. Smith. Minneapolis: University of Minnesota Press.

Stengers, Isabelle. 2005. "The Cosmopolitical Proposal." In *Making Things Public: Atmospheres of Democracy*, edited by Bruno Latour and Weibel Peter, 994–1003. Cambridge, MA: MIT Press.

Stengers, Isabelle. 2014. *Thinking with Whitehead: A Free and Wild Creation of Concepts*. Cambridge, MA: Harvard University Press.

Stengers, Isabelle. 2018. *Another Science Is Possible: A Manifesto for Slow Science*. Translated by Stephan Mueck. Cambridge: Polity Press.

Stoller, Paul. 1997. *Sensuous Scholarship*. Philadelphia: University of Pennsylvania Press.

Strathern, Marilyn. [1988] 1990. *The Gender of the Gift: Problems with Women and Problems with Society in Melanesia*. Berkeley: University of California Press.

Strathern, Marilyn. 1991. *Partial Connections*. Savage, MD: Rowman and Littlefield.

Strathern, Marilyn. 1992a. *After Nature: English Kinship in the Late Twentieth Century*. Cambridge: Cambridge University Press.

Strathern, Marilyn. 1992b. *Reproducing the Future: Essays on Anthropology, Kinship, and the New Reproductive Technologies*. New York: Routledge.

Strathern, Marilyn. 1996. "Potential Property: Intellectual Rights and Property in Persons." *Social Anthropology* 4 (1): 17–32.

Strathern, Marilyn. 1999. *Property, Substance and Effect: Anthropological Essays on Persons and Things*. London: Athlone.

Strathern, Marilyn. 2001. "The Patent and the Malanggan." *Theory, Culture and Society* 18 (4): 1–26.

Strathern, Marilyn. [1991] 2004. *Partial Connections*, updated ed. Walnut Creek, CA: AltamMira Press.

Strathern, Marilyn. 2006. "Useful Knowledge." *Proceedings of the British Academy* 139: 73–109.

Strathern, Marilyn. 2009. "Outside Desk-work." In *Writers on Writing*. Writing across Boundaries series. Durham: Durham University. https://www.dur.ac .uk/writingacrossboundaries/writingonwriting/marilynstrathern/. Accessed on February 20, 2020.

Suchman, Lucy. 2011. "Anthropological Relocations and the Limits of Design." *Annual Review of Anthropology* 40: 1–18.

Suchman, Lucy. 2013. "Consuming Anthropology." In *Interdisciplinarity: Reconfigurations of the Social and Natural Sciences*, edited by Andrew Barry and Georgina Born, 141–60. Abingdon, UK: Routledge.

Suchman, Lucy, Endre Dányi, and Laura Watts. 2008. "Relocating Innovation: Places and Material Practices of Future Making." Lancaster, UK: Centre for Science Studies, Lancaster University. https://sand14.com/relocating -innovation-places-and-practices-of-future-making/. Accessed on February 20, 2020.

Suhr, Christian, Ton Otto, and Steffen Dalsgaard. 2009. *Ngat Is Dead: Studying Mortuary Traditions*. Boston: Documentary Educational Resources, and London: Royal Anthropological Institute.

Suhr, Christian, and Rane Willerslev, eds. 2013. *Transcultural Montage*. New York: Berghahn.

Takaragawa, Stephanie, Trudi Lynn Smith, Kate Hennessy, Patricia Alvarez Astacio, Jenny Chio, Coleman Nye, and Shalini Shankar. 2019. "Bad Habitus: Anthropology in the Age of the Multimodal." *American Anthropologist* 121 (2): 517–24.

TallBear, Kim. 2019. "Feminist, Queer, and Indigenous Thinking as an Antidote to Masculinist Objectivity and Binary Thinking in Biological Anthropology." *American Anthropologist* 121 (2): 494–96.

Tambiah, Stanley J. 1990. *Magic, Science, Religion, and the Scope of Rationality*. Cambridge: Cambridge University Press.

Taussig, Michael. 2011. *I Swear I Saw This: Drawings in Fieldwork Notebooks, Namely My Own*. Chicago: University of Chicago Press.

Tilley, Helen. 2011. *Africa as a Living Laboratory: Empire, Development, and the Problem of Scientific Knowledge, 1870–1950*. Chicago: University of Chicago Press.

TILT Collective. 2013. *Codesigning Space: A Primer*. London: Artifice.

Timmermans, Stefan, and Iddo Tavory. 2012. "Theory Construction in Qualitative Research: From Grounded Theory to Abductive Analysis." *Sociological Theory* 30 (3): 167–86.

Trüper, Henning. 2013. "Wild Archives: Unsteady Records of the Past in the Travels of Enno Littmann." *History of the Human Sciences* 26 (4): 128–48. https://doi.org/10.1177/0952695113501094.

Tsing, Anna L. 2015. *The Mushroom at the End of the World: On the Possibility of Life in Capitalist Ruins*. Princeton, NJ: Princeton University Press.

Verdery, Katherine. 2018. *My Life as a Spy: Investigations in a Secret Police File*. Durham, NC: Duke University Press.

Verran, Helen. 2001. *Science and an African Logic*. Chicago: University of Chicago Press.

Verran, Helen. 2010. "Number as an Inventive Frontier in Knowing and Working Australia's Water Resources." *Anthropological Theory* 10 (1–2): 171–78.

Verran, Helen W., the Yirrkala Yolngu Community, and David Wade Chambers. 1989. "Exhibit Two: Talking of the Word: A Frame Up Job." In *Singing the Land, Signing the Land*. http://singing.indigenousknowledge.org/exhibit-2 .html. Accessed on September 29, 2020.

Vilca, Aparecida. 2015. *Praying and Preying: Christianity in Indigenous Amazonia*. Berkeley: University of California Press.

Vium, Christian. 2018. "Temporal Dialogues: Collaborative Photographic Reenactments as a Form of Cultural Critique." *Visual Anthropology* 31 (4–5): 355–75.

Viveiros de Castro, Eduardo. 2004. "Perspectival Anthropology and the Method of Controlled Equivocation." *Tipití: Journal of the Society for the Anthropology of Lowland South America* 2 (1): 3–22.

Viveiros de Castro, Eduardo. 2007. "The Crystal Forest: Notes on the Ontology of Amazonian Spirits." *Inner Asia* 9 (2): 153–72.

Viveiros de Castro, Eduardo. 2014. *Cannibal Metaphysics: For a Post-Structural Anthropology*. Translated by Peter Skafish. Minneapolis: University of Minnesota Press.

Vogel, Else. 2016. "Subjects of Care: Living with Overweight in The Netherlands." PhD diss., University of Amsterdam. https://dare.uva.nl/search?identifier =f7c8d692-24c3-49b0-8c21-bd94b3e2119a. Accessed on February 20, 2020.

Vogel, Else. 2018. "Metabolism and Movement: Calculating Food and Exercise or Activating Bodies in Dutch Weight Management." *BioSocieties* 13 (2): 389–407.

Vogel, Else, and Annemarie Mol. 2014. "Enjoy Your Food: On Losing Weight and Taking Pleasure." *Sociology of Health and Illness* 36 (2): 305–17.

Vonderau, Asta. 2017. "Technologies of the Imagination: Locating the Cloud in Sweden's North." *Imaginations: Journal of Cross Cultural Image Studies* 8 (2): 8–21.

Wagner, Roy. 1981. *The Invention of Culture*. Chicago: University of Chicago Press.

Wagner, Roy. 1986. *Symbols That Speak for Themselves*. Chicago: University of Chicago Press.

Wagner, Roy. 2001. *An Anthropology of the Subject: Holographic Worldview in New Guinea and Its Meaning and Significance for the World of Anthropology*. Berkeley: University of California Press.

Wagner, Roy. 2010. "Depersonalising the Digression." In *Writers on Writing*, Writing Across Boundaries series. Durham, UK: Durham University. https://www.dur.ac.uk/resources/anthropology/writingacrossboundaries /RoyWagner.pdf. Accessed on February 20, 2020.

Walford, Antonia. 2015. "Double Standards: Examples and Exceptions in Scientific Metrological Practices in Brazil." *Journal of the Royal Anthropological Institute* 21 (S1): 64–77.

Waltorp, Karen. 2013. "Public/Private Negotiations in the Media Uses of Young Muslim Women in Copenhagen: Gendered Social Control and the Technology-Enabled Moral Laboratories of a Multicultural City." *International Communication Gazette* 75 (5–6): 555–72.

Waltorp, Karen. 2015. "Keeping Cool, Staying Virtuous: Social Media and the Composite Habitus of Young Muslim Women in Copenhagen." *MedieKultur: Journal of Media and Communication Research* 58: 49–67.

Waltorp, Karen. 2016. "A Snapchat Essay on Mutuality, Utopia and Non-innocent Conversations." *Journal of the Anthropological Society of Oxford* 8 (1): 251–73.

Waltorp, Karen. 2017. "Digital Technologies, Dreams, and Disconcertment in Anthropological Worldmaking." In *Anthropologies and Futures: Researching Emerging and Uncertain Worlds*, edited by Juan F. Salazar, Sarah Pink, Andrew Irving, and Johannes Sjöberg, 101–16. London: Bloomsbury.

Waltorp, Karen. 2018a. "Fieldwork as Interface: Digital Technologies, Moral Worlds and Zones of Encounter." In *Experimental Collaborations: Ethnography through Fieldwork Devices*, edited by Adolfo Estalella, and Tomás Sánchez Criado, 114–31. London: Berghahn.

Waltorp, Karen. 2018b. "Intimacy, Concealment and Unconscious Optics: Filmmaking with Young Muslim Women in Copenhagen." *Journal of Visual Anthropology* 31 (4): 394–407.

Waltorp, Karen. 2020. *Why Muslim Women and Smartphones: Mirror Images*. London: Routledge.

Waltorp, Karen, and Christian Vium, dir. 2010. "MANENBERG: Growing Up in the Shadows of Apartheid." Documentary distributed by DR International sales/ Royal Anthropological Institute.

Waltorp, Karen, Christian Vium, and Christian Suhr. 2017. "Witnessing and Creating the World Audio-Visually: Aesthetics, Politics, Anthropology." *Visuel Arkivering* 10: 46–51.

Warren, Jason. 2017. *Creative Worlds: How to Make Immersive Theater*. London: Nick Hern Books.

Watts, Laura. 2012a. "OrkneyLab: An Archipelago Experiment in Futures." In *Imagining Landscapes: Past, Present and Future*, edited by Monica Janowski and Tim Ingold, 59–76. Oxford: Ashgate.

Watts, Laura. 2012b. "Sand14: Reconstructing the Future of the Mobile Telecoms Industry." *Fibreculture Journal* 20 (139): 33–57.

Watts, Laura. 2014a. "Future Archaeology: Re-Animating Innovation in the Mobile Telecoms Industry." In *Theories of the Mobile Internet: Materialities and Imaginaries*, edited by Andrew Herman, Jan Hadlaw, and Thom Swiss, 149–67. London: Routledge.

Watts, Laura. 2014b. "Liminal Futures: A Poem for Islands at the Edge." In *Subversion, Conversion, Development: Cross-Cultural Knowledge Exchange and the Politics of Design*, edited by James Leach and Lee Wilson, 19–38. Cambridge, MA: MIT Press.

Watts, Laura. 2019. *Energy at the End of the World: An Orkney Islands Saga*. Cambridge, MA: The MIT Press.

Watts, L., C. Howe, G. C. Bowker. Forthcoming. *Unda: A Graphic Novel of Energy Encounters*. Manchester, UK: Mattering Press.

Watts, Laura, James Maguire, and Brit R. Winthereik. Forthcoming. *Energy Worlds in Experiment*. Manchester, UK: Mattering Press.

Whitehead, Alfred North. [1920] 2013. *The Concept of Nature*. Mineola: NY: Dover.

Wilden, Anthony. 1972. *System and Structure: Essays in Communication and Exchange*. London: Routledge.

Winnicott, Donald W. 1986. *Holding and Interpretation: Fragment of an Analysis*. New York: Grove.

Winthereik, Brit R. 2019. "How to Reinvent ANT with Ethnography?" In *A Companion to Actor-Network Theory*, edited by Anders Blok, Ignacio Farias, and Celia Roberts, 24–33. London: Routledge.

Winthereik, Brit R., and Helen Verran. 2012. "Ethnographic Stories as Generalizations Tthat Intervene." *Science Studies* 25 (1): 37–51.

Winthereik, Brit R., Laura Watts, and James Maguire. 2019. "The Energy Walk: Infrastructuring the Imagination." In *digitalSTS: A Field Guide for Science and Technology Studies*, edited by Janet Vertesi and David Ribes, 349–63. Princeton, NJ: Princeton University Press.

Wittgenstein, Ludwig. 1953. *Philosophical Investigations*. Trans. G. E. Anscombe. Oxford: Blackwell.

Wolfe, Audra J. 2018. *Freedom's Laboratory: The Cold War Struggle for the Soul of Science*. Baltimore: Johns Hopkins University Press.

Wright, J. Lenore. 2006. *The Philosopher's I: Autobiography and the Search for the Self*. Albany: SUNY Press.

Yates-Doerr, Emily, and Annemarie Mol. 2012. "Cuts of Meat: Disentangling Western Natures-Cultures." *The Cambridge Journal of Anthropology* 30 (2): 48–64.

Zeitlyn, David. 2000. "Archiving Anthropology." *Forum Qualitative Sozialforschung / Forum: Qualitative Social Research (Sozialforschung)* 1 (3). doi.org/10.17169/fqs-1.3.1034.

Zeitlyn, David. 2012. "Anthropology in and of the Archives: Possible Futures and Contingent Pasts. Archives as Anthropological Surrogates." *Annual Review of Anthropology* 41 (1): 461–80.

Zuiderent-Jerak, Teun. 2015. *Situated Intervention: Sociological Experiments in Health Care*. Cambridge, MA: MIT Press.

PATRICIA ALVAREZ ASTACIO is an anthropologist and filmmaker whose scholarly research and creative practice develops in the folds between ethnography, critical theory, experimental methods, and the documentary arts. She is an assistant professor in the Anthropology Department at Brandeis University. Patricia is currently working on her book manuscript *Moral Fibers: Making Fashion Ethical*, which explores the Peruvian alpaca wool supply chain, analyzing how, through the intervention of development projects, indigenous women artisans and their aesthetic traditions are interpolated into "ethical fashion" manufacturing networks. Her latest film, *Entretejido*, weaves together the different sites and communities involved in this supply chain, bringing viewers into contact with the ways objects we wear are entangled in national racial politics and histories.

ANDREA BALLESTERO is an associate professor of Anthropology at Rice University. She is also the founder and director of the Ethnography Studio (https://ethnographystudio.org/). Her research examines spaces where the law, economics, and technoscience are so fused that they appear as one another. Her areas of interest include the politics of knowledge production; economic, legal, and political anthropology; water politics; subterranean spaces; and liberalism. She is the author of *A Future History of Water* (Duke University Press, 2019).

ALBERTO CORSÍN JIMÉNEZ is a reader in the Department of Social Anthropology at the Spanish National Research Council in Madrid. His interest in the organization of ethnography and anthropological knowledge as descriptive and theoretical forms led to the publication of *An Anthropological Trompe l'oeil for a Common World* (2013). He is also the editor of *Culture and Well-being: Anthropological Approaches to Freedom and Political Ethics* (2008), *The Anthropology of Organisations* (2007), and *Prototyping Cultures: Art, Science and Politics in Beta* (2017). He is currently writing an ethnographic history of the free culture movement in Spain.

IVAN DA COSTA MARQUES graduated in electronic engineering from the Instituto Tecnológico de Aeronáutica (1967) and obtained a master's degree (1970) and doctorate (1973) in electrical engineering and computer science at the University of California Berkeley. Upon returning to Brazil, he was a professor-researcher in the graduate school of engineering at the Universidade Federal do Rio de Janeiro (UFRJ). From 1977 to 1980 he was the coordinator for industrial and technological policy of CAPRE and the technical director of Digibrás (agencies of the Ministry of Planning). From 1981 to July 1986 he was the CEO of Embracomp, a small private manufacturer of terminals and other computer products in Rio de Janeiro. From August 1986 to July 1990 he was the CEO of the state-owned computer manufacturer COBRA. For two decades he obtained experience in economics and production engineering. He sought to be technically and politically active in the Brazilian scenario, especially on issues related to technological development, education, international division of labor, and the computer industry. From August 1990 to July 1992 he joined the Historical Studies Committee of the New School for Social Research in New York as a visiting scholar, focusing on the history of science and technology. In 1995 he returned to UFRJ as a full-time professor-researcher in the Graduate School of Engineering and the Department of Computer Science. In the past two decades he has been dedicated to the development of science studies in Brazil, associated with the UFRJ's Graduate Program in History of Science and Techniques, and Epistemology.

STEFFEN DALSGAARD holds a PhD in anthropology and ethnography from Aarhus University and is currently an associate professor in the Business IT Department at the IT University of Copenhagen. He has carried out more than two years of ethnographic fieldwork in Papua New Guinea about a range of topics including canoe craftsmanship and tradition, state and leadership, and perceptions of nature and value seen through the commodification of carbon. His publications have mainly appeared in anthropology journals such as *Anthropological Forum, Ethnos, HAU, Social Analysis,* and *Social Anthropology.* He is the editor, with Morten Nielsen, of the volume *Time and the Field* (2015).

ENDRE DÁNYI is a guest professor for the Sociology of Globalisation at the Bundeswehr University in Munich, Germany. The project discussed in this book was Endre's PhD research, which was a material-semiotic analysis of the rise and fall of liberal democracy in Hungary. In his habilitation project he is examining the European refugee crisis, the "War on Drugs," and Indigenous initiatives in northern Australia as instances where parliamentary politics reaches its limits, thereby generating productive tensions. In addition to research and teaching, Endre is busy corunning Mattering Press, an open access book publisher.

MARISOL DE LA CADENA teaches at the University of California Davis; she was trained as an anthropologist in Peru, England, France, and the US. The Andes of Peru have been her field site, and she has recently been working in Colombia. Thinking through ethnographic concepts, she has published extensively on race and indigeneity; her current work is on multispecies political economies. She is the author of *Indigenous Mestizos: The Politics of Race and Culture in Cuzco, Peru,*

1919–1991 (Duke University Press, 2000); *Indigenous Experience Today*, edited with Orin Starn (2007); *Earth Beings: Ecologies of Practice across Andean Worlds* (Duke University Press, 2015); and *World of Many Worlds*, edited with Mario Blaser (Duke University Press, 2018).

RACHEL DOUGLAS-JONES is an associate professor at the IT University of Copenhagen, where she is the head of the Technologies in Practice research group and codirector of the ETHOSLab. She conducts research at the intersection of medical anthropology and computational cultures, cultivating interests in forms of ethical governance over technological change. These interests developed through studies of NGO networking and the capacity building of ethics review processes in the Asia-Pacific region, out of which she has published a number of articles attending to the form of ethics review in global health. She has also followed committee work into the contentious domain of embryonic stem cell research ethics committees in the US, examining the vestiges of voluntary governance mechanisms. Recent publications include an analysis of tech manifestos, a chapbook made out of data protection legislation erasure poetry, and a bestiary of digital monsters.

CLÉMENT DRÉANO is a PhD candidate at the University of Amsterdam in the program group Anthropology of Health, Care and the Body. He studied sociology, philosophy, and musicology at the universities of Nantes and Frankfurt am Main. His doctoral research involves ethnographic fieldwork in Ghana and the Netherlands, where he seeks to explore ideals and practices of good living with sickle cell disease and how bad surprises and moments of crisis participate in shaping them. His interests are in ethnographic methods, science and technology studies, medical anthropology, and feminist approaches to care.

JOSEPH DUMIT is the chair of performance studies and a professor of science and technology studies and of anthropology at the University of California Davis. He is an anthropologist of passions, brains, games, bodies, drugs, and facts. His research and teaching constantly ask how exactly we came to think, do, and speak the ways we do about ourselves and our world, and what are the actual material ways in which we come to encounter facts, conspiracies, and things and take them to be relevant to our lives and our futures. He is the author of *Picturing Personhood: Brain Scans and Biomedical America* (2004) and *Drugs for Life: How Pharmaceutical Companies Define Our Health* (Duke University Press, 2012), and coeditor of *Cyborgs and Citadels*, *Cyborg Babies*, and *Biomedicine as Culture*. He has written articles about neuroscience and play, irrational computers, patient experiences, difficult-to-define illnesses, and the history of medicine, and he was the managing editor of *Culture, Medicine and Psychiatry* for ten years. He holds a BA degree from Rice University and a PhD in the history of consciousness from the University of California Santa Cruz. His current research includes comparative anatomies and fascia via improvisation practice as research, the infernal alternatives of capitalism and health, three-dimensional visualization (virtual reality) environments for science, game studies, and data studies. Visit his website at http://dumit.net.

MELANIE FORD LEMUS is a PhD candidate in the department of anthropology at Rice University. Her dissertation research focuses on architectural interventions in the deep ravines (*los barrancos*) that compose nearly half of Guatemala City's terrain. Interested in the relationship between form, environment, and design, Melanie researches moments of encounter between ravine residents, urban planners, and architects to understand how they negotiate designs for a more socially and environmentally conscious urban future. Her research aims to strengthen insight into how Guatemala City attempts to reckon and ameliorate social and environmental issues that result from the instability, marginality, and violence of the twentieth century. At Rice University, Mel is a co-coordinator of the Ethnography Studio with Katie Ulrich and Dr. Andrea Ballestero, and a predoctoral fellow at the Center for Energy and Environmental Research in the Human Sciences (CENHS) at Rice University.

ELAINE GAN is an artist-scholar who teaches at the Center for Experimental Humanities and Social Engagement at New York University, where she also directs the Multispecies Worldbuilding Lab. Her practice engages with the fields of feminist science and technology studies, environmental arts and humanities, multispecies ethnography, and digital media. She is coeditor of an anthology titled *Arts of Living on a Damaged Planet: Ghosts and Monsters of the Anthropocene* (2017).

GRAHAM M. JONES is a cultural and linguistic anthropologist who explores how people use language and other media to enact expertise in practice, performance, and interaction. An associate professor of anthropology at the Massachusetts Institute of Technology, he teaches classes on a range of subjects including magic, science, and religion; education; play and games; communications technologies; and ethnographic methods. Jones's two monographs constitute a diptych: *Trade of the Tricks* (2011) describes day-to-day life and everyday talk within the insular subculture of contemporary French illusionists; *Magic's Reason* (2017) examines the meaning of magic in Western modernity, bridging the intellectual history of anthropology and the cultural history of popular entertainment.

TRINE MYGIND KORSBY is a postdoctoral researcher at Stanford University, where she works on a project on transnational crime and criminal livelihoods in Romania. She completed her PhD in anthropology with the Department of Anthropology, University of Copenhagen. Her recent publications include *The Brothel Phone Number: Infrastructures of Transnational Pimping in Eastern Romania* (2017), and the chapter "In the Workshop: Anthropology in a Collaborative Zone of Inquiry," cowritten with Anthony Stavrianakis and Paul Rabinow (in *The Composition of Anthropology*, 2018).

JUSTINE LAURENT, Oliver Human, Carolina Domínguez Guzmán, Els Roding, Ulrike Scholtes, Marianne de Laet, and Annemarie Mol are an Amsterdam-based team of researchers brought together by a shared sensitivity to contrasting as an analytical technique. They work on situated cases concerned with eating and bodies, excreting, sensing, and cleaning houses and cities, and relating to more-than-humans, caring for clean water, and botanical gardens. They all engage with their cases, methods, and theories differently, but they share a practice of thinking through the specificities of their ethnographic spaces while resisting a clear division between theory and practice. They collaborate through conversations, workshops, supervisions and intervisions, walking seminars, cowriting, collective fieldwork, and dinners and lunches. During these collaborations, and outside of them, they cultivate their specificities, sometimes also through noting and discussing contrasts among themselves. While discussing potty training practices they noted not only contrasts within and between the stories but also contrasts between their takes on these stories. Calibrating such distinctions without erasing them is what the analytic technique of contrasting is about.

JAMES MAGUIRE is an anthropologist and assistant professor at the IT University of Copenhagen. His work has focused on the political, temporal, and environmental consequences of energy extraction, with a particular ethnographic focus on northern Europe. His current research examines the interrelationship between the digital and the environmental, paying particular attention to the production of digital infrastructures through the appropriation of environmental forms.

GEORGE E. MARCUS has been Chancellor's Professor of Anthropology at the University of California Irvine since 2005, when he inaugurated the Center for Ethnography (which he has since directed). For the twenty-five years preceding that, he was the chair of the Anthropology Department at Rice University, which in effect was for that entire period a sustained research/debate circle regarding anthropology's research practices and the momentum it received from the lively debates across disciplines about culture, language, and representation. *Writing Culture, Anthropology as Cultural Critique, Ethnography Through Thick & Thin*, and the *Late Editions* series of fin-de-siècle annuals are the participatory publications that mark that heady period. His interest in anthropological writing and research practices morphed in the early 2000s into the relationship between ethnographic methods and studio/design practices of various kinds and, more recently, digital technologies. His experimentation with intermediate forms of fieldwork, the nature of collaborations, the fate of "field notes," and the evolution of research careers beyond rite of passage projects of ethnography, and their forms of writing, have been his continuing concerns.

SARAH PINK is a professor and the director of the Emerging Technologies Research Lab at Monash University, Melbourne, Australia. Her research seeks to develop a dialogue between her academic scholarship, applied practice, and interdisciplinarity. Her recent team ethnography projects have been in Australia, the United Kingdom, Sweden, Spain, Brazil, and Indonesia. Publications from these projects include books, journal articles, an ethnographic film, and websites. Some examples of this work can be seen at www.laundrylives.com and www.energyanddigitalliving .com. Her recent collaboratively written and edited books include *Uncertainty and Possibility* (2018), *Refiguring Digital Visual Techniques* (2017), *Anthropologies and Futures* (2017), *Making Homes* (2017), and *Digital Ethnography: Principles and*

Practice (2016). In 2015 she codirected the ethnographic documentary *Laundry Lives*.

MARKUS RUDOLFI studied sociology, psychology, and human geography at the University of Jena and Goethe University Frankfurt, and he is a former member of the editorial board of the student-led magazine *Soziologiemagazin*. After his studies he worked as a lecturer in political education, as a high ropes instructor, and as a temporary helper at a mountain cottage in the Alps. In 2018 he joined the chair of cultural psychology and anthropology of knowledge at Ruhr-University Bochum, where he helped to build up the RUSTlab. He currently works as a research associate at the chair for interpretative social research at Goethe University Frankfurt, where he is engaged in a PhD project about conservation practices at a central European transboundary park.

ANTHONY STAVRIANAKIS is a researcher at the Centre National de la Recherche Scientifique, France. He is the coauthor, with Paul Rabinow, of *Demands of the Day: On the Logic of Anthropological Inquiry* (2013) and *Designs on the Contemporary: Anthropological Tests* (2014). He is currently engaged in two field projects: on assisted suicide in Switzerland and on care for people diagnosed with amyotrophic lateral sclerosis in Paris and San Francisco.

LUCY SUCHMAN is a professor of anthropology of science and technology in the Department of Sociology at Lancaster University. Before taking up her present post she was a principal scientist at Xerox's Palo Alto Research Center, where she spent twenty years as a researcher. She is the author of *Human-Machine Reconfigurations* (2007). Her current research extends her long-standing engagement with the fields of human-computer interaction and artificial intelligence into the domain of contemporary warfare, including the figurations that animate military training and simulation, and problems of "situational awareness" in in the context of increasingly automated weapon systems. She is concerned with the question of whose bodies are incorporated into these systems, how they are incorporated, and with what consequences for social justice and the possibility for a less violent world.

KATIE ULRICH is a PhD candidate in the Department of Anthropology at Rice University. Her research focuses on petrochemical replacements made from sugarcane and other plant sources, including not only biofuels but also biobased plastics, synthetic fabrics, solvents, specialty chemicals, and more. She is working with scientists and industry actors in Brazil who are researching new biotechnologies to expand the scope and scale of sugar-based alternatives to petrochemicals. Her project follows the technical practices of scientists, industry actors, and funding agents within and beyond the laboratory that reconfigure sugarcane molecularly, socially, and politically—and to what extent these practices ultimately transform sugarcane from a crop with a violent history into a feedstock for new environmental and industrial futures. At Rice she is a co-coordinator of the Ethnography Studio and a former predoctoral fellow at the Center for Energy and Environmental Research in the Human Sciences.

HELEN VERRAN considers that in ethnographic analysis is it often useful to refuse the Western commonsense understanding that the author in the flesh is ineluctably ontologically distinct from the author in the text. As an author in the flesh she is an old woman, University Professorial Fellow at Charles Darwin University in Australia's Northern Territory, and currently a visiting scholar at the Max Planck Institute for the History of Science in Berlin. As author in the text? Well, it is up to readers to judge. She is author of the prize-winning book *Science and an African Logic* (2001).

ELSE VOGEL works at the intersection of anthropology and science and technology studies. In her research she combines philosophical reflection with the empirical study of care practices, particularly those aimed at lifestyle change. She currently works as a postdoctoral researcher at the University of Amsterdam, the Netherlands, and as a research fellow at the University of Linköping, Sweden. In addition to teaching courses in anthropology and philosophy of science, she is conducting research on human-animal relations in intensive livestock production, with a focus on how veterinarians in this industry negotiate diverse values in caring for farm animals.

ANTONIA WALFORD is a lecturer in digital anthropology at University College London. Her work critically engages with the social and cultural implications of data and digitization practices, with a particular focus on the scientific data economy in the Brazilian Amazon. She previously held a position at the Centre for Social Data Science, University of Copenhagen, and was a research associate at the ESRC Centre for Research on Socio-Cultural Change (CRESC). She has published articles in journals including the *Journal of the Royal Anthropological Institute* and *Social Analysis*, and several book chapters, and she has coedited a number of collections on various topics, including one with Francis Dodsworth on the contemporary consequences of globalization, and one with Hannah Knox for *Cultural Anthropology* on whether there is an ontology to the digital.

KAREN WALTORP is an assistant professor of anthropology at Aarhus University and an award-winning filmmaker. Her research focuses on gender, Islam, visual and digital technologies, and new configurations of space and personhood related to new technologies. She works with long-term projects grounded in an experimental approach and collaborative methodologies and carries out fieldwork primarily in South Africa and Denmark. Waltorp is the author of *Why Muslim Women and Smartphones: Mirror Images* (2020), and her work has appeared in a range of anthropological and interdisciplinary journals including *Ethnos*, *Visual Anthropology*, and *International Communication Gazette*. She is the co-convener of the FAN: European Association for Social Anthropologists' Future Anthropologies Network, and is a coinvestigator on the three-year Aarhus University Research Foundation NOVA grant "ARTlife: Articulations of Life among Afghans in Denmark" (2017–20), working on collaborative filmmaking and web presence with a collective of Danish-Afghan women.

LAURA WATTS is a writer, poet, ethnographer of futures, and a senior lecturer in energy and society at Geography and the Lived Environment, Geosciences, University of Edinburgh. As a science and technology studies scholar, she concerns her research with the effect of "edge" landscapes on how the future is imagined and made and on methods for writing futures otherwise. For the past decade she has been working with people and places around both energy and data futures in the islands of Orkney, Scotland. Her latest book, *Energy at the End of the World: An Orkney Islands Saga*, was published in 2019.

BRIT ROSS WINTHEREIK is a professor of ethnography and science and technology studies, head of the Center for Digital Welfare, and affiliated with the Technologies in Practice research group at the IT University of Copenhagen. Her research focuses on digital data, welfare, infrastructures, data, energy, and accountability. She is cofounder of the Danish Association for Science and Technology Studies (www.dasts.dk), and the ETHOSLab (https://ethos.itu.dk). She is the coauthor, with Casper Bruun Jensen, of *Monitoring Movements in Development Aid: Recursive Infrastructures and Partnerships* (2013) and has published broadly across anthropology and STS.

abduction, 235, 239–40, 244
Aboriginal Australians, 235–38
aboutness, 262–64
Abrahamsson, Sebastian, 194
absences, 79–80, 253
absolute metaphors, 181
Agar, Michael, 198
agriculture, 107–10, 113–17
Ahrens, Sönke, 157
Albert, Bruce, 215
alpacas, 16, 28n1
alpaca wool: interactive installation, 22, 24–25; touch, 15–18, 20; visual anthropology, 16, 19, 21, 23–24
Amerindian mythology, 214–15
analogy: categorization use, 157–61; descriptive transformations, 211; exercises, 160–61; measurement and myth, 215–17; protocol, 217–18; Strathern, Marilyn's use, 210–11, 218n3
analysis: overview, 1–3; collaborative, 32–33; comparative, 37; as craft, 6–7; creative techniques, 9–10; difficulties, 265; discussions of, 3–5; enlivening concepts, 3–4; interdisciplinary, 33; openings for, 2; singularity, 3–5; and theory, 32; timespace of, 5–7, 11; transcription, 33; and writing, 32, 134–35
analytic protocols: overview, 10–11; analogy, 217–18; categorization, 161–62; contrast analysis, 196–97; diagrams,

118–20; drafts, 131–32; drawing, 105; ethnographic hunches, 39–40; ethnographic story writing, 244–45; as experimentation, 259, 261; juxtaposition, 64–65; knowledge device decolonization, 233–34; limits, 11; multimodal analysis, 149; not knowing, 254–56; object exchange, 93; para-sites, 50–51; podcasting, 172; postcards, 80–81; substance as method, 184–85; touch, 26–28
anechoic chambers, 163
archives: free culture activist processes, 124–25, 127; Indigenous, 127; online, 126–29; peasant, 246–47, 249–50; wild, 126, 128–29
assemblages, 106
assisted suicide, 86, 88–90, 92

Ballestero, Andrea, 259
Barad, Karen, 21, 111–12, 118, 218n1
Bataille, Georges, 248
beliefs: cosmological, 148–49; procreation, 204–5; translating, 247–48, 251
Benjamin, Walter, 141, 256
Bennett, Jane, 21, 176, 181–82
binaries, 182
Blumenberg, Hans, 181
Boas, Franz, 12n1
both/and situations, 254
Bradley, Richard, 81n2

Brazil: knowledge devices received, 220;
Large-Scale Biosphere-Atmosphere
Experiment, 209, 211–14; technology
use while commuting, 36–37
Brazilian graduate education: disciplinary
divisions, 227–32; evaluation, 222–27;
funding, 222; knowledge device list,
220; structures, 221–22
breakdowns, 198
Brent, T. David, 48
"bringing forth" role of anthropology, 147
bromides, 176–79, 184
Buck-Morss, Susan, 73, 74
Budapest, Hungary, 71, 73, 74, 78–80
Burke, Tom, 83

Cadena, Marisol de la, 17
calibration, 213
Castro, Eduardo Viveiros de, 215
categorization: analogy, 157–61; of
categorizing practices, 161; exercises,
156–57, 160–61; filing systems, 152–57;
importance, 152–53; protocol, 161–62;
roles of, 151; tools, 152, 156
Center for Ethnography, University
of California Irvine, 41–42. See also
para-sites
Chavez, Leo, 45
Cheng, Jesse, 43–46, 51n1
Christen, Kimberly, 127
Classen, Constance, 28n2
collaboration: contrast analysis, 186–88,
190, 197n3; discussion, 82; epistemic
partners, 42, 50; fieldwork, 41, 44, 199;
free culture activism, 128; spaces for,
83; team ethnography, 32–34; thinking
about objects, 82. See also exchanges of
perspective; object exchange
commuting and technology use, 36–37
companionship, 7–8
concept-metaphors, 38–39
Conklin, Harold, 109–10, 118
contrast analysis: overview, 186–87, 195;
academic literature, 193–95; advantages,
186, 195; distinctions resulting from,
187–88; excretion practices analysis,

186–94; informant *versus* researcher
concerns, 196; language, 192–93, 196;
norms, 190–91; protocol, 196–97; team,
186–88, 190, 197n3; techniques, 189–90;
theoretical tension emphasis, 195–96;
things, 191

Das, Veena, 3–4
data, 38, 140–41, 165
data centers, 164–65
the dazzle, 6, 170, 260
death penalty mitigation activists, 43–47,
52n2
defamiliarization, 141–42, 150n3
Deleuze, Gilles, 29n5, 179
Denmark, 164–66, 201–3. See also Muslim
immigrants in Denmark
Dewey, John, 82–83, 85, 245n4
diagrams: advantages, 106–7, 117;
analogies, 159–61; anthropological use
survey, 96; class exercises, 120; crops,
107–9; limitations, 101, 108; multispecies ethnography use, 107–8; phrenol-
ogy, 112–14; protocol, 118–20. See also
diagram temporality
diagram temporality: overview, 106;
disruption and emergence, 112, 116–17;
halting, 96; iterative reconfiguring,
111–12; multispecies, 112–17; one-point,
108–9, 111, 117–18; oscillations, 112,
114–15, 116; recursive, 109–11
disclosure contexts, 147
discreteness, 212, 214–15
displacement, 249
disruption, 116–17
Doing Visual Ethnography, 31
drafts: and anthropological description,
125–26; archives as, 127; ethnographic
practices as, 128–31; free culture activism, 124–25, 127–28; as material vectors,
123; oral, 242; protocol, 131–32; as social
relations, 123; triplex model, 125; as wild
archive, 126
drawing: advantages, 104–5; anthropological uses, 96–97; everything technique,
98–100; goals, 95; organizational

techniques, 102–4; origins, 95, 97; protocol, 105; scale, 99–100; separating-and-distinguishing technique, 100–101; thinking with, 94–95; *versus* writing, 95, 104

driving, 37

Dumit, Joe, 10, 20

Duque, Melisa, 38

empiricism, 262–64, 266

Engelmann, Lukas, 96–97

entertainment magic, 153–55, 158–60

epistemic partners, 42, 50

epistemological right, the, 251–52, 256n1

ethics, 89, 100, 165

ethnographic hunches. *See* hunches

ethnographic knowing, 33–34, 205, 239–40, 242

ethnographic reading, 239, 242, 244, 245n2

ethnographic story writing: abduction, 235, 239–40, 244; aporia negotiation, 243; "Bus Passenger" text, 236–38; generalizations, 239; knowers, 239–40; ontological constitution, 235, 239–40; oral drafts, 242; physical stuff, 235–36, 240–42; protocol, 244–45; word deployment, 236, 242–44

ethnographic subjects, 41, 48–49. *See also* informants

ethnography: agency of, 49; classical, 48; dialogic aspects, 47; experimental ethos, 49; goals of, 48; of knowledge-making processes, 48–49; in the middle of things, 264–66; multimodal approaches, 21, 23, 49–50; multispecies, 106–8, 112–17; sensorial engagement, 19–20; standard procedures, 257; team, 32–34; third impact areas, 47; training in, 48–49, 257–58, 261–63, 266

etymologies, 182

Evans-Pritchard, E. E., 96

events, 89

excess, 248

exchanges of perspective: overview, 200; breakdowns, 198; informant coana-lysts, 199; informant reciprocal visits, 199–206; protocol, 207–8; shared projects, 203–7; Strathern, Marilyn on, 200

excretion practices, children learning: bodily control, 187–88; contrast analysis, 186–94; independence tropes, 188–89, 193; informant accounts, 186–87; language, 192–93, 197n1; parental concerns, 190–91; techniques, 189; things, 191

experiments, 49, 258–61

Fabian, Johannes, 126–27

feminist objectivity, 210

feminist theory, 9, 42, 106, 111, 252

fieldwork: anxieties, 199; collaboration, 41, 44, 199; cosmological beliefs, 148–49; iterative approaches, 149; limitations, 49, 263–64; para-sites, 52n2; rule use, 86, 88–90, 92; social media use, 136–39, 148. *See also* para-sites

"Figuring Out Ethnography" system, 10

filing systems, 152–57

filmmaking, 23, 29n6

Fischer, Michael, 150n3

Fors, Vaike, 37

Fortun, Kim, 10, 98, 100, 259

Foucault, Michel, 181, 252

free culture activism, 124–29

Freire, Paulo, 226–27, 234n9

Geertz, Clifford, 159

generative words, 234n9

Gentner, Dedre, 159–60

gift exchanges, 200

globalization, 42

Glöss, Mareike, 37

Goffman, Erving, 156–57

Gomes, Alex, 36

graduate education. *See* Brazilian graduate education

grounded theory, 152

Guattari, Félix, 29n5

Guha, Ranajit, 248

Guyer, Jane, 3

Haraway, Donna: feminist objectivity, 210; Implosion exercises, 10; on relationality, 106; on stories, 76; on visual production, 140–41
Hayward, Eva, 29n7
Herzfeld, Michael, 160
Hodson, Elizabeth A., 96–97
Holdman, Scharlette, 43, 52n2
Human Expectations and Experiences of Autonomous Driving (HEAD), 37
Humphrey, Caroline, 96–97
Humphrey, Robin, 95
hunches: overview, 30–31; comparative analysis, 37; concept-metaphors, 38–39; protocol, 39–40; serendipity, 33–36; team ethnography, 33; and theory, 35
hygrometers, 211–12

iconoclash, 74
immersement, 135, 149, 164, 166, 260
immersion, 4
Implosion exercises, 10
improvisation techniques, 20
Indigenous peoples: Aboriginal Australians, 235–38; Amerindians, 214–15; Andean, 247; illusionism, 154
informants: analyzing ethnographers, 200; as coanalysts, 199; feedback from, 143, 146–47, 150n4; reciprocal visits, 199–206
inter-embodiment, 193–94
internet, the, 136
intimacy, 164, 266
invisible architectures, 35
Irigaray, Luce, 246, 250
'Isawa, the, 154, *155*, 157–58, 160

juxtaposition: overview, 53; as active process, 63–64; defamiliarization, 141–42; health expert ethnography, 54–56, 59–64; katachresis, 69, 78–80; multimodal sorting, 141–42, *143–44*, *145–46*; protocol, 64–65

Kant, Immanuel, 100
katachresis, 69, 78–80

Kelly, José, 215
knowing: ethnographic, 33–34, 205, 239–40, 242; ways of, 30–31
knowledge device decolonization: differences and resemblances, 232–33; inhabitant lists, 219–20; limit situations, 232–33; panoramic views, 221; protocol, 233–34; territory choice, 221. *See also* Brazilian graduate education
knowledge devices: overview, 220; generative, 226; names, 220–21; stabilization as facts, 231; Western dominant, 232
knowledge-making process ethnography, 48–49
Kofman, Sarah, 245n7

Labinar, the, 83
language: contrast analysis, 192–93, 196; storytelling impact, 242–43
Large-Scale Biosphere-Atmosphere Experiment in Amazonia (LBA), 209, 211–14
Latour, Bruno, 74, 99, 210, 216
Law, John, 254
LBA (Large-Scale Biosphere-Atmosphere Experiment in Amazonia), 209, 211–14
Leder Mackley, Kristin, 33, 35
Leenhardt, Godfrey, 101
Lévi-Strauss, Claude, 214–15
Libraria, 129
Luhmann, Niklas, 157
Lynteris, Christos, 96–97

Madrid, Spain, 123–25. *See also* free culture activism
Marcus, George, 150n3
Marks, Laura, 17
material semiotics, 55
Maurer, Bill, 46
Mazzio, Carla, 28n1
McCarthy, Tom, 151
measurement: anthropological perspectives, 209–10; calibration, 213; construction-representation dilemma, 210–11, 216; continuous-to-discrete transformations, 212, 214; conventional

true value, 213, 218n4; myth analogy, 215–17; scientific perspectives, 210; uncertainty, 213–14, 216

La Mesa collective, 123–25. *See also* free culture activism

metaphors, 38–39, 126, 181

methodological messiness, 265–66

Mills, C. Wright, 152–53

Minh-Ha, T., 29n6

Mol, Annemarie, 61–62, 254

Moore, Henrietta, 38

Morgan, Jennie, 32

mortuary ceremonies, 204

movement, 257–59

multimodal sorting: overview, 133, 135–36; defamiliarization, 141–42, 150n3; feedback from informants, 143, 146–47; image juxtaposition, 141–42, *143–44, 145–46*; procedures, 139–40; protocol, 149; representation's role, 146; technologies enabling, 148; unconscious optics, 141

multispecies ethnography, 106–8, 112–17

Murphy, Michelle, 19, 258

Muslim immigrants in Denmark: overview, 133–34; image collages, *143–44, 145–46*; social media use, 136–38, 148

Myers, Fred, 153

Myers, Natasha, 20

Nalo, Joe, 202

Natural User Experience project (NUX), 36–37

nonlinearity, 257

not knowing: advantages, 251–52, 254; beliefs, 247–48; displacement, 249; epistemological right prevention, 251–52; excess, 248–49; *versus* knowing, 250; "not only" device, 253–54; presence, 246; protocol, 254–56. *See also* Turpo, Mariano

obesity epidemic, 53–56

obesity epidemic ethnography: overview, 56; care practices, 56–60; context awareness, 60; fieldwork sites, 56–57;

goods/bads discourses, 60–61; health-pleasure oppositions, 61–63; juxtaposition applications, 54–56, 59–64; material ordering, 57–58; overweight living practices, 59; responses to, 63

object exchange: overview, 84–85; assisted suicide fieldwork rule, 86, 88–90, 92; conceptual origins, 83–84; efficacy, 92–93; ethical dimensions, 87–88; interconnected problem analysis, 83–84; judgment concerns, 87; pimp interview, 86–87, 90–92; protocol, 93; psychological relations, 85; violence, 90

objects, 82–83, 85

O'Dell, Tom, 33

Okri, Ben, 3

onto-epistemic assertions, 253–54

optics, 141

Orkney, Scotland, 74, 75, 76, 78–80

Otto, Ton, 208n1, 208n3

Papua New Guinea, 204–5

Papua New Guinean informants, 201–3

para-ethnography, 46

para-site experiments: overview, 43; death penalty mitigation activists, 43–47, 52n2; as fieldwork training, 52n2; stakes of, 46–47

para-sites, 42–43, 50–51

Partridge, Tristan, 96–97

perspective exchanges. *See* exchanges of perspective

phenology, 113–17

photography, 34

Pink, Sarah, 23, 33

podcast creation: academic authority, 168–69; academic uses, 166; and access, 165; analytic power, 169–71; audience considerations, 168–69, 171; awkwardness, 167; dazzle, 170; equipment, 171–72; ethnographic methods, 166–67; field-desk dichotomy collapse, 170; jingles, 167; linguistic considerations, 167–68; protocol, 172; *versus* written analysis, 167–68

politics of invention, 23

postcards method: advantages, 80; Budapest example, 71, 73, 74, 78–80; inspiration to use, 70; internet use, 71, 76; katachresis reading, 69, 78–80; Orkney example, 74, 75, 76, 78–80; as pieces of places, 70, 81n2; protocol, 80–81; reading, 76; theme development, 76–78

protocols, 10. *See also* analytic protocols

questions *versus* experiments, 259

Rabinow, Paul, 82–84
radical difference, 17
reading, ethnographic, 239, 242, 244, 245n2
reciprocal visits, 199–206
reflexive knowledge, 46
relationality, 106, 163, 180. *See also* diagrams
"Relocating Innovation" project, 69, 76–80. *See also* postcards
Rice University Ethnography Studio, 259
Romanian sex industry, 86–87, 90–92
Rouch, Jean, 141
Ruckenstein, Minna, 38
rules, 89

SAM. *See* substance as method
Sanjek, Roger, 126
Schwartz, Theodore, 205
science, 209–10, 258
senses: engagement, 19; Enlightenment definitions, 18; fingereyes, 24, 29n7; flavor, 29n4; and knowledge, 18–19, 28n3, 169–70; sight, 17, 29n5. *See also* touch
serendipity, 33–34
Serres, Michael, 169–70
Shank, Michael, 69, 78
sight, 17, 29n5
Simpson, Bob, 95
size, 99
skin, 20–21
Skyspace, 7–9
smartphones, 36–37, 134, 141

socialism, 71, 73, 74
social media: disclosure, 147; and ethnographic writing, 135; immigrant use, 136–38, 148; reciprocal visits, 206; temporalities, 135–36; ubiquity, 134
software politics, 129
Solok, Kalou, 198, 204
sound and landscapes, 166
sound recording, 163–66, 168, 171. *See also* podcast creation
Stengers, Isabelle, 120n2, 183, 246, 251, 266
storytelling as aporia negotiation, 243
story writing. *See* ethnographic story writing
Strathern, Marilyn: absences, 253; *After Nature*, 160; analogy use, 210–11, 218n3; analysis and writing, 134–35, 260; coloniality of power, 223; culture, 159, 161; displacement, 249; gift exchange, 200; immersement, 164; Leenhardt's diagram, 101; negativities, 253; new projects, 104; partial connections, 254; personhood theories, 205; social constructivism, 244. *See also* the dazzle
subjects. *See* ethnographic subjects
substance as method (SAM): overview, 175–76; implicit substances, 179; protocol, 184–85; relationality, 180; specialist texts, 177–79, 183–84; specification, 180–81; specificity, 176–77; surprise of others, 177, 179–80; theoretical term reassessment, 179–82; ways of living and working, 182
Suhr, Christian, 208n1
Sweden, 37

team ethnography, 32–34
temporality, 264. *See also* diagram temporality
textiles, 18. *See also* alpaca wool
tirakuna, 247, 250, 252
touch: alpaca wool, 15–18, 20; Barad, Karen on, 21; context's impact on, 17–18, 20–21, 24; as field notes, 18; and filmmaking, 21, 23–24; functions of, 20; interactive exhibitions, 22, 24–25;

pathways, 20–21; protocol, 26–28; recollection, 18; representation resistance, 17, 28; and sight, 17; workshops, 25–28
truth as absolute metaphor, 181
Tsing, Anna, 264
Turell, James, 8
Turpo, Mariano and Nazario: archive, 246–47, 249, 252, 254; belief translation, 247–48, 251; co-laboring, 247–51; communication, 251; excess (ethnographic mode), 248, 252; and history, 249; "not only" device, 253–54; and *tirakuna*, 247, 250, 252

unconscious optics, 141
unremarkable events, 9
unruly companions, 265–66

Visual anthropology, *16*, *19*, *21*, 23–24

Wagner, Roy, 95, 158
wearable technology, 38
Weibel, Peter, 74
Whitehead, Alfred North, 175, 183
wild archive metaphor, 126
wild archives, 126, 128–29
Willim, Robert, 33, 38
Witmore, Chris, 78
Wittgenstein, Ludwig, 245n3, 245n5
workshops, 25–28, 264
writing, 32, 95, 104, 134–35; and analysis, 32, 134–35; *versus* drawing, 95, 104; ethnographic moments, 135; as thought, 95, 104

Xerox PARC, 70–71, 72, 78–80

Zeitlyn, David, 126–27
Zettlekasten filing, 157
Zilse, Renata, 36